PRASE FOR
PEOPLE WITH PURPOSE

'Another great book by the author of the bestselling *The Language of Leaders*. This book brings together the "best of the best" when it comes to research and best practice on purpose, leadership, engagement and performance. It is exactly the right book to read to seize the huge opportunity for productivity improvement across the UK. It is a masterpiece on values, the value of purpose and the importance of inspirational leadership in creating successful enterprise. Kevin offers a reminder of the immense power of audacious goals and the huge attraction of thriving over survival. A book full of great ideas, great examples and practical advice. This is a textbook on how to succeed as a leader in the 21st century, and is fun to read.'
Paul Drechsler, CBE, President of the Confederation of British Industry

'Kevin Murray's new book is needed now more than ever. In uncertain times the best way for leaders to navigate is to find their own "North Star" and help their people to do the same. *People with Purpose* shows you how to do just that. A must-read.'
Ann Francke, Chief Executive of the Chartered Management Institute

'Wow. What a tour de force! I couldn't put it down and have re-read it a second time with so many great ideas to implement. If you want to lead with purpose, gain competitive advantage, and have a highly engaged workforce, this is the book for you!'
Sir Eric Peacock, Chairman, Just Loans plc and Buckley Jewellery

'I have never been a great reader of books on management as I've always found them heavy on theory and short on real-world experience. To thrive today you need people with purpose. This book shows you how effective leaders develop people with purpose. It's not a book of theory... it's a book of practice from the mouths of leaders who have done it. It's a practical guide to leadership and empowerment. It's a book I wish I could have read 30 years ago.'
Lord Rose, Chairman of Ocado

'Purpose is a very fashionable word in marketing today, but what is really meant by it, and how do you make it work for your brand? Kevin Murray's book uncovers its many layers of meaning and gives a valuable practical guide to making it work for your organization. As he says, a well-crafted purpose will act as a guiding star for your brand and give it an unfair competitive advantage in three ways: it will focus the company on serving the customer, it will motivate staff to deliver the customer benefit, and it will give it an unfair competitive advantage with holders.'
Hugh Burkitt, Chief Executive of the Marketing Society

'The 21st century has truly begun with the realization that shareholder value long-term can only be created through stakeholder value – so purpose matters and value can only be created by people driven and energized by purpose. Kevin impressively brings this all together linking value and values with engagement and behaviours, bound by purpose.'
Tony Manwaring, Executive Vice President of the Chartered Institute of Management Accountants

'Kevin has once again produced a well-researched, thoughtful and stimulating contribution which enriches our understanding of good management and brilliant leadership. As Chair of the All-Party Parliamentary Group, I would love to be able to use this as compulsory reading for all parliamentarians.'
Barry Sheerman MP, UK Parliament

'All my experience from 40 years of leadership across multiple organizations, large and small, plcs and private equities, charities as well as corporates, in the UK, the US and elsewhere, tells me that Kevin's messages in this book are fundamental and absolutely right. It's a must-read for all leaders, current and aspiring, who want to deliver superior performance. It remains deeply depressing how few leaders really do understand the concepts discussed by Kevin.'
Philip N Green, CBE, Chairman, Carillion and BakerCorp

'*People with Purpose* is an inspiring, fresh and lucid account of how strong values can be transformative of the performance of diverse organizations, improving profitability of businesses, increasing effectiveness of service delivery and nurturing unrealized talent. It is an optimistic book that is even more relevant amid national and global uncertainty. *People with Purpose* serves as a challenging route map to more resilience by doing and being better.'
Baroness Tessa Jowell

'Profit alone isn't enough. *People with Purpose* brings alive the need for clear and consistent application of purpose, values and goals in enabling businesses to realize their potential and prosper far into the future. Kevin's assessment is a very practical one, draws on the experience of many business leaders and provides a framework to help leaders motivate and inspire their people. This is an upbeat book, full of insights which will be indispensable to business leaders grappling with profound changes in society and committed to building great businesses for the long term.'
Ian Durant, Chairman, Greggs and Capital & Counties Properties plc

'Kevin serves up a secret sauce for 21st-century business in a rich read that inspires and equips. In the process, he reminds us all that even, and especially, in the business world, it's our humanity that wins. This timely read advances the global purpose movement from talk to walk.'
Valerie Keller, Global lead, EY Beacon Institute, Executive Director, Global Markets, Ernst and Young

People with Purpose

How great leaders use purpose to build thriving organizations

Kevin Murray

KoganPage

Publisher's note

Every possible effort has been made to ensure that the information contained in this book is accurate at the time of going to press, and the publishers and authors cannot accept responsibility for any errors or omissions, however caused. No responsibility for loss or damage occasioned to any person acting, or refraining from action, as a result of the material in this publication can be accepted by the editor, the publisher or the author.

First published in Great Britain and the United States in 2017 by Kogan Page Limited

2nd Floor, 45 Gee Street	c/o Martin P Hill Consulting	4737/23 Ansari Road
London	122 W 27th St, 10th Floor	Daryaganj
EC1V 3RS	New York, NY 10001	New Delhi 110002
United Kingdom	USA	India

www.koganpage.com

ISBN   978 0 7494 7695 3
E-ISBN   978 0 7494 7696 0

British Library Cataloguing-in-Publication Data

A CIP record for this book is available from the British Library.

Library of Congress Cataloging-in-Publication Control Number

2016046149

Typeset by Graphicraft Limited, Hong Kong
Print production managed by Jellyfish
Printed and bound by CPI Group (UK) Ltd, Croydon CR0 4YY

Purpose

Noun

1. the reason for which something is done or created or for which something exists.
   Synonyms: Motive, Motivation, Cause, Reason, Basis.

2. a person's sense of resolve or determination.
   Synonyms: Determination, Resoluteness, Resolve, Backbone, Drive, Enthusiasm, Ambition, Commitment, Conviction, Dedication.

Verb

1. have as one's intention or objective.
   Synonyms: Intend, Mean, Aim, Plan, Design.

CONTENTS

PART TWO People with purpose: How leaders use purpose in their own organizations   105

07   From surviving to thriving: The importance of a long-term vision   107

08   Authentic purpose: Start with the customer to truly engage with people inside and outside your organization   123

13   **The purpose framework: How to create the tool that gives everyone in your team a sense of purpose**   227

The resources   245

PREFACE

This book is about how great leaders use purpose to power super performance. It is not only about purpose, or the importance of purpose, it is also about the wider concept of what it takes to give people a *sense of purpose*.

It shows how leaders create value when they align purpose with culture and stretching goals, and it explains why a sense of purpose is derived from the *combination* of values, purpose and goals.

Leaders who make purpose the beating heart of their organizations create more engaged employees, more committed customers and more supportive stakeholders. By doing this, they create greater value, as well as thriving businesses, communities and environments. In the following chapters you will learn how to think about purpose, articulate purpose and use purpose to align your organization and create the conditions for success.

If you have to lead, then this book is for you. It is for leaders of large businesses, divisions of those businesses, and small teams in those businesses. It is for people who aspire to be leaders in any organization, big or small. It is for entrepreneurs who are setting out in business, for people leading teams in the public sector, and leaders in the world of charity.

As you will see in various chapters in this book, leaders everywhere are paying more attention to purpose, and increasingly understand how and why their purpose must be more widely beneficial than simply to make a profit and provide a return to shareholders. Of course, making a profit is crucial, but awareness is growing that today you have to create value for a wider range of stakeholders, and clearly communicate what that value is, if you want to continue to grow.

You will see that businesses that express their purpose in a way that shows how they improve people's lives do much better than their peers. One study shows that companies that have done this have outperformed their peers by 400 per cent. One reason is because employees with purpose are more motivated, and deliver better results. Leaders who make people's work meaningful, and make their people feel worthy, inspire their people to be more passionate, engaged and flourishing employees, driven to make a difference.

Giving people a sense of purpose *is* a leader's role – no matter whether you lead a small team or a global organization. Employees want this most of all. However, all my research tells me that most leaders are poor at doing this.

The book provides research behind why purpose is so effective – for individuals, teams and organizations. It looks at the work of neuroscientists, brings together the evidence from around the world that proves purpose powers performance, and shows why purpose matters more in a digitally connected and transparent world. You will see how employee engagement is key to better results, and how much there is to gain by improving your ability to engage people and create a positive culture. Organizations with a shared sense of purpose outperform those with no sense of purpose, on both hard, financial measures and soft, intangible measures. Businesses with top-quartile engagement scores deliver growth that is 2.5 times greater than those with scores in the bottom quartile.

More than 30 chief executive officers (CEOs) from a wide range of companies have been interviewed for this book, and they tell their own stories about how they have used a purpose framework as a 'North Star' for long- and short-term decision making. They talk about how purpose has encouraged their people to look for solutions that deliver durable value and returns. These are leaders who have used powerfully articulated purpose statements to bring companies back from the brink of collapse, or rapidly grow businesses into global giants, or simply enable their organizations to thrive over long periods of time.

They describe how purpose has helped them to transform performance, motivate people through meaning, not fear, and create cultures of high energy and high performance, often from the very edge of disaster. These leaders share how they have articulated their purpose, their values and their goals.

I find that when you combine purpose, values and goals into an integrated framework, and communicate it all on a single page, you create a powerful tool that can help you to deliver a more agile, empowered, energized and aligned organization – the prerequisites of high performance.

At the end of the book, I provide a framework that you can use to better articulate your vision, values and purpose, and create your own compelling purpose framework. With this framework, you can communicate purpose in ways that inspire super performance.

Every leader, at whatever level, needs this tool to succeed.

Introduction: Lives transformed by purpose

From people in prison to people with purpose

My first meal in jail was an extraordinary affair, and a great deal more tasty than I had been anticipating.

Apart from the fact that it was behind a heavily locked door, in a windowless room, behind several layers of high-security fencing, as well as a daunting number of bars and secure gates, it was just like being in a restaurant! The decor in the room was elegant and quietly understated. The tables were perfectly laid. The room felt clean, bright and comfortable. There were views of the kitchen so that we could watch the food being prepared and cooked.

I was served by other occupants of the jail, and ordered a full three-course meal. The food had been prepared by the inmates themselves and, from the taste and appearance of the meal, they were talented chefs. They were also courteous and attentive waiters. It very much felt like a top contemporary restaurant.

The menu provided around five choices for the starters, the main course and dessert, with a choice of meat, vegetarian and fish dishes. Many of the ingredients were grown in the prison as part of a project teaching horticultural skills to prisoners. The only differences that I could detect from a normal restaurant were the fact that we had to use plastic cutlery and, of course, there was no wine or alcohol, and no cash.

Before entering the prison, we were searched for anything that might be a weapon. For the same reason, no metal cutlery is allowed, and this complicates the menu. Nothing that requires a metal knife can be served, so the chefs concentrate on slow-cooked dishes such as shoulder of lamb and mutton hotpot.

Some of the prisoners who were cooking and dishing up the food were serving sentences of 5–10 years. I was in HM Prison High Down, a Category B local prison on the outskirts of Banstead in Surrey, England. Its catchment area comprises Croydon and Guildford Crown Courts and surrounding magistrates' courts.

Category B prisons in Britain house people serving sentences for offences involving violence, threat to life, firearms, robbery, drugs and sex crimes. They will be sent here, rather than to a Category A jail, because it will have been judged that, for a variety of reasons, they do not require the highest level of security but still need a high level in order to make any chance of escape from prison extremely difficult.

Lest there be any confusion, I was there as a guest, taken to experience a unique dining occasion by some close friends who kept it a surprise from me until we arrived. They had intrigued me by insisting that I bring with me my passport, which we had to show on arrival. Our mobile phones and other items that posed a security risk were taken from us and kept in a secure locker while we went in to the prison. Our friends had to book at least 72 hours prior to arrival, and were warned that we might need to have our fingerprints and photographs taken.

I must admit that the process of entering the prison and getting to the restaurant was a daunting experience. We were led, slowly, through a series of fences, gates, heavily bolted doors and containment areas, across a court-yard and into a room where we were invited to take our seats at a table. The door was locked behind us.

We were in The Clink, a fine-dining restaurant run by The Clink Charity and HM Prison Service, following a concept proposed by renowned chef Alberto Crisci, who previously worked at the Mirabelle restaurant in London. The Clink launched in May 2009 and is one of four training restaurants run by The Clink Charity, along with a horticulture scheme and an event caterer.

At the time of writing, more than 500 prisoners have graduated from The Clink's training projects, after working and training for at least 40 hours per week during the last 18 months of their detention. Through all of these schemes, the charity has more than 150 positions available each year, with the express design of rehabilitating prisoners through training them in cooking, cleaning and front-of-house service, and then placing graduates into the hospitality industry upon their release from prison. The project has received many different awards.

As a training centre, each restaurant offers prisoners training in true-to-life work experience while gaining nationally recognized City and Guilds qualifications. The Clink at HM High Down currently holds the Best Overall

Restaurant award in *Time and Leisure* magazine. You can find restaurant reviews on TripAdvisor.com.

Chris Moore is chief executive of The Clink Charity, which is based at HMP High Down. He says that what inspired him to join was the role in reducing reoffending rates, which in 2009 were still running at 57 per cent. He says:

> 'The restaurant environment is very different from normal prison life, which means the prisoners don't act like they are in prison. They work eight hours a day over a 40-hour week. They have to wear a uniform, and they have to learn to work together. It is about challenging public perception – prisoners look like you and I.
>
> Because of the success of The Clink, we now have other restaurants at HMP Cardiff and HMP Brixton and a fourth has just opened at HMP Styal in Cheshire – the first in a woman's prison. By 2017 we aim to have 10 sites in the UK, releasing more than 500 prisoners a year.'

The Clink Charity runs a five-step programme: they recruit, train, support, employ and mentor. Trainees are carefully recruited from prisoners with 6–18 months left on their sentence. They work towards qualifications in food preparation, front-of-house service and industrial cleaning. The Clink puts them in contact with potential employers, helping them with their CVs and disclosure letters. They have a pool of about 200 employers with whom they work, from contract caterers and high-street chains to hotels and high-class restaurants.

Most importantly, members of the charity meet their trainees at the gates of the prison when they are released and mentor them afterwards. They are with them for the 18 months before their release and the first 12 on the outside. This, says Chris Moore, is key to the success of the programme.

Lives transformed

Case studies published on The Clink's website demonstrate just how much of a positive effect their work has on individuals, whose lives might otherwise have run an entirely different, and negative, course.

One example is that of Michael, 25 years old, who was serving his second sentence. The first was for common theft at the age of 17, and the second was for burglary. After a troubled childhood and a life of petty theft as a teenager, Michael found his salvation through The Clink Charity. The support that he received transformed his life. This ranged from workshops designed to improve his confidence and motivation, interview practice and techniques, and knowledge of the hospitality industry, to tours or taster days at top London hotels, and group activities and events that enabled students to network and engage with top hoteliers within the industry.

Given a second chance at life, Michael's enthusiasm and determination to make a better life for himself, his girlfriend and his son was exceptional. Michael's current boss says of him: 'I do not want to lose Michael. He is fantastic and just what I'm looking for. I want to employ him permanently for sure, 100 per cent absolutely fantastic!'

Tony, whose story is also published on the charity's website, says that as a direct result of all the help and support he received at The Clink he now has confidence, direction, social skills and is much more comfortable in intense social situations. His plan is to use the training he has had in order to learn as much as he can and progress within the catering and hospitality industry: 'I hope one day to open my own restaurant and club, now that I have seen what is achievable through hard work.'

Both Michael and Tony have had their lives transformed. Latest reports show that reoffending rates among prisoners who have gone through The Clink's programme have dropped to 5 per cent from the original 57 per cent. That is not only good for them but it is also good for society. Reoffending is one of the most pressing challenges facing society today. If you can reduce reoffending rates, you reduce the number of crimes committed and the associated costs to society. Less crime means fewer victims. Everyone wins.

As the prisoners themselves say, going through the programme represents a new life, a new direction and a new purpose.

A new purpose

My visit to HMP High Down inspired me. After having written two books about inspiring leadership communication, it struck me during my visit that the power of having a purpose in life was transformative. If individuals could have their lives so dramatically and positively changed, what could having a powerful purpose do for businesses?

If The Clink Charity has the power to transform lives and provide such a benefit to society, could inspiring purpose deliver the same effect for companies and for the economies of countries?

What would that mean for the leaders of companies who took the time and effort to articulate and share an inspiring purpose with all employees and with all external stakeholders? Would it help to create long-term value?

Would it give companies a competitive edge? How, exactly, would it engage employees to work harder, be more empowered and achieve more?

I have now found that most organizations do have a purpose, and for the vast majority it tends to be a profit-based purpose. While this may be engaging for shareholders, and perhaps for company boards, such a purpose is highly unlikely to motivate the workforce and encourage the right behaviours and culture in the organization. Far from it, sometimes a pure profit-based purpose can encourage destructive short-term behaviours that damage the long-term interests of the organization and its shareholders.

After my visit to HMP High Down, the more I thought about it the more I became intrigued with a simple question: what is the value of purpose, and what, really, is the purpose of values? In the months since then I have interviewed more than 30 CEOs of a wide range of organizations, asking them about how purpose and values have helped them in their leadership. These are leaders who have used powerfully articulated purpose statements to bring companies back from the brink of collapse to rapidly grow businesses into global giants, or to enable their organizations to thrive over long periods of time.

In addition, I have spent months researching the subject, exploring neuroscience, speaking to a wide range of think tanks, leadership institutions, management organizations, accountancy associations, talent development and workplace organizations, and employee engagement specialists. I have invested my own money in researching more than 2,000 employees and 1,800 managers on the subject.

Purpose delivers business value

From the research I have undertaken I conclude that, when articulated and communicated the right way, a compelling purpose that is truly shared by all employees delivers significant business value, for large and small companies alike. When also aligned to strong and true values, the right purpose enables leaders to create cultures that will help them to thrive now and well into the future.

Whether you are the CEO of a large organization, a leader of a division of that business, or a leader of a small team, the benefits are the same and the principles are the same. Shared purpose and powerful values help to deliver mutually beneficial relationships, strong reputations and more trust and credibility – all endangered species at a time of hyper-transparency and lightning speed, brought about by the digital revolution and social media.

In a world in which intangible assets are now the most critical drivers of future value, how should leaders at all levels and seniority think about purpose and communicate it in ways that will inspire super performance? We have a global productivity challenge and, in Europe, with the impending exit of Britain from the European Union, this now becomes one of the most important economic challenges to solve. This can be done only through more engaged and committed employees, inspired to do so because they have a compelling sense of purpose.

In my research I have discovered that there is a growing conversation about the importance of purpose, and about the importance of finding ways to measure and manage intangible assets such as company culture, relationships, reputation, talent, knowledge and engagement. Leadership itself is a vastly valuable intangible asset.

What can we learn from leaders who started and are now growing their businesses with a strong sense of purpose? What do we learn from leaders who have brought their companies back from the brink? And what about those leaders who have managed to sustain their success for decades?

Perhaps the most inspiring quote I found on the subject came from Dee Hock, the founder and former CEO of Visa International, a giant in the credit card industry. The business he created in 1970 is now 10,000 per cent bigger, and continues to expand at more than 20 per cent per year. Today it operates in some 200 countries worldwide and includes 22,000 member banks and 750 million customers. Its annual transactions reach US$1.25 trillion.

Dee says: 'Money motivates neither the best people, nor the best in people. It can move the body and influence the mind, but it cannot touch the heart or move the spirit; that is reserved for belief, principle and morality.'

Dee has huge faith in the power of purpose. He says: 'Simple, clear purpose and principles give rise to complex, intelligent behaviour. Complex rules and regulations give rise to simple, stupid behaviour.'

He's right. Too many rules and regulations kill off initiative and that, in turn, leads to employees behaving in ways they know are unproductive, unhelpful or wrong, because they know it is impossible to free themselves of the constraints that chain them to those behaviours. In contrast, a powerful purpose and a strong set of values liberates people throughout your organization to be leaders. It enables them to make decisions when their own leaders are not around, confident that they are on mission and sticking to the principles of the organization. They need this framework if they are to perform at the very highest level.

With the right purpose, values and goals your people will be more engaged, more committed and much more likely to give of their discretionary effort in helping you to achieve your goals. Every metric that I have seen shows that companies that create shared purpose, and then communicate regularly about purpose and values, with engaging leaders, outperform their competitors by some margin.

So, how can you think about purpose, values and goals and best deliver them in your team or organization? How can you best give your people what they need to help you succeed? That is the purpose of this book.

Next: why you need to think more about the chemistry of the brain.

PART ONE
Why purpose is central to performance

'Simple, clear purpose and principles give rise to complex, intelligent behaviour. Complex rules and regulations give rise to simple, stupid behaviour.'

DEE HOCK, FOUNDER AND FORMER CEO
OF VISA INTERNATIONAL

Effective leadership

01

It's all in the mind

Leaders who put relationships and purpose before results enable their people to perform better. Why? Because having a sense of purpose and belonging, and being respected, makes you feel worthy, changes your brain chemistry and that changes everything – from your perception of pain, your ability to handle difficult and challenging environments, and even your health and well-being.

Understanding more about how our brains work will help leaders to be more inspiring.

When people find a sense of purpose, and begin to dream and chase positive goals, the benefits are limitless. They change themselves, they better their families, they improve their communities, they help their organizations and companies to perform better, they help to create wealth and prosperity, and they contribute to society in a wide range of ways.

It was for this reason that I became obsessed with the question: how is it that prisoners who spent time on The Clink's programme were able to transform their lives so radically, and achieve such positive effects all around them?

Yes, I know it was because they had a renewed sense of purpose, and were given a lot of help. But *what* was it about having a purpose that had such a positive effect on these individuals? I have always understood that how we feel determines how we perform. But isn't how we feel an emotion? And isn't an emotional mental state a biological reaction to stimuli? Who would know more about this? Who could I go to for a better understanding?

The answer, of course, is neuroscientists – the people who study the nervous system and the brain, especially in relation to behaviour and learning.

Why? Because research being done around the world in neuroscience is beginning to piece together connections between the brain and behaviour, especially at work. This research is providing valuable insights into how to be a more effective leader. Understanding how our brains function, and the chemicals they release, is vital to delivering our strategies successfully.

More specifically, what do scientists know about our brains and giving people a sense of purpose? Do they have insights that we can take into our own organizations and the teams we lead? These are the questions that led me to Dr Duncan Banks, a lifetime honorary member of the British Neuroscience Association and also director of work-based learning at the Open University in Milton Keynes. Why him? Because Dr Banks is one of Britain's leading neuroscientists.

Dr Banks says:

> 'Purpose is most often derived from a willingness to take part in activities for the greater good of the community. It is all a matter of whether you feel worthy or worthless.
>
> Jails are places of minimal engagement and minimal enrichment, so any effort to give people a greater sense of purpose, and a greater sense of a positive role in society, will be more enriching and have a positive effect. Make them feel worthy and they will try harder.'

We are, he says, communal animals and we became even more communal as we developed communication skills:

> 'We know that enrichment has a big part to play in brain development from an early stage, even for babies. Give them a rich environment in which they develop and you'll find they develop into better individuals. If you put someone into an un-rich, worthless environment, they are very likely to go downhill and not be able to contribute, whether this is in a business or in a community.'

Purpose changes your brain chemistry

'When you have a sense of purpose, especially a sense of common purpose, your brain chemistry changes. These chemicals change everything – from your perception of pain, your ability to handle difficult and challenging environments, and even your health and well-being', says Dr Banks.

One such chemical is a hormone called oxytocin (released by neurons in the brain), which goes into the bloodstream following positive social interactions and has a positive effect on the whole body. Studies have shown that oxytocin has the potential to improve wound healing, by reducing inflammation. Increased levels of oxytocin can decrease feelings of anxiety and protect against stress, particularly in combination with social support. It has a powerful effect on prosocial behaviours and has also been proved to increase levels of trust and reduce levels of fear.

'For all these reasons, leaders need to think about whether they make their employees feel worthless or worthy', says Dr Banks:

> 'Do they make their employees feel a sense of common purpose, and part of a community? Do leaders communicate in the right way, involving people and listening to them, as well as persuading and encouraging them? Only by communicating effectively, can leaders make their employees feel worthy and respected.
>
> The positive side effect will always be an increase in performance, because people who feel worthy are much more likely to give of their discretionary effort when called on to work harder.'

Striving to find a meaning in one's life is the most primary and most powerful motivating and driving force in humans. But how do you measure this?

In 1964, psychologists James Crumbaugh and Leonard Maholick developed a 'Purpose-in-Life' scale, probably the most widely used measure of purpose in the world.

Purpose – values – goals

Crumbaugh and Maholick's Purpose-in-Life scale is based on three dimensions. First, it is about believing that life does have a purpose. Second, it is about upholding a personal value system. Third, it is about having the motivation to achieve future goals and overcome future challenges.

Questions in the Purpose-in-Life test are designed to discover whether a person has an 'existential void' – a lack of meaning or purpose in their life, or high levels of motivation and a strong sense of being worthy.

There are many other scales produced by psychologists to measure whether people have a sense of meaning in life, including, for example, the Ryff Scales of Psychological Well-Being, formulated by researcher Carol Ryff of the University of Wisconsin Madison. She says: 'As a psychologist, I approach optimal ageing in terms of what key ingredients comprise healthy mental functioning. Our studies focus on six dimensions of well-being: autonomy, environmental mastery, personal growth, positive relations with others, purpose in life and self-acceptance.'

Her Purpose-in-Life scale has been demonstrated to relate consistently to a wide variety of well-being and other psychological variables, including life satisfaction, morale, happiness and self-esteem.

Why all this scientific interest in purpose?

Scientists now say that having a higher purpose in life can have dramatic effects on your health in a number of ways. It prevents strokes, reduces the risk of heart attacks and protects from Alzheimer's and other forms of dementia. It is linked to reducing depression and has many positive health benefits including better mental health, happiness, personal growth and self-acceptance, better sleep and even longevity.

One particular study, by Dr David Bennett, director of the memory and ageing unit at the Rush Medical Centre in Chicago, found that a person with a high Purpose-in-Life score was approximately 2.4 times more likely to remain free of Alzheimer's disease.

Purpose also matters to the young

The so-called millennial generation now rank finding work that is meaningful as one of the top three factors determining their career success, with 30 per cent of millennials ranking purpose as the most important factor. The word 'millennials' applies to the cohort of people born between 1980 and the mid-2000s, most of whom are at the beginning of their careers and so will be an important engine of the economy in the decades to come. They are willing to make less money and work longer, non-traditional hours, as long as their work is personally meaningful. This was the finding of a study by the career advisory board at De Vry University, an online university in the United States.

So, being happy and purposeful at work really matters. Happy and engaged people are much more productive workers and will work both harder and smarter. That's the leader's job – to engage people and give them a greater sense of purpose. How well are leaders doing this job?

Alarmingly, studies in the UK and the United States, backed up by studies in other countries of the world, show that large numbers of employees are disengaged from their work. These people are toxic at work and create havoc among their colleagues and for their leaders. Studies by Gallup show that employee engagement has remained largely constant over the years despite economic ups and downs. Too few people are really engaged with their work and too many have not been for a very long time.

And yet, as Dr Banks says, if you can give people a sense of purpose that inspires them, and help them to feel part of a group that has a common interest, you can work wonders as a leader.

Neuroscience is all about what helps our brains to perform at their best. It brings essential insights to any leader with an interest in hitting targets, improving innovation and collaboration, and creating a high-performance culture in the organization.

So, what will help our brains to think and perform at their best at work? The answer: more inspiring and engaging leaders, who have a much greater focus on how their employees feel. I am a huge fan of the work of David MacLeod and Nita Clarke, who produced a report called 'Engaging for success'. Their work is on display at engageforsuccess.org.

In 2008, John Hutton, the UK's then Secretary of State for Innovation and Skills, commissioned David MacLeod and Nita Clarke to write a report answering three questions: what is employee engagement? Is there evidence to suggest it matters? And what were the things present in organizations that were successfully engaging their people?

As it turned out, there were four things:

1 A powerful strategic narrative that provided line of sight between the employee's activity and the organization's goals. (Organizations that have a sense of purpose, a strong narrative and have spent time communicating this have more engaged employees.)

2 Engaging managers who facilitate, empower, recognize and respect their employees.

3 Employees who are encouraged to speak up and contribute and whose views are respected and acted on by their bosses.

4 Integrity, which means that the espoused and actual values match at all levels in the organization.

Avoid threat, find reward

Leaders who encourage their people to work for a positive purpose are aligning themselves with how the brain works, and this increases their chances of success. Our brains are wired to either avoid threat or move to reward. Avoiding threat produces all the wrong brain chemicals and behaviours. And yet leaders put their people in this situation every day, either inadvertently or deliberately.

Hilary Scarlett, a UK-based consultant and author on change management and neuroscience, is currently conducting research into applied neuroscience with four major organizations in the private and public sectors in the UK. Hilary has also been working with Professor Walsh of University College

London to apply cognitive neuroscience to practical management tools. Her work has spanned Europe, the United States and Asia and concentrates on the development of people-focused change management programmes, coaching and employee engagement.

She says that the fundamental organizing principle of the brain is to avoid threat and find reward. Although our brains have evolved, we still fundamentally have the same brain as our prehistoric ancestors. Their brains were wired to help them survive. When faced with the choice of facing a threat or achieving a reward, it is much more important to avoid threats:

'Our brains are prediction machines. They want to be able to predict and make sense of what is going on around us. Change, by its very nature, prevents our brains from predicting, and ambiguity is even worse: our brains really don't know what to make of it.

All this means that the brain moves away from threats and towards rewards. When confronted with a threat, you become distracted, anxious, you see colleagues as more hostile, deliver a poor performance, and have a weakened immune system. When you are more positive and moving towards reward, you are more focused, more willing to collaborate, more able to learn, more innovative and creative, more willing to get involved and make a difference and, physically, you have increased resilience.'

How does Hilary's work relate to the four drivers of engagement espoused by David MacLeod and Nita Clarke? These are:

1 a powerful, purposeful narrative;

2 engaging managers;

3 an employee voice;

4 strong, consistent values.

A powerful, purposeful narrative

Having a strong sense of purpose and a clear set of goals enables people to make more sense of what to expect, and therefore predict better, says Hilary:

'Aligned to the need to predict, our brains crave certainty. It matters that we have a line of sight between our activity and the organizational purpose as it provides a sense of being valued and of status, because our work matters and makes a difference. Feeling valued puts our brains into a positive mind set.

Research has demonstrated that for most people, doing something meaningful means doing something meaningful *for others*. Strategic narrative is important to employee engagement, but one that describes how employees are helping others is all the more powerful.'

Engaging managers

Our survival instinct drives our need to connect, Hilary explains, which is why engaging managers are crucial:

> 'From our first moments out of the womb, we are wired to check that there is someone to look out for us. This need to connect stays with us throughout our lives and this includes in the workplace. Our brains are constantly checking whether we are accepted or rejected, whether we are part of the in group or the out group. When we are accepted, our brains are in the towards state and are able to do all the good things that the state enables. It is in the interest of every manager to make sure members of the team feel part of the group. Most organizations pay far too little attention to the fact that our brains are wired to be social.'

An employee voice

One of our deepest needs is to have some control, or at least a perception of control, over our environment, says Hilary. If we have no control, we are helpless and, in prehistoric times, unlikely to survive. In our 21st-century brains, lack of autonomy leads to higher levels of stress: 'There are many studies that show that we have better health and live longer when we have some influence. This is how neuroscience provides evidence as to why having a voice matters, and is essential to employee engagement. Employees who are given a voice feel that they have some influence over their environment.'

Strong, consistent values

Finally, Hilary explains why organizational integrity – where espoused and actual values match – is another crucial element for employees:

> 'Neuroscience identifies the negative impact of uncertainty on our brain. If we are told one thing, but see action supporting a contrary value, this creates uncertainty which leads to a threat state. Having integrity is about fairness, and having a fair share of food and of warmth from the fire, is a basic survival instinct.
>
> Neuroscience underpins the importance of a higher purpose for companies. But it also makes the case for engaging managers who make employees feel part of a team, who explain why employees are important, who live the values of the organization and respect how employees contribute to the organization's goals.
>
> One of the benefits of neuroscience is that it brings the language of science to managers who might otherwise think that employee engagement is soft and fluffy stuff. The challenge for leaders is how to create a brain-friendly workplace – one in which employees are excited by their work and willing to give greater discretionary effort.'

Inside the brains of leaders

Richard Boyatzis is an American organizational theorist and a distinguished professor of organizational psychology and cognitive science at Case Western Reserve University in the United States. He is an expert in the field of emotional intelligence and behaviour change.

He says that advances in functional magnetic resonance imaging (fMRI) have made it possible to venture physiologically inside leaders and followers to understand what is happening in their brains during leadership interactions:

> 'Such studies have shown the first and most important thing that leaders need to do is build relationships and, through those, inspire and motivate others to do their best, to innovate and adapt. Leaders who build resonant relationships with others around them will perform far better than dissonant leaders, who seem to turn people off and alienate them and cause them to lose their motivation. These neuroscience findings suggest a basic reason why these inspiring relationships are important – they help activate openness to new ideas and a more social orientation to others.'

Professor Boyatzis hopes these insights may move the emphasis of many leaders' actions away from the often used 'results orientation' leadership towards a greater focus on relationships: 'This does not preclude a concern with the results, but is focused first and foremost on one's relationships that enable others to perform better and more innovatively – and lead to better results.'

He explains that the emotional state of leaders is like a contagion that affects all of those around them, even when leaders are trying their best to hide their negative emotions. Negative emotions are far stronger than positive ones and ignite a stronger neural sequence in followers:

> 'If you believe that leadership involves inspiring others and motivating them to be their best and develop, learn, adapt and innovate, then activating the parts of their brain that will help requires arousing what we call the positive emotional attractor (PEA). To arouse their PEA, our studies are suggesting that we need to be social and engage our followers in positive, hopeful contemplation of the desired future.
>
> Positive emotions might also be stimulated when discussing core values and the purpose of the organization. All too often, people in leadership positions begin with conversations about the financial metrics and dashboard measures of the desired performance. Our research findings suggested that

while important, this sequence confuses people and actually results in them closing down cognitively, emotionally and perceptually.'

Measures follow purpose, and must not become the purpose, he suggests: 'If you want them to open their minds, you need to discuss the purpose of the activity (not merely the goals) and the vision of the organization. Then, you can lead a discussion about the financial metrics and measures. But you have to make it clear that the measures follow the purpose, they have not become the purpose.'

The big take out from this research? Measures follow purpose, and must not become the purpose. Profit is a measure of success, not the purpose of all enterprise.

How to build inspired motivation

Marcelo Manucci has a doctorate in communication sciences. He is a psychologist based in Turin, and also has postgraduate training in cognitive neuroscience and in systemic therapy and psychodrama. He says leaders should focus on achieving an emotional stake in employees that he calls 'inspired motivation'.

Dr Manucci says that when employees are in this state they have a positive outlook and are keen to open up possibilities and even greater inspiration. They believe their initiative and engagement will influence the course of events at the company. This is the face of creativity and commitment, he says.

His research suggests that managers need to use a four-part approach to building inspired motivation. First, you have to communicate the goals and purpose of the organization and the value of coexistence with each employee. Second, you have to build emotional capital and the level of trust and security with each other in order to cooperate and collaborate effectively. This is why the need to strengthen diversity and integrate points of view from different genders, ages and philosophies (while maintaining an environment of respect) is critical.

Thirdly, he says, it is crucial to share the value of contributions. The work must have meaning beyond just making money and the employee's contribution needs to be seen as valuable by others in the company, especially the direct manager. It is vital to recognize the employee's participation and contribution in the development of the company's corporate purpose.

Finally, he says, it is important to encourage employee perceptions that they can be agents of change, contributing significantly to the transformation of the life of others.

Words can change your brain

Leaders who are more emotionally intelligent also understand the need to choose their words with care when communicating. Neuroscience is now showing that our brains are wired to respond to certain kinds of speech, and ineffective or negative communication may change neural pathways in our brains and foster long-lasting negativity. Equally, positive language can transform our reality and encourage high levels of motivation.

Words can literally change your brain, say Dr Andrew Newberg and Mark Robert Waldman. Dr Newberg is a leading neuroscientist and a physician at Jefferson University Hospital in Philadelphia. Mark Waldman is one of the world's leading experts on communication, spirituality and the brain. He is on the faculty at Loyola Marymount University's College of business in Los Angeles.

In their book *Words Can Change Your Brain*, they write: 'Positive words can help promote the brain's cognitive functioning. They propel the motivational centres of the brain into action and build resilience.'

Conversely, hostile language disrupts genes that play a key part in the production of neurochemicals that protect us from stress. Humans are hardwired to worry, they say. This is part of our primal brains protecting us from threats, so our thoughts naturally go there first. Thus, even a single word can increase the activity in the fear centre of our brain and send alarm messages, which then shut down the logic and reasoning centres located in the frontal lobes.

Newberg and Waldman say that if you were to be put into an fMRI scanner and the word 'NO' was flashed in front of you for less than one second, there would be a sudden release of dozens of stress-producing hormones and neurotransmitters. These chemicals immediately interrupt the normal functioning of your brain, impairing logic, reason, language processing and communication.

The more you were shown negative words, the more stress would be put on key structures in the brain that regulate memory, happiness feelings and emotions. This would disrupt your sleep, your appetite, and your ability to experience long-term happiness and satisfaction.

Their advice: choose your words wisely and speak them slowly. This will allow you to interrupt the brain's propensity to be negative and, as recent research has shown, the mere repetition of positive words like love, peace and compassion will turn on specific genes that lower your physical and emotional stress. You will feel better, you will live longer, and you will build deeper and more trusting relationships with others – at home and at work.

Neuroscience is a great liberator for managers. It brings the language of science to their work and validates the need to pay greater attention to the 'soft' part of their jobs – because getting those soft things right makes it far, far easier to achieve their 'hard' measures and targets. The science shows that the more leaders focus on a purpose beyond profit, and the more they respect employees and give them a voice, as well as create a sense of community with a strong culture, the more likely they are to succeed.

Next: the growing global conversation on the benefits of purpose.

Key points from Chapter 1

1 Neuroscience is piecing together connections between the brain and behaviour, especially at work. Understanding how our brains function provides insights into how to be a more effective leader and is vital to achieving goals.

2 Any effort to give people a greater sense of purpose, and a greater sense of a positive role in society, will be more enriching and have a positive effect. Science says that if you make them feel worthy they will try harder.

3 Having a sense of purpose changes your brain chemistry, and has massively positive effects on your health, your relationships and even on your lifespan.

4 The best effects are achieved when you give employees a higher purpose, strong values and stretching goals. The three work together.

5 When you feel worthy you are more focused, more willing to collaborate, more able to learn, more innovative and creative, more willing to get involved and make a difference and, physically, you have increased resilience.

6 Neuroscience suggests that, for most people, doing something meaningful means doing something meaningful *for others*. Strategic narrative is important to employee engagement, but one that describes how employees are helping others is all the more powerful.

7 Having line of sight between what work we do, and the organizational purpose, matters. It shows how our work makes a difference, makes us feel valued, and puts our brains in a positive mind set.

▶

8   When leaders begin conversations about the metrics of an enterprise, they confuse people and cause them to close down cognitively, emotionally and perceptually. Start with purpose, THEN metrics.

9   Our brains are wired to respond to certain kinds of speech, and negative communication fosters long-lasting negativity. Positive language transforms our reality and encourages high levels of motivation. How purpose is phrased makes an enormous difference.

The purpose movement

02

A growing global conversation

More and more companies, governments, investors, institutions and think tanks are turning their attention to the benefits of purpose-led business. Research shows that having a purpose beyond profit improves performance and improves the way business is perceived by stakeholders – thus improving the conditions for long term success. At the same time, a global survey of citizens shows that 80 per cent of people believe businesses can both increase profits and improve the economic, social and environmental conditions in the communities in which they operate. Sadly, a majority of businesses still have a profit-based purpose, which does little to enthuse employees or customers.

In 2014, a concerned group of politicians from all parties in the UK got together with a range of business people and academics to look at the future of management and leadership, amid growing concerns about the country's productivity challenge.

They recognized that there was a global challenge to business around this issue – one in which billions of dollars were being lost because of low levels of engagement among employees, which not only cost companies in profits, but also cost governments and citizens of those countries. In the UK, the problem was acute and experts were saying that the country was losing £20 billion per year.

The All Party Parliamentary Group on Management (APPGM), working with the Chartered Management Institute (CMI), set up 'the commission on the future of management and leadership' to find solutions to a problem that weakened the UK's competitiveness and, if not tackled, threatened to curb economic growth rates.

The CMI is the leading authority on management and leadership in the UK, with a 130,000-strong membership. All party parliamentary groups are informal, cross-party interest groups that have no official status within Parliament and are not accorded any powers or funding by it. They are, however, hugely influential.

After the financial crisis of 2007–8 had plunged the UK economy into the doldrums and shattered trust in business leaders, companies that looked like world beaters teetered on the brink of collapse and a ferocious cost-cutting agenda was unleashed. This only reinforced the short-term outlook that seemed to have got the country into trouble in the first place. It was against this backdrop that the APPGM decided to found the commission.

The task? Investigate how management and leadership in the UK would need to change by 2020 to deliver sustainable economic growth.

The commission brought together members of both houses of Parliament, drawn from across the main parties, and united them with leaders from a wide range of business sectors. These members of the commission considered evidence from academic experts, vibrant entrepreneurs, up-and-coming young managers, and world-renowned business leaders. The commission was chaired by Peter Ayliffe, then president of the CMI, still chairman of the financial services company Monetise, and former chief executive of Visa Europe. It was co-chaired by Barry Sheerman, MP for Huddersfield and chair of the APPGM.

Peter Ayliffe said:

> 'From the evidence seen by this commission, it is clear that we are faced with a ticking time bomb of myopic management. We neglect the importance of sustainable growth in the long term in favour of cutting costs to deliver profits in the short term. Our managers are not encouraged to take risks or given space to be innovative. They bear a heavy responsibility for driving economic growth yet they are not given the training or coaching that they need to do their jobs properly. As a result, the UK falls short in the leadership stakes.'

The APPGM and the CMI published their report in July 2014: 'Management 2020: leadership for long-term growth'. It now provides the basis for a new campaign for a Better Managed Britain. It revealed the need for 1 million more, better skilled managers by 2020. When their report was launched the commission published an open letter to the media. In it, the two chairs said:

'We are at a tipping point. We must raise our sights to a longer-term global agenda. Those who cut costs and overheads seem to earn more respect for such hard-nosed decisions than those who take the riskier, more innovative paths that lead to growth in revenue, jobs and profits. This approach infects the public sector and social enterprise too, when financial targets are put before service delivery and creating social value.'

While cost and profit are important, said the commission chairs, we need management to create value for all stakeholders: shareholders, society and staff alike. Our future prosperity and global competitiveness depends on this: 'Boards must refocus on their organization's longer-term purpose, beyond just making money or meeting targets – and to set measurable commitments to customers, suppliers, employees, communities and the environment, as well as to investors.' The leaders' role: give employees a greater sense of purpose.

'Employees need to understand what their leaders are trying to do, why they are trying to do it and what it will achieve not only for the organization itself but also for the organization's wider stakeholders, including society in general', the commission said 'Only then will employees truly buy into a leader's vision.'

The commission found that employees were increasingly sceptical of their leaders' motivations and were increasingly inclined to demand higher levels of integrity than ever before. For this reason leaders and managers – even at a junior level – needed to demonstrate purpose and strong values and conduct themselves with high levels of integrity. Crucially, the commission found that even at a junior level, management was a leadership role. Individual managers need to take responsibility for the morale and sense of purpose of each person reporting to them. To do this they needed to develop a coaching style that was collaborative, open and fair, and supported the career development of their team.

Having the ability to communicate with a wide range of people was crucial to good leadership, the commission heard again and again. Managers did not just set the strategy and give guidance and instructions. They needed continually to engage with everyone who had to make the strategy happen. It meant communicating why something needed to happen, especially what difference proposed actions would make to end customers. Communication took place not just through words, but through actions.

It was the commission's view that high-performing organizations were characterized by a focus on long-term growth, a sense of purpose and strong values: 'Our evidence shows that companies that are committed to long-term growth, serve the customers effectively and treat their staff well, typically generate excellent returns for shareholders.'

The better they deliver purpose, the more profits

Ann Francke, chief executive of the CMI, comments:

> 'Purpose creates meaning and is essential for engaging your employees. It gives your customers a connection to your company and creates ties to communities. Purpose can be found in the smallest places. It is also found in the biggest.
>
> You don't want to lose your purpose. When you do, you might lose a lot more. Look at all the once-great organizations that have become tarnished by blunders. They lost their sense of direction because profit became more important than purpose, and their moral compass fell apart.
>
> Purpose works better than corporate social responsibility programmes, because rather than being an add-on, it is what they live for. It is also hooked up to the business model – the better they deliver the purpose, the more profits they make. So get your organization a purpose and make sure you do two more things. First, communicate your purpose often. Second, measure your progress against your purpose for each of your stakeholder groups every year.'

The CMI now has a wide range of resources available online to help leaders consider how well they are delivering purpose, developing their people and releasing potential (www.managers.org.uk/management2020).

How purpose-led business can help restore trust

All my research tells me that the purpose challenge is not confined to the UK. Across the world, organizations are investigating how a greater sense of social purpose can deliver better business results, while also creating thriving communities and helping to sustain the planet. In order to be given the licence to operate, business needs to do more to restore trust. Greater trust encourages collaboration, creativity, innovation and growth. A lack of trust encourages more rules and regulations, extra costs, complexity and slows decision making. Purpose has a critical role to play in regenerating trust.

Every year, Edelman, a leading global communications marketing firm, publishes a trust barometer. The company undertakes a survey of more than 33,000 respondents, across 28 countries. In January 2016, Edelman published the 16th annual trust and credibility survey. The global survey asks respondents how much they trust the four institutions of government, business, non-governmental organizations (NGOs) and the media, to do what is right.

Richard Edelman, president and CEO of Edelman, says that despite the general population's scepticism of business, it is business that has the best opportunity to bridge the trust chasm. Overall, respondents in the Edelman trust barometer view business as the institution most likely to keep pace with rapid change, far more than they do government and NGOs. Business is significantly more trusted than government in 21 out of 28 countries.

A decisive 80 per cent of people surveyed believe business can both increase its profits AND improve economic and social conditions in the communities in which it operates. 'The public is responding positively to CEOs trying to realize the dual mandate of profit and societal benefit, as CEO trust has risen substantially in the past five years to 48 per cent', says Richard.

A lack of trust has many negative consequences, but it also presents an opportunity for businesses that want differentiation and sustained growth. Trust is earned through common purpose. Having a purpose beyond profit clearly can improve the way a business is perceived by stakeholders and encourage support and collaboration. The trust barometer shows that 68 per cent of people surveyed reported having bought products or services from companies that exhibited trustworthy behaviours; 59 per cent recommended trusted businesses to friends or colleagues and more than 40 per cent shared positive opinions about them online; 37 per cent said they voluntarily paid more to buy from trusted companies and 18 per cent were motivated by shares in those businesses.

Purpose: an underutilized asset

Building trust is not the only benefit of purpose-led leadership. Global surveys of CEOs show that most now believe in the power of purpose to grow and transform their organizations. What they find hard is embedding purpose from top to bottom in their companies.

The World Economic Forum (WEF) is a Swiss non-profit foundation based in Cologny, Geneva. It is recognized by the Swiss authorities as an international institution for public and private cooperation. It is dedicated to improving the state of the world by engaging business, political, academic and other leaders of society to shape global, regional and industry agendas. The forum is best known for its annual winter meeting in Davos, a mountain resort in the eastern Alps region of Switzerland. The meeting brings together some 2,500 business, political and intellectual leaders with a range of journalists to discuss the most pressing issues facing the world.

It was in Davos that the EY Beacon Institute was launched in 2015. Designed as a collaborative, catalytic force to transform business, it is made up of a diverse community of executives, entrepreneurs and thought leaders. Its own purpose is to transform business through the science and execution of purpose.

Research commissioned by the EY Beacon Institute among 500 global business leaders, and conducted by Harvard Business Review Analytic Services (HBRAS), highlighted how global executives view the power of purpose to grow and transform their organizations. It also realized that purpose was a powerful but vastly underutilized asset.

The institute found that:

- *Most executives believe purpose matters*:
  - 89 per cent of executives surveyed said a strong sense of collective purpose drives employee satisfaction;
  - 84 per cent said it can affect an organization's ability to transform;
  - 80 per cent said it helps increase customer loyalty.
- *However, only a minority of executives said their company currently runs in a purpose-driven way*:
  - 46 per cent said their company has a strong sense of purpose;
  - 44 per cent say their company is trying to develop one.
- *Importantly, companies with a strong sense of purpose are able to transform and innovate better*:
  - 53 per cent of executives at companies with a strong sense of purpose said their organization is successful with innovation and transformation efforts;
  - just 19 per cent report transformation success at companies where leaders have not thought about purpose.

Valerie Keller, strategy executive director of Ernst and Young (EY is a global leader in assurance, tax, transaction and advisory services) and global leader of the EY Beacon Institute, says: 'The business environment today is in a permanent state of disruption. Far-reaching trends, disruptive challengers, rapidly changing consumer and employee expectations and declining levels of trust are changing the way business does business. There is a growing dialogue among business and thought leaders that a strong shared sense of purpose can help companies to meet these new challenges and transform their organizations.'

The EY Beacon Institute, in a report with the University of Oxford Said Business School, says there are five key trends at work. They are:

1 *An evolving view of the role of business as a partner for societal well-being.*

   'Business is both a source of shareholder value and a tool for addressing challenges', says their report. 'Across industries and geographies, this focus is a move beyond harm reduction – or the corporation taking responsibility for externalities – to now having an active role in creating well-being.' This tracks key shifts: from 'value creation for its own sake' to 'value creation without harm', to now actively 'building value for and with a wider set of stakeholders'.

2 *The corporate dialogue on purpose is louder and is changing.*

   While 'purpose' is certainly not new to conversations about commercial activity, more than ever it is dominating the conversation. There is an expansion from the traditional mission statement that predominantly focused on products and services (what companies do) and attributes such as trustworthiness and timeliness (how they do it) to corporations also articulating a broader purpose that is their reason for being (why they exist).

3 *Executives are using a common language of purpose to engage stakeholders.*

   Pioneering CEOs and other senior leaders are speaking a language of purpose that engages employees and customers in new ways, inviting their insights for innovation. This is a language of open-sourced value creation among diverse constituents. It foregrounds 'meaning' with an appeal to shared values that invite the extended group of stakeholders – employees, customers, suppliers, regulators and others – to recognize a stake in the growth path of a corporation. Making (shared) meaning in this way is critical work for leaders today.

4 *Purpose can be a lever driving innovation and transformation for growth.*
   These pioneering senior leaders are initiating purpose-led transformation journeys in their organizations, spanning from the brand identity through the business model, across business units and functions.

5 *There is an implementation gap: purpose is underleveraged to drive transformation.*

'A broad cross-section of business professionals report a gap between stating a shared purpose and the policy and practice in their organizations. Our research points to still uncharted territory where purpose reinforces innovation in offerings, business models and governance', says the EY Beacon Institute.

Purpose brings wide-ranging benefits

In the run-up to the 2016 meeting in Davos, Valerie Keller said there was mounting evidence of a strong and growing business case for purpose. Why? Valerie said:

'First, a clearly articulated aspirational purpose instills strategic clarity in a business. In our volatile, rapidly changing world, purpose serves as a "North Star" – a fixed point guiding both short- and long-term decision making, which helps determine what activities the business should, and should not, consider.

Second, when focused on a compelling bigger picture, purpose can encourage people to look beyond short-term considerations to look for solutions and innovations that will deliver durable value and returns. In this way, purpose helps channel innovation and keeps people focused on what matters.

Thirdly, purpose helps organizations transform themselves, motivates people through meaning, not fear, and helps people understand the need for change rather than feeling alienated by imposed change.

Fourthly, humans have an innate desire to contribute to something bigger; to find meaning in their lives and their work. Articulating a business's purpose helps people to see that they are working for something, rather than simply against the competition, tapping into a powerfully motivating universal need.

Finally, by showing where people and organizations share common ground, purpose also helps to build bridges, across business functions within organizations and between different organizations. This helps to create the collaboration that businesses so need in order to succeed in the 21st century.'

However, she says, moving purpose from aspiration to action is not easy: 'In many areas of a business there is still a wide gap between aspirations and action. We are now helping leaders to shift from why purpose matters, to how we create purposeful organizations that create sustainable value – and how to measure that value beyond only the short-term financial motives.'

The gap between future leaders and current leaders

Implementing purpose inside a company has its challenges, but how are companies doing when it comes to combining a duty to shareholders to drive profit with a broader social purpose? And how do current and future leaders see the challenge? This was the question that Coca-Cola Enterprises (which manufactures, distributes and markets Coca-Cola products in Western Europe) commissioned Cranfield School of Management's Doughty Centre for Corporate Responsibility to explore during 2014.

Uniquely, in order to find the answers the Doughty Centre surveyed current CEOs as well as a future generation of business leaders. Working with the *Financial Times*'s FT Remark, the Doughty Centre spoke with 50 CEOs and almost 150 MBA and MSc students and graduates from across Europe.

It found that:

- 88 per cent of current CEOs and 90 per cent of future leaders surveyed believe businesses should have a social purpose.

- However, only 19 per cent of future leaders think businesses already have a clear social purpose, compared to 86 per cent of CEOs.

- CEOs and future leaders hold different beliefs on the biggest barriers to businesses adopting a social purpose, with current leaders citing external factors such as government and regulation, while future leaders believe current management attitudes play a larger role.

The research showed that both current and future leaders agree that business profit and the ability to provide shareholder value are the best barometers of business success today. However, the groups disagreed on how that may change in the future. While the overwhelming majority of current CEOs felt that profitability and shareholder value would remain key in the future, future leaders had higher expectations of the role that business should play, claiming that societal and environmental impact, innovation and development of future talent will be more important indicators of business success in the years to come.

The Doughty Centre suggests that three key developments could accelerate the shift of business towards adoption of social purpose:

- *The first of those is to make sure that environmental and social costs were fully incorporated in company's profit and loss statements.*
  However, the Doughty Centre states that until this is corrected through government intervention of some kind, it would be irrational for investors

to incorporate such costs since they do not affect financial figures nor appear on the balance sheet and therefore do not affect company profitability. This means that the corporate cost of capital does not reflect the true sustainability of the firm.

- *The second accelerator would be greater corporate transparency and accountability.*

  For this to happen, however, companies would need to state their purpose and their values clearly, and use the mandate they have defined to measure and report on how well they have filled this purpose, including the social, environmental and economic impacts, as well as their financial performance.

- *The third accelerator, says the Doughty Centre, would be the finding and sharing of more examples of business success from social purpose*:

  'Today's and tomorrow's business leaders need to be inspired by what is already being successfully achieved by leading sustainable businesses around the world. More good practice examples are needed, not least to drive change in the world's 13,000 business schools, which have assiduously promoted shareholder value theory. Business leaders who have successfully and profitably embedded social purpose and sustainability need to share their stories and experiences. There needs to be a dramatic scaling-up of the conversation and the sharing of good practice to catalyse large-scale change.'

Why leaders should focus on relationships, purpose and values

For more than two decades, Tomorrow's Company, a not-for-profit think tank that exists to inspire and enable companies to be a force for good, has been quietly and relentlessly advocating an inclusive approach as key to enduring successful business. It says an inclusive approach focuses on relationships, purpose and values.

In 1993, the Royal Society for the Encouragement of Arts, Manufactures and Commerce (RSA) initiated a business-led enquiry into the role of business in a changing world. The objective was to develop a shared vision of the company of tomorrow. Findings of the inquiry, published in 1995, introduced the concept of an inclusive approach to business success in which a company:

- defines and communicates its purpose and values;
- develops a unique success model;

- places a positive value on each of its relationships;
- works in partnership with stakeholders;
- maintains a healthy reputation.

Mark Goyder is Tomorrow's Company's CEO and founding director. He says:

'We believe businesses can and should be a force for good. Our work today will restore the licence for business to operate and for businesses to be successful tomorrow. We succeed in our goal by convening leaders, investors, policymakers and NGOs to participate in a uniquely thoughtful process and to set new agendas. Our impact has included changes to company practice, policy and regulation.

Most fundamentally, our conviction is that it is not organizations that have relationships – it is the people within and between those organizations. This means that the relationship with another person cannot simply be a means to an end, but is a worthwhile aim in itself; and that a stakeholder is not an object, but the subject with whom mutual respect unlocks value that is created together.

All too often business processes erode relationships, increasing risk, reducing resilience, destroying value. Good relationships are about creating an environment in which everyone can thrive.'

By 'effective relationships', Tomorrow's Company means a relationship that satisfies the goals of both parties. Happiness or satisfaction is a beneficial but not essential side-effect.

What stops leaders at all levels from implementing a more purpose-led approach? It is often said that the greatest barrier is the short-termism of investors – the people who provide business with the capital to grow and who expect a healthy return on their investment, now! Mark is keen to ensure that capital markets recognize the role they have in helping businesses to move to a more purpose-led motive:

'Directly or indirectly the capital in our capital markets comes from our savings, or those of people like us, around the world. So it is logical for us as human beings to want to see that capital used and mobilized to tackle the huge problems of tomorrow. We describe our capital markets as a hydra. An ugly beast maybe. But one that has proven successful over generations at fuelling growth and prosperity. The beast is not out of control. By our actions we can steer it.

Provided we give it the right instructions, create the right boundaries and rules and standards of behaviour, and provided we don't imagine we can do it all through financial incentives such as long-term incentive plans, based on dubious and excessively short-term criteria, or share options that create incentives to manipulate the current share price rather than build a better company. That's the thing about markets. They are good servants, but they are bad masters. We need to unlearn some of the economics that we have been taught.

People set up companies for all sorts of reasons – rarely, in fact, just to make money. It is sometimes assumed that shareholders and stakeholders are different people, to be thought of in different compartments. Not true. You and I and many like us, are both shareholders and stakeholders. We need our investments to reflect the totality of what we value, not just the short-term financial side. Capital markets exist to serve wealth creation and societal health. Let us take every step we can to ensure that they are attuned to that purpose.'

More communication needed between leaders and investors

So how do investors respond? Do asset managers see themselves as the problem?

Saker Nusseibeh is chief executive of Hermes Investment Management, which manages almost £30 billion in assets across specialist equities, fixed income, real estate and alternatives on behalf of a global clientele of institutional and wholesale investors. He is a Palestinian with a doctorate in medieval history from the University of London, and a powerful advocate for 'correcting the failings of the business I have worked in since I started as a graduate trainee with Mercury Asset Management in 1987'.

Saker is founder of The 300 Club, a group of senior industry participants that includes Alan Brown, Schroeder's former chief investment officer, and Bob Maynard, chief investment officer at the Public Employee Retirement System of Idaho. The purpose of the group is to raise uncomfortable questions about their business. His desire is that fund management is and is seen as a much more honourable business – with behaviours guided by ethics that earn trust.

The members of the club – named after the 300 Spartans who held off the Persians at the Battle of Thermopylae – are campaigning to challenge the beliefs of the asset management industry. Saker has an important position of leadership not only at Hermes but also for the City of London, one of the great financial service centres of the world.

I interviewed him in his London office, and it soon became clear that he has a compelling sense of purpose rooted in a deep recognition of whose money he is managing. He has a passionate sense of responsibility about what Hermes and other fund managers should do with the hard-won savings of the citizens who entrust their money to him.

The profit motive encourages bad behaviours

Pension funds' obsession with short-term financial returns and an out-of-control bonus culture, he argues, have destroyed a sense of the interconnectedness of society: 'We are moving towards an industry that is just about returns and absolute numbers. This encourages some very bad behaviours.'

He says there needs to be fundamental changes in the way the financial markets are run, and that government should change the rules of the game and threaten executives in the industry with prison if they act irresponsibly:

'We have authority but no responsibility. The first thing I would do is to remove the legislation that stops investment bankers from being unlimited liability partners in businesses that they're in. It would control the risks in the system far better. We've created a financial system where the risk takers, the investment banks, have unlimited upside individually but no downside when they make mistakes, and that is absurd.'

Saker argues that a lack of accountability has also meant that decision makers using other people's money have lost any sense of connection with ordinary people, and that along with wealth should come a sense of service:

'When I was very young and very arrogant I had to give a speech to retirees about how we had outperformed the market because our fund had fallen only by 6 per cent compared with the benchmark 12 per cent decline. I looked at them and thought, here I am telling them I did a good job because I lost them money, and I saw the difference between the clothes I was wearing and what they had on.

That was an epiphany. People in the city need more empathy and need to understand how difficult it is for everyone else. When they make a mistake they feel gutted because it knocks money off their bonus, but actually it knocks a huge amount of someone else's income, on which their lives depend.'

Saker argues that the old definition of the purpose of business – to maximize profits for shareholders – has not worked: 'It has failed and the failure is palpable and clear for all to see. I believe that business serves a purpose and that its purpose is to serve society.'

Business has to serve all stakeholders in society but in particular, he says, three primary stakeholders – shareholders, the people who work in the company, and customers:

'A sustainable business is a business that grows and repeats and does not go bust, it is as simple as that. They employ people for a long time and serve customers for a long time because those customers can afford to keep coming back time and again. Government gets a good deal because it is taking the right sort of tax from the system. The community that the businesses operates in benefits as well. As a result of the business and its stakeholders thriving, shareholders are rewarded. That is the right model to think about.'

Create value for all

It is only when you think about creating value for all of these stakeholders that you create a business able to thrive for the long term. Saker says:

'The problem is the lack of real communication between business leaders and fund managers. Business leaders say they want to talk about the long term but that all fund managers want to talk about is the short term and the next quarter's earnings. Fund managers I speak to say they want to talk about the long term but that all business leaders ever talk to them about is the next quarter's earnings. Business leaders need to have the courage to talk about long-term issues and better define their five-year plans and 10-year visions. If you define your purpose as serving your customer base, you have to understand how you fit within it and have a view of where you want to be in 10 years' time. Unless you have a long-term vision you cannot do great things.

For me the purpose of asset management is to act as a pipe between a nation's savings and the future growth of its economy. It's as simple as that. For the savers who have entrusted their money to us we have to provide them with the right environment to retire that allows them to enjoy the fruits of their labour. That is a different purpose from returns and beating benchmarks.

I want to see the profits for my company made in a world I'm happy to live in. I offer the same standard to my investors: you want fair return on your investment, and you want to see an improvement to the world in which you will spend it.'

Because of this, Hermes has become part of the Blueprint For Better Business movement. Does Saker believe that this change will happen quickly? No. He thinks that his 300 club will begin to move pebbles that will move rocks that will create an avalanche, but it will take time: 'I believe we are at the cusp of something that could become one of the great social movements. The timing is right, the need is there. Find your company's social purpose, live it and talk about it.'

Fund managers must encourage better corporate cultures

Saker is not alone in his thinking. Although not in the majority, there are more influential fund managers beginning to talk about the need for more purpose-led business. One such person is Helena Morrissey, chief executive at Newton Investment Management and chair of The Investment Association. Newton investment Management is a London-based, global investment management subsidiary of BNY Mellon. It has assets under management approaching £50 billion and serves institutional investors, charities, corporations and individuals. Its policy is to provide long-term orientation. She says:

'I don't believe that companies face a choice between delivering for investors and behaving well – these are entirely compatible aims.

Maximizing shareholder returns is often cited as a reason for the poor behaviours that ultimately led to the financial crisis. Such a focus can indeed result in irresponsible actions and corrosive cultures, but many long-term investors firmly believe that responsibly managed companies are the ones that will achieve sustainable competitive advantage. Those better managed companies will, in turn, deliver better returns over the years or decades – not months, weeks, days or hours – and it is with them that we want to hold our investments. Much of the UK fund management industry now regards strong, positive corporate culture and behaviours as inextricably linked to delivering good long-term returns for our clients.

But it's clear many people still believe companies are only focused on serving their shareholders. We have not made our views clear and I believe fund managers should speak up more. We need to raise our voices because shareholders can and must drive a real breakthrough in the pace of change towards better corporate cultures.'

Euan Munro is CEO of Aviva Investors, a global asset manager that currently invests £267 billion on behalf of its customers. It has expertise in real estate, fixed income, equity and multi-asset. He says the asset management industry has a responsibility to ensure that an investing public are spared the worst consequences of short-term thinking: 'We live in an age of ever increasing volumes of data, and markets feed on data. Our apparently insatiable appetite means that we have tied listed companies to a gruelling quarterly-reporting regime. Asset managers are part of the problem because we can be guilty of being distracted by our own short-term performance metrics, rather than pursuing long-term sustainable returns.'

Euan has called for companies to be required to report less frequently, but has asked that they report on a wider set of issues. These would include the company's employment practices, the state of its reputation and greater disclosure on non-financial information, such as environmental, social and corporate governance issues. 'Using the power that comes with voting rights attached to the shares we manage can help us in another influencing role. We can use our votes to shape better and longer-term behaviour in the companies we invest in', he says.

Sadly, he adds, engagement with companies on such issues is declining because investors tend to vote with their wallets and exercise their view by selling their stock, rather than engaging in dialogue: 'We believe that with stewardship of assets comes a responsibility to engage in dialogue. Within our company we place significant store on our investors taking in wider environmental, social and governance issues as these can be the matters that lead to catastrophic loss of value for long-term investors.'

The golden thread that delivers short- and long-term success

Although still a minority, many fund managers are now advocating the merits of purpose- and values-driven companies. They are convinced these businesses will grow faster and last longer. But do companies with a strong purpose perform better? This was the question that the Chartered Institute of Personnel Development (CIPD) tried to answer in a study conducted in 2010.

The starting point to the research was that most organizations tended to have a 'profit-based' purpose. Despite being a common purpose, the CIPD research found that making profit for investors and owners did not fire up the workforce – in fact, those with a profit-based purpose tended to have employees less in sync with day-to-day operations.

The CIPD research showed that organizations with a sense of shared purpose that went beyond profit outperformed those with no sense of purpose, on both soft and hard measures. Among public and third-sector organizations, there were indications from the research that the greater the sense of shared purpose, the greater the perception that service delivery was more timely and more cost-effective.

The CEO of the CIPD is Peter Cheese, who is passionate about the need of business to find new ways of measuring the value of human talent and reporting this to shareholders. He says that the CIPD's research showed that having a strong sense of organizational purpose that is shared by all employees, and often beyond, to include external stakeholders, is linked with engagement, satisfaction and sustainable business performance. 'Shared purpose is the "golden thread" to which an organization's strategy should be aligned', he feels.

The CIPD report explored the findings of a survey of 2,000 UK employees to understand their views on shared purpose and how it impacts them. 'In addition to improving performance, our research indicated that having a sense of shared purpose also improved employee engagement, but only if that sense of shared purpose was achieved throughout the organization', explained Peter.

Purpose, values and goals must be aligned

The CIPD says that alignment was the key issue. Alignment between an organization's purpose, its values and its goals was more important than the specific purpose of the organization – as indeed was the alignment between an employee's goals and the values of the organization and ultimately understanding where they fit.

Respondents were asked about how engaged they were with their work, where employee engagement was described as a combination of commitment to the organization and its values and a willingness to help out colleagues. It went beyond job satisfaction and was not simply motivation.

Peter Cheese, CEO of the CIPD, comments: '69 per cent of respondents stated that they were engaged with their work, compared with 13 per cent who said they were not engaged. Respondents working for organizations where a sense of shared purpose existed throughout, seemed far more likely to be engaged (84 per cent) than those employees who worked for an organization without a set of shared purpose (32 per cent).'

Where there was alignment between the purpose, values and goals of an organization, levels of engagement and satisfaction increased. Arriving at that requires that the people not only understand the purpose and values of the organization, but also see where they fit into it:

'The emphasis here is on understanding; an employee can only share the purpose of the organization if they understand what that purpose is. Similarly, a greater sense of purpose is achieved if their goals are aligned with the organization's values.

The problem is that for most employees we surveyed, the sharing of purpose stopped short (and in some places considerably short) of the whole organization. What this highlights is the importance of communication and leadership in achieving a greatest sense of shared purpose in their organizations.'

So, purpose-led business is a growing movement, but has it yet reached a critical mass that will make it unstoppable and produce greater good for people all over the world? Not yet. While most top business leaders believe in its importance, and future leaders even more so, it will take the efforts of managers and leaders at all levels of all organizations to make it work. That means you!

Articulating a more compelling purpose, embedding it in your team or organization and then communicating it more effectively with stakeholders, including shareholders and investors, is what is required.

The benefits are potentially huge: more committed employees; greater productivity; faster, more reliable growth; more support from customers, investors, regulators, and communities – the list goes on and on. The real point is that being purpose led is no longer just desirable, it is crucial in a more connected, transparent and complex world.

Next: the evidence proves that employees with purpose deliver better results.

Key points from Chapter 2

1 Poor management could be costing businesses hundreds of billions a year in lost working hours. Low levels of engagement are damaging productivity. A greater sense of purpose drives up engagement and delivers better results.

2 Employees need to understand what their leaders are trying to do, why they are trying to do it and what it will achieve not only for the organization itself but also for the organization's wider stakeholders. Purpose helps organizations to transform themselves, motivates people through meaning, not fear, and helps people to understand the need for change.

3 Boards must refocus on their organization's longer-term purpose, beyond just making money or meeting targets – and set measurable commitments to customers, suppliers, employees, communities and the environment, as well as to investors. Our future prosperity and global competitiveness depends on management creating value for all stakeholders.

4   In a global survey 80 per cent of people surveyed believe that business can both increase its profits AND improve economic and social conditions in the communities in which it operates. Having a purpose beyond profit improves the way business is perceived by stakeholders and thereby improves performance.

5   High-performing organizations are characterized by not only a focus on long-term goals and a social purpose, but also by strong values that drive culture.

6   Alignment is the crucial issue – managers at most companies are poor at ensuring that all employees are aligned with the purpose, values and goals.

7   To be effective, companies should report on purpose, including the social, environmental and economic impacts, as well as their financial performance. Sadly, a majority of businesses still have a 'profit-based' purpose, which does not engage employees.

8   An increasing number of business leaders, investors and institutions now believe that the old definition of the purpose of business – to maximize profits for shareholders – has not worked. Organizations with a shared sense of social purpose outperform those without one, on all hard and soft measures.

Purpose and employee engagement

Why giving employees a greater sense of purpose is every leader's job

When leaders give their teams a greater sense of purpose, more respect, and a positive culture, they drive up levels of engagement. Learning to be a more engaging manager is truly the low-hanging fruit of the productivity tree. Engagement delivers better performance, faster growth and more wealth for nations. And there are other benefits – its win-win – because employees live longer, have fewer illnesses, happier lives, and they feel fulfilled in terms of having meaning and purpose.

Your job as a leader is to give everyone in your team or your organization a greater sense of purpose.

In much of the debate about purpose-led leadership, the concept of purpose centres on the idea of explaining why your organization exists. What is it here to do? In Chapter 2 we saw that there is a growing debate and movement to make business more about serving a higher purpose than simply to make profit. Business people should make their purpose about creating value for a wider range of stakeholders.

To me, purpose is wider even than this. Purpose is not only about why we exist, it is also about resolve and determination, drive and ambition, commitment and dedication.

And, of course, it is about intent – what is it you are trying to achieve? At the beginning of this book you will see a dictionary definition of purpose. This is what I mean by giving employees purpose – the reason we exist; the plans and goals we need to achieve; the culture in which to thrive; and the resolve, energy, commitment and drive to achieve the impossible.

This is what engaged employees have – and the evidence is overwhelming that people with that sense of purpose achieve a great deal more than those who don't have it. They are people with purpose, and it makes a HUGE difference.

According to the McKinsey Global Institute, the business and economics research arm of McKinsey and Co, there are about 2.9 billion workers currently active around the world. That is projected to be around 3.5 billion by 2030. In the UK, there are about 30 million.

Sadly, it appears that being classified as an active worker does not necessarily mean that you are *actually* very active. The evidence is that there are an awful lot of people who are not working very hard. The latest surveys on trends in employee engagement around the world, conducted by Aon, a leading global provider of risk and people solutions (that operates in more than 120 countries), suggest that only 62 per cent of all those 2.9 billion people are 'engaged' at work.

By 'engaged' they mean people who have purpose; people who want, and are able, to give their best at work each and every day, bringing energy, commitment and creativity to their jobs and helping their employers to be successful.

Really? More than one-third of all workers are not engaged? Hang on a minute. Let's do the maths. Hmmm. That means that more than 1.1 billion people go to work and do as little as possible before packing up and going back home again? They simply go through the motions at work, but do not really exert the full force of their creativity, intelligence or effort. Can that be right?

The cost of disengagement

How much is that costing the world's economy? How much is it costing us here in the UK? How much is it costing your company? Or the division you head up, or the team you lead? How badly is that affecting your attempts to achieve your goals – to win more customers, create more revenues, keep your customers satisfied, save costs and improve profits?

According to Aon, engagement levels vary widely around the world. The highest levels of engagement during 2014, they say, were in Latin America, which can boast that 71 per cent of its employees are engaged. (Bear in mind that Latin America is home to the growingly important economic powers of Brazil and Mexico.) Alarmingly, some of the lowest levels of engagement are in Europe, where the average is just 57 per cent.

The economic uncertainty arising from the British vote to exit the European Union makes it even more important to tackle the productivity challenge. Like every other country, the UK has an employee engagement deficit. Survey after survey indicates that one-third of UK workers say they are actively engaged, and one-third say they are positively disengaged. These figures leave the UK ranked ninth for engagement levels among the world's 12 largest economies ranked by gross domestic product (GDP). That makes sense. As we saw from the CMI's Management 2020 Report, the UK also has a productivity challenge. Output per hour in the UK is said to be some 15 percentage points below the average for the rest of the G7 industrialized nations.

Billions being lost globally

The CMI and the Commission on the Future of Management said that disengagement among the workforce was conservatively costing the UK £20 billion a year. How many billions are we losing globally?

Engage for Success, a voluntary not-for-profit movement promoting employee engagement in the UK, says that the employee engagement deficit and the UK's productivity deficit are clearly related. 'There is a firm correlation between employee engagement and high organizational productivity and performance, across all sectors of the economy', says the organization.

As we learned in Chapter 1, Engage for Success was founded by David MacLeod and Nita Clarke. David is a visiting professor at Cass Business School and a fellow of Ashridge Business School. He is an associate of the Institute for Government, and a fellow of the Institute of Marketing. Nita Clarke is the director of the Involvement and Participation Association (IPA). Nita was the vice chair of the MacLeod Review on employee engagement and is co-author of the report 'Engaging for success' (also known as the MacLeod Report), and continues to work with David MacLeod and the Department for Business, Innovation and Skills on implementing the report's findings.

They say: 'Employee disengagement is clearly contributing to our disappointing productivity figures. Analysis indicates that were the UK to move its engagement levels to those of, say, the Netherlands, this would be associated with a £26 billion a year increase in GDP.'

That would represent an improvement in productivity of just 10 per cent. What would a productivity improvement of just 10 per cent mean to your company? Or, if you lead a department or small team, what impact would that have on your annual targets? For this reason, a groundswell of support is starting to push the issue of engagement out of the office of the hard-pressed human resources professional, and into company boardrooms. Why? The answer seems fairly obvious.

'There is money sitting on the table here, in terms of growth and organizational performance', says Wendy Leedham, until recently the programme director for Engage for Success (Wendy was loaned to the movement by Lloyds Banking Group). She says: 'That translates into GDP for our country. And there are other benefits – it's win-win – because employees live longer, have fewer illnesses, happier lives, and they feel fulfilled in terms of having meaning and purpose.'

Wendy adds that the main document underpinning the Engage for Success movement – a paper entitled 'The evidence', published in partnership with the University of Bath as a follow-up to the government's MacLeod Review on employee engagement – provides more than enough evidence for even the most sceptical of boards or management teams: 'You could slap that on to any board table and say: "Read this, and tell me this thing doesn't matter and shouldn't be a key priority".'

Disengaged employees cause catastrophes

Over three decades of working in public relations, for some of the world's biggest companies, I have often seen the dreadful fruits of the labours of disengaged employees. These have sometimes been catastrophic – nuclear accidents, aircraft disasters, rail crashes. Distressingly often, they are a result of carelessness and lack of engagement by employees.

At the other end of the spectrum, and far more difficult to see, is the worker who does as little as possible to get through the day. These people are insidiously costing their companies in wasted time and effort, alienating customers and falling short of promises to citizens – whether it be in health care or in public services. Nothing annoys us more then the employee at the other end of the line who just doesn't seem to care about our custom.

Whatever the case, these disengaged employees make excuses for their actions (or lack of action), fail to help their colleagues, are lacking enthusiasm or initiative, are constantly distracted, and usually are opposed to learning and growing.

More visible, is the toxic worker. They are the ones helping to destroy morale by constantly gossiping, forming poisonous cliques within the company, constantly complaining and often telling lies that are dangerous for team morale. They are frustratingly irresponsible, lacking any sense of accountability whatsoever.

Truly engaged employees display vigour, dedication, absorption in their work, and a willingness to go the extra mile (discretionary effort.) They also have an awareness of the business context in which they operate – a line of sight between their tasks and the goals of their employer.

How engagement helps you as a leader

If you are a leader, at any level in an organization, what are the key performance indicators that are likely to occupy your mind?

You are going to be worried about income growth and, with it, productivity and profitability. You are going to be worried about customer satisfaction and customer acquisition, without which you cannot grow revenues. You hope that your employees are constantly innovating, finding new and better ways of doing things that create extra value. You will worry about absenteeism and employee well-being, because lots of sick days can cause havoc with your schedules. Of course, you will also worry about health and safety, for all sorts of legal and moral reasons. And you will worry also about staff retention. High turnover rates of staff are not only massively disruptive, but also take a big chunk of money out of your profits.

How will creating more engaged employees help with all of those performance goals? The evidence is fairly overwhelming.

More than 70 per cent of business leaders now believe that engagement is critical for their businesses, citing it as a key element to the success of any organization.

Here are some of the statistics published in the 'Engage for success' report:

1 *Income growth*:
   – Businesses in the top quartile of engagement scores demonstrate revenue growth 2.5 times greater than those organizations in the bottom quartile.
   – Listed companies with engagement levels of 65 per cent or greater outperform the total stock market index and post total shareholder returns 22 per cent higher than average.

- Companies with engagement levels of 45 per cent or less have a total shareholder return 28 per cent lower than the overall average return in 2010.

- Companies with high and sustainable engagement levels had an average one-year operating margin that was close to three times higher than those with lower engagement.

- Organizations with a highly engaged workforce saw a 13.7 per cent improvement in net income growth compared to a decline of 3.8 per cent in low engagement companies, over the study period.

2 *Productivity and performance*:

- 85 per cent of the most admired companies believe that efforts to engage employees have reduced employee performance problems.

- Gallup data in 2012, from 24,000 business units, demonstrated that those units with engagement scores in the top quartile averaged an 18 per cent higher level of productivity than those units in the bottom quartile.

- Research linking employee survey data to performance ratings showed that highly engaged employees were 10 per cent more likely to exceed performance expectations.

3 *Customer/client satisfaction*:

- 70 per cent of the more engaged have a good understanding of customer needs against only 17 per cent of the disengaged.

- Several companies were able to demonstrate that there is a direct relationship between engagement and their net promoter scores (NPSs) – a measure of customer loyalty. Those contracts serviced by employees whose engagement had improved over the year had NPSs of 24 per cent higher than those employees whose engagement had declined.

- An analysis of data from four UK and Irish banks showed that as a result of an increase in engagement – by one standard deviation – it led to increases in customer satisfaction that cascaded into corresponding improvements in sales achievement, such as a 6 per cent improvement in branch sales to target.

- Employees themselves share a similar view; 78 per cent of highly engaged employees in the UK public sector said they could make an impact on customer service, while just 29 per cent of the disengaged felt the same way.

4 *Innovation*:

- Encouraging shop-floor input and creating a more engaged workforce at BAE – a global defence, aerospace and security solutions business – has reduced the time it takes to build fighter planes by 25 per cent.

- Gallup data in 2013 found that 59 per cent of engaged employees said that their job brings out their most creative ideas, against only 3 per cent of disengaged employees.

5 *Absence and well-being*:

- According to the Confederation of British Industry, sickness costs the UK economy more than £17 billion per year. They found that engaged employees take an average of 2.69 days per year, while disengaged employees were taking 6.19 days each year.

- Those employees in highly engaged companies report significantly less workplace stress, 28 per cent versus 39 per cent.

6 *Retention*:

- Replacing employees who leave can cost up to 150 per cent of the departing employee's salary. The Corporate Leadership Council (CLC) reports that highly engaged organizations have the potential to reduce staff turnover by 87 per cent – the disengaged are four times more likely to leave than an average employee.

- Companies with high levels of engagement show staff turnover rates of 40 per cent lower than companies with low levels of engagement – so an organization with 20,000 employees can save upwards of £16 million per year in employee turnover, by moving from a low engagement to a high engagement environment.

7 *Health and safety*:

- Organizations with engagement in the bottom quartile averaged 63 per cent more accidents than those in the top quartile.

- It has been identified across National Health Service (NHS) hospitals that where there is more engagement amongst staff there are lower mortality rates – patient mortality rates were 2.5 per cent lower in those trusts with high engagement levels than in those with medium engagement levels.

What are the attributes of an engaged employee?

Engaged employees show higher levels of well-being all round, meaning that they are more likely to enjoy their work, are able to cope with work-related problems and are less likely to lose sleep over work-related issues. Those who are absorbed in their work have positive emotions at work – enthusiasm, cheerfulness, optimism, contentment and calmness. Those who are not are three times more likely to feel miserable, worried, depressed, gloomy, tense or uneasy.

Engaged employees care about the future of the company and are willing to invest discretionary effort. This means more committed staff who willingly go beyond their job specification to deliver exceptional service to benefit the business. They show greater understanding of the job, the team, the organization and how their role aligns to strategy. They never tell you that they cannot do something because it is 'outside my job description'. Instead of expecting recognition or reward to come first, they simply do the right thing, confident that they will be rewarded later but not particularly concerned if they are not.

They speak up when they have to and challenge processes that are not effective. They champion customer needs and are never satisfied – they are driven to improve, which is why they recognize when things are broken and are more than happy to take the initiative to fix problems. They often counteract the toxic people in your organization, and chivvy up those whose get-up-and-go has got up and gone. Most of all, they are happy to be accountable for their actions and their performance.

Willing to work does not necessarily mean able to work

Does having an engaged workforce mean they will always go the extra mile? No. A lot depends on whether they have the energy.

In 2015, Opinium, a strategic insight agency based in the UK, asked more than 2,000 people how they were getting on at work. Worryingly, more than one-third of respondents said they were too tired to enjoy life outside of work as a result of their job. They said they had regularly to work beyond their contracted hours, sacrificing valuable work–life balance in the process.

While they felt they were either being paid fairly or that their pay was moving in the right direction, a high proportion were tired of getting home tired.

Fatigue can halt even the most engaged of employees in their tracks. Only mindful and caring management can ensure that employees do not burn themselves out. Engagement that can be sustained is critical to success.

A 2012 global workforce study of 32,000 employees by the consulting company Towers Watson found that the traditional definition of engagement was no longer sufficient to fuel the highest levels of performance. 'Willing, it turns out, does not guarantee able', they said.

The company sought to understand what impact fatigue had on operational performance and found that companies with high engagement scores measured in the traditional way had an operating margin of 14 per cent. By contrast, companies with the highest number of 'sustainably engaged' employees had operating margins of 27 per cent.

Sustainably engaged employees were encouraged to take breaks, were given work environments where they could focus in an absorbed way on their most important tasks, given flexible working conditions so that they could determine when and how they got their work done, were made to feel valued and appreciated for the contribution, and felt connected to a higher purpose at work.

Wanted in leaders: purpose, vision, values and stretching goals

The UK government's MacLeod Report determined that there are four enablers of engagement:

- First, visible and empowering leaders who can explain the purpose of the organization, where it has come from and where it is going.

- Second, engaging managers who focus on their people and give them scope, treat them as individuals and coach and stretch them.

- The third key factor is that employees have a voice throughout the organization, and are enabled and encouraged to contribute ideas or challenge views. Employees need to be seen as central to solutions.

- Finally, organizational integrity is essential. The values on a poster on the wall need to be reflected in day-to-day behaviours – at all levels of the organization.

Engage for Success is a British organization, so their views reflect those of British workers. Are the drivers of engagement similar globally?

Kenexa is part of IBM and is a global employment and retention solutions organization. Their global research has found that there are commonly four things that drive high levels of engagement. These are:

- leaders who inspire confidence in the future;
- managers who recognize employees and motivate their teams for peak performance;
- exciting work and the opportunity to improve skills;
- a genuine responsibility by leaders to employees and the communities in which they operate.

Consulting and accountancy firm Deloitte surveyed 7,800 'millennials' across 29 countries worldwide (millennials applies to the cohort of people born between 1980 and the mid-2000s).

The vast majority said that the best leaders possessed an overarching sense of purpose, which included a commitment to employees as well as making a contribution to local communities. As far as individual leaders went, the millennials placed the most value on qualities such as strategic thinking, the ability to inspire, interpersonal skills, vision and passion. Sadly, this same group thought that most current leaders focused on profit and personal reward rather than people, and were failing to deliver on their purpose.

All of the above strongly suggests that the evidence for engagement and what drives engagement is now fairly conclusive. One thing stands out clearly above all else: how well leaders give people a sense of purpose at work profoundly influences how well those people perform. And it all starts with respect.

A study led by Christine Porath, associate professor at Georgetown University's McDonough School of Business, working with *Harvard Business Review*, researched 20,000 employees globally, and found that civility and respect enhanced the influence and performance of leaders, because it had a powerful effect on commitment and engagement.

The power of respect: the most important ingredient in leaders

'No other leadership behaviour had a bigger effect on employees across the outcomes we measured', said Christine Porath:

'Being treated with respect was more important to employees then recognition and appreciation, communicating an inspiring vision, providing useful feedback – or even opportunities for learning, growth and development.

Those who get respect from their leaders reported 56 per cent better health and well-being, 1.72 times more trust and safety, 89 per cent greater enjoyment and satisfaction with their jobs, 92 per cent greater focus and prioritization, and 1.26 times more meaning and significance. Those who felt respected by their leaders were also 1.10 times more likely to stay with their organizations than those who did not.

Respect also had a clear impact on engagement. The more leaders give respect, the higher the level of employee engagement: people who said leaders treated them with respect were 55 per cent more engaged.'

As Dr Duncan Banks, a leading UK neuroscientist, said in Chapter 1, it's all a matter of whether leaders make their people feel worthless or worthy.

Many other studies show a gap between what employees want, and what managers think employees want. We know that employees want to be made to feel worthy, want meaningful work, want to be appreciated and stretched, and want to feel part of a community working to a common cause. Most managers, however, think employees want good wages, job security and promotion before all else. It never fails to amaze me that all of the soft factors are often stripped out of a manager's view of their staff. They think that commitment and energy can simply be bought for cold cash and promises of a step up the work ladder.

Intrigued by the idea that clever leaders with a brilliant plan could still fail spectacularly (I have been a first-hand witness to more than my fair share of those), I began my own journey of discovery in 2010. I went to speak to as many leaders as I could to ask them what it took to be inspiring. I managed to get in front of more than 70 CEOs and chair persons of a wide range of businesses, public sector organizations and charities. The result was my first book, *The Language of Leaders*, published by Kogan Page in 2011.

Since then, I have devoted myself to trying to understand more and more about what it takes to be an engaging, inspiring leader – and I wrote a second book, *Communicate to Inspire: A guide for leaders*, published by Kogan Page in 2014. Both books are now published in many languages around the world.

Whether you lead a major organization or a small team, my focus has been on trying to understand what you need to do to bring out the very best in other people. After five years of research, I have now interviewed more than 120 CEOs, surveyed 3,000 managers and 6,000 employees, and read just about every book there is on leadership and communication.

I strongly believe that the most successful leaders use a system of communication that enables them to be engaging. By following just 12 principles, leaders can have a dramatically positive effect on the engagement and commitment of their teams, and deliver the respect that is such a prerequisite of employee engagement.

What, then, is the *system* of communication used by leaders?

The leaders I interviewed said that the purpose of leadership communication is to influence and inspire in order to achieve great results. In that context, they talked about:

- Why trust is essential to leadership, why that means you have to be authentic and why you have to learn to be more passionate in your communication.

- Why you need to articulate a purpose that goes beyond profit as a motive.

- How they created leaders throughout their organizations by relentlessly communicating a framework of values that enabled action and decision making. When they talked about 'leaders', they meant empowered people everywhere, able to make decisions without going up and down the chain of command.

- Why they put into words a vision of the future that powered all their communication and empowered others.

- How they brought external views of their organization into the organization in order to drive change, especially those of customers, and made the building of trust in all relationships a strategic goal.

- How they made employee engagement another strategic goal, and systematically used powerful conversations to engage and motivate people.

They said that if you want to be a more effective communicator, you have to:

- Address the concerns of your audience BEFORE delivering your own messages, in order better to connect with people.

- Learn to listen better and master the most difficult communication skill of all, asking the right question.

- Develop strong points of view on key issues, to provide powerful standpoints that support your purpose and values.

- Use more stories to capture hearts and imprint messages on memories, to inspire the right behaviours.

- Be aware of the power of the unintended signals you send through your body language and all your behaviours.

- Prepare properly when appearing before groups of people or on public platforms.
- Be humble and keep reviewing and honing your communication skills and effectiveness.

The 12 principles of inspiring leadership communication

The 12 principles below are dealt with more fully in my previous two leadership books but, in summary, let's look at them one by one.

1 *Be yourself better.*

Authenticity as a leader is crucial. Followers will not commit if they do not trust you and believe that you have integrity. So, even if you are a highly introverted individual, you will have to learn to speak with more passion, talk to your values, and stand up more often to speak for your beliefs and values. Followers must *feel* your passion, and believe that you believe. When you are clear with yourself about the things you really care about, you cannot help but talk to them with passion. Most leaders have not spent the time articulating those beliefs, yet the ability to draw on and display that passion and commitment, consistently and predictably, counts for more than skills at oratory, and communicates more effectively than even the most perfectly crafted words. You have to be true to yourself, but you also have to learn to 'perform' yourself better.

2 *Have a powerful purpose and strong values.*

As we have already seen in Chapter 2, leaders too often use financial or numerate goals to motivate people. They are more comfortable being rational and objective. Too often, followers say they don't get out of bed in the morning to achieve financial or other numerate objectives. They come to work and want to be inspired by a sense of doing something important, something that makes a difference. A strong sense of purpose can help shape decisions to be made throughout the organization, and is even more empowering when coupled with a set of values that your people know to be true. In this world of radical transparency, values have assumed far greater importance, for many reasons. Values define how people in the organization behave in pursuit of their objectives, and their actions define a business to the outside world. Those intangible values – often dismissed as 'soft and fluffy' – translate into actions on the ground, which translate into hard numbers in the annual report. How you articulate purpose and values is crucial.

3 *Formulate an uplifting future that creates value for all stakeholders.*
Every leader I spoke to used the future to drive the present. They knew precisely where they wanted to be in a given timescale, even if they did not know exactly how to get there. They were never satisfied with the status quo, and their restlessness was a tangible force. Every question they asked had to do with how people were progressing towards the goals, and they kept those goals under constant review. They painted a vivid picture of success, often describing the future both in rational terms (the numbers) and emotive terms (how it would feel for all concerned). This bringing together of the rational and the emotional was key to inspiring people. Fusing the future vision (what success will look and feel like) to the purpose (what important thing we are here to do) to the values (how we do it) was what stirred hearts and minds. This future, though, had to be expressed in *benefit* terms for all the people with a vested interest in the performance of the organization – customers, shareholders, local communities, suppliers and partners and, most importantly, employees.

4 *Bring the outside in and give people a purpose that benefits others.*
Leaders have to live outside their organizations, constantly bringing stories of success and failure in external relationships into the organization in order to keep everyone fixed on what needs to improve. Successful leaders know that relationships are the engines of success, and they keep a close eye on the state of all key relationships, and keep their enterprise focused on those relationships as well. You have to set up 'quivering antennae', as one leader described it – a radar system that keeps you in touch with the outside world. Too often I heard about the 'reputation gap' – the difference between the promise the business made and the experience customers or stakeholders actually received. Narrowing that gap, or even managing it away, is the goal, if you want to be trusted. And you *do* want to be trusted. Trust is now the most valuable but most hidden asset on your balance sheet. Leaders are increasingly looking to make trust a strategic goal, measured and managed as preciously as any other key asset. Research shows that employees are much more motivated by seeing how what they do delivers a positive benefit to customers than by anything a manager can do to inspire.

5 *Engage through more powerful conversations.*

More and more leaders are now measuring levels of employee engagement, and using this measurement as a strategic tool to find the ways to keep people motivated and committed to the cause. As we have already seen, study after study has shown that companies with high levels of engagement outperform their competitors, by some margin. Engagement is achieved through conversations – structured, potent conversations that allow employees to fully understand the big objective, and work out with their leaders what they have to do to help achieve the goals. It is in these conversations that the rubber hits the road, where the plan gets traction. Too often, these conversations are neglected, and middle managers are neither trained for, nor measured on, their ability to hold these critical conversations. Nor are they shown how to link local actions to the organization's higher purpose, and make them relevant and clear to every employee. Worse, too often top management does not check on the quality of those conversations, or seek to get the feedback from those conversations in a systematic way. The more regularly these conversations are held, the more engaged and motivated the employees will be.

6 *Be more audience-centric; start with them.*

Let us be clear: you have NOT communicated well if people have not heard you, understood you and feel motivated to think differently and act differently as a result of your words. You may have stood up and talked *at* them, but communication has only taken place when your words have had an impact. In any enterprise, leadership communication is all about achieving big goals. It is about changing behaviours. People listen from behind their own filters – filters that may be cultural or emotional, or they may be in place because of their unique perceptions or even misunderstandings. You have to talk to them about *their* concerns, their issues, before you can be understood on your own. Every leader I have interviewed, without exception, spoke to the need to be audience-centric in your communication, and to recognize that, when it comes to communication, it is all about *them*. You have to set out to achieve change in how they think, feel and act, but that requires you to know how they think, feel and act NOW.

7 *Be an outstanding listener.*

Quite often, the people I interviewed treated the subject of listening as if it were somehow distinct from communicating. They rated it an essential skill of leadership, possibly the hardest to perfect. Sometimes the simple act of listening, they said, is an act of inspiration in itself: 'You have to give people a damn good listening to.' There is something more fundamental at work here, though, and I call it The Listening Contract – first you have to listen, if you want to be heard. When you listen and then respond with actions that remove barriers, or pick up on good ideas, you create enormous goodwill, and demonstrate you are on their side, particularly when you encourage people to open up, and create an environment where people can bring you bad news, express their frustrations, and voice their concerns, without fear of repercussions. It is by listening that you show you care, and make them feel worthy. You have to listen beyond the words, into the motives and agendas, into the context, into the key performance indicators (KPIs) and the financial numbers and the mood, and you have to show you understand, even if you don't agree. You have to ask great questions, and learn to unleash your curiosity and interest in people. It really makes a difference.

8 *Have a powerful point of view.*
The best leaders have a potent point of view, and it is always the person with the strong point of view who influences the group, who wins the day. As a leader, you are going to have to stand up and give your point of view, time and time again. You will have to take a position on issues, be courageous, and stand up for what you believe to be right. Too few leaders think about developing points of view – yet when well articulated, they can help you to win friends and influence people, and gain a stronger voice in shaping the future. Not having a point of view, and not standing up for it, creates confusion and a vacuum, which toxic employees will quickly rush to fill. In a world where people trust the motives, judgement and competence of business leaders less now than just five years ago, shouldn't we be talking to those issues more often, with more transparency, more conviction and, yes, passion? The ideal point of view should therefore bring together your purpose and your values, highlight your behaviours and draw attention to the benefits of doing things your way. And it should call people to action. Powerful stuff.

9 *Use stories and metaphor more.*
Getting people to listen to you is tough enough, but getting them to sit up and take notice, and then remember what you have to say, is a supreme challenge. Every leader uses stories, knowing that we are wired to listen, imaginatively, when we are told stories. Good stories get under the cynical radar and touch hearts. Backed up by facts to cover off the mind, stories have the power to *move* people. The best stories tell us about customer experiences, good and bad, or make heroes out of

employees delivering the values of the organization, or show up the frustrations of workers unable to do their best because of the system, or vividly portray the future, or reveal aspects of the leader to the audience. They deliberately avoid the tyranny of PowerPoint, and are the more memorable because of it. Some leaders I spoke with were uncomfortable with the word stories, and preferred the word anecdotes, saying this was factual rather than fictional, as some stories can be. But they all used them and loved hearing them, then retelling them, over and over.

10 *Be more aware of the signals you send.*
Actions speak louder than words. A cliché, you might say, but nevertheless one of the hardest truths for a leader to grasp. Being a leader means looking, acting, walking and talking like a leader. Countless times, leaders forget that they are in a fishbowl and are being watched all the time. A look of frustration here, a preoccupied walk through an office without speaking to anyone, a frown of frustration when someone is talking – all of these send powerful signals that staff take away and dissect for meaning. Great leaders communicate positivity and optimism, and they often do it through a smile, or by walking with energy, or by standing straight and tall. Equally, there is nothing more corrosive than the conflict between saying one thing and doing another. For example, saying that bullying is offensive, but then doing nothing about a high-earning bullying manager. That says one thing, and one thing only: money matters more than staff welfare. Leaders who clearly love what they are doing, who show it in everything they do, in every expression, are hugely infectious.

11 *Prepare properly for public platforms.*
Many a leader has had their reputation dented, or even shattered, because they have not prepared properly for speaking to groups of employees, or to external gatherings. Employees like it when their boss is good on their feet. They really do. And it can make a huge difference to motivation, as we shall see. Employees want to be proud of their bosses, especially when they speak on public platforms. The more senior leaders get, the more likely it is they will have to appear on highly public platforms. Done well, such appearances can do enormous good, and drive up sales or the share price, calm nervous investors or unhappy customers, or persuade talented people to the cause. Proper training or coaching is highly recommended, but is not enough by itself. Practice makes perfect, and rehearsal is the best practice. Never get complacent – it is just not worth the risk.

12 *Learn. Rehearse. Review. Improve.*

Humility is one of the things that followers most want in their leaders, as we shall see from my research in the next chapter. Being self-aware, and humble, inspires more discretionary effort from employees. If you strive to be an excellent communicator, you will become a better, more effective leader. This is why all the leaders I spoke with focused on continuous improvement, fuelled by full and frank feedback on each and every performance. Brilliant leadership can be the difference between outstanding performance and disappointing failure. Great leaders steer organizations to success, inspire and motivate followers, and provide a moral compass for employees to set direction. They spearhead change, drive innovation, and communicate a compelling vision for the future. The ability to motivate and inspire others is the characteristic most commonly cited as important when recruiting senior leaders. Communication is the tool that enables inspiring leadership. The simple truth is that you have to get better at it.

These 12 behaviours, if delivered well, can have a dramatic effect on employees, and are the cornerstones of engagement. They are the way you can become a more engaging leader. They help you to construct a more powerful strategic narrative for your team or company, they help you to give employees a voice, and they help you to deliver your values consistently in your leadership. This is how you make people feel worthy, part of a community, working towards a higher purpose, understanding how they contribute, and willing to give of their very best.

How effective are these 12 principles? Can they truly have an impact on performance? Can they encourage employees to deliver the holy grail of engagement – greater discretionary effort? This was the question I put to YouGov, an international internet-based market research firm, headquartered in the UK but with operations in Europe, North America, the Middle East and Asia-Pacific. Stress-test what I have learned from all the leaders I interviewed, I said. Find out from managers and employees whether they agree. Their findings are covered in the next chapter.

Next: how well do leaders give employees a greater sense of purpose?

Key points from Chapter 3

1 How well leaders give their people a sense of purpose at work profoundly influences how well those people perform.

2 How engaged employees are depends on their sense of purpose. Employee engagement is the low-hanging fruit of performance improvement.

3 There is a firm correlation between employee engagement and high organizational productivity and performance, across all sectors of the economy.

4 Understanding the line of sight between one's job role and the purpose and objectives of the organization is central to productivity.

5 More than 70 per cent of business leaders now believe that engagement is critical for their businesses, citing it as a key element to the success of any organization.

6 Those who have a sense of purpose at work have more positive emotions – enthusiasm, cheerfulness, optimism, contentment and calmness. Those who do not are three times more likely to feel miserable, worried, depressed, gloomy, tense or uneasy.

7 Being treated with respect is more important to employees than anything else. People who say that leaders treat them with respect are 55 per cent more engaged.

8 Wanted in leaders: purpose, vision, values and stretching goals.

How purpose powers better results...

04

and the leadership behaviours that
do most to unlock discretionary effort
from employees

*Employees who derive meaning and significance from their work
(purpose) are more than three times as likely to stay with their
organizations, and are significantly more engaged at work.
Sadly, a large percentage of managers say that defining and
communicating purpose is one of the things they are weakest at
doing. Employees agree. Special research by online polling company
YouGov points to what you need to do to inspire super performance
from your team.*

In spite of the fact that I am a passionate advocate of greater employee engagement, I would never declare that this alone *causes* better share price returns
for investors.

What I will say is this: engaged employees will help you to deliver better
results than competitors who have less engaged workers. In other words,
they help to deliver competitive advantage. Greater levels of engagement
and a greater willingness to go the extra mile translate into significant business
benefits, and these will translate into better shareholder returns.

It is also clear that the intangible asset that is called culture can contribute
to the value of a firm. So too can leadership. Where investors perceive that
a company's leadership is high quality and that its culture is strong and

employees highly engaged (assuming other factors are also favourable), they tend to reflect that in how highly they value the company.

I am also not going to try to claim that purpose delivers great results and long-term value by itself. However, it is a major factor in determining how employees feel and therefore in determining how they perform.

But purpose alone is not enough. There are a multitude of other factors that will determine how leaders make employees feel, and how well they inspire them to super performance. This has been my quest – to understand what behaviours management need skilfully to exhibit that will enable them to inspire their people and encourage greater levels of engagement, higher levels of commitment, more happiness and greater discretionary effort.

How you need to behave as a leader to inspire more effort from your team

How do you actually behave as a leader in ways that will induce the right neurochemicals in people and encourage more of the right behaviours? How do you create the win-win of happy and fulfilled employees, as well as high-performing teams or organizations?

This is what I have written about in my previous two books and this is what I have spoken about on platforms around the world. To do this, I have drawn on the hard-won experience and wisdom of more than 120 CEOs who granted me their time and willingly shared their wisdom and learning. I distilled this into the 12 principles I outlined in Chapter 3. Since then, managers at all levels have rated themselves on those 12 skills and I now have a database of more than 1,000 leaders who have ranked their performance in these areas.

Given below are the questions I use to understand a manager's performance against the 12 principles. When surveyed, leaders are asked to rate themselves on a scale of 0–10, where 10 is excellent, against the following:

1 On the whole, to what extent would you say you inspire people by communicating with authentic passion and integrity?

2 Overall, how often do you talk about the organization's purpose and values, and how the team's work connects to it?

3 How frequently do you talk about the future and use that to help people understand what they need to do to make it happen?

4 Overall, how often would you say you have an outside-in focus, bringing in customer views and fostering good relations?

5 How frequently do you have really deep and meaningful conversations about the organization, where it is going, and what people need to do to deliver?

6 In general, how often do you take time to truly understand the audience perspective and discuss issues important to them?

7 How frequently would you say you really take time to deeply listen to people to understand their situation?

8 To what extent would you say you speak out clearly and strongly on issues that are important to you and the organization?

9 How often do you use stories and anecdotes to get a message across?

10 Overall, how often would you say there is consistency between your words, actions and body language?

11 How effective are you when speaking in front of a large audience/public platform?

12 How often do you review your communication performance and seek training to improve?

Distressingly, the area where leaders rate themselves lowest is purpose and values – feeling they either don't know how to deliver the corporate purpose and values in their department, or that they have not thought about defining it for their unit. Yet another reason for this book, then – as leaders feel they do not do this well, and all our research shows that it is one of the most important factors in delivering engaged, super-performing employees.

This is how the leaders who have done my survey rated themselves, with their scores aggregated, from lowest to highest:

Purpose and values (Q2)	5.96
Learn, improve (Q12)	6.11
Public platforms (Q11)	6.13
Bringing the outside in (Q4)	6.22
Future focus (Q3)	6.30
Stories (Q9)	6.36
Engage, through conversations (Q5)	6.63
Signals (Q10)	6.63
Audience centricity (Q6)	6.69
Be yourself better (Q1)	6.96
Listening (Q7)	6.99
Point of view (Q8)	7.24

How would you rank if you rated yourself using the 12 questions?

I think it is perfectly understandable that so many leaders rank speaking to groups of people as low as they do – who really relishes the idea of doing this? Not many. But, as you will see, your ability to do this is crucial to effective leadership. The three areas that leaders rate themselves highest are: being themselves, better (authenticity); listening; and having a strong point of view (top rated).

Terrible listeners

Most employees I have spoken to say that their leaders are not very authentic, are terrible listeners, and often give strong opinions that they are just as likely to change the next day. That can be confusing and destroy morale. The thing they wanted most, employees said, was a sense of purpose, strong values and a culture within which they felt cared for, and plenty of conversations with their bosses, in which their views and input were encouraged and respected. They would often tell me that they simply didn't get enough of this from their bosses.

No surprise, then, that the 1,000+ managers surveyed did not on average rate themselves very highly in the area of engaging with their staff, scoring themselves only middling against the comment 'My team and I are having enough conversations with our employees so that they feel engaged, motivated and committed to what we are doing'.

These leaders also ranked themselves low on the ability to articulate an inspiring vision – an area that we have seen employees around the world think is one of the most important attributes of leadership. This is a significant gap, and a worrying one.

(By the way, you can do the test yourself and see how you compare with 1,000 other managers from around the world. The questionnaire is available for you to rate yourself now at www.leadershipcommunication.co.uk/the-test – should you wish to get a top-line assessment of your own 'inspiration quotient'. The online test not only shows where your strengths and weaknesses lie, but also offers relevant practical tips on areas where you can improve. Managers who have already done this test have come from all over Europe, the United States, South America, Australia and the Far East.)

Intrigued by these apparent gaps in thinking between managers and employees, I commissioned research two years ago to understand more about how employees felt about the inspiration quotient of their bosses. We surveyed a nationally representative sample of more than 4,000 workers in Britain and found that only 21 per cent rated their bosses as very good at inspiring them, with just 5 per cent rating their bosses as 'extremely inspiring'.

This means that only 1 in 20 employees would give their leaders the top score for inspiration. At the other end of the spectrum, 33 per cent rated their bosses uninspiring, with a further 12 per cent rating them as 'extremely uninspiring'. This research showed there was a huge inspiration deficit, one that leaders and managers everywhere ignored at their peril. Such an inspiration deficit will lead directly to an engagement deficit, which quickly leads to a performance deficit in your appraisal.

Now it was time for the acid test. I had learned all I could from leaders and distilled their experience into 12 principles. I had tested more than 1,000 managers on their own views of how they perform against those principles. I had asked 4,000 employees how inspiring their bosses were.

The important manager behaviours: as seen by employees

Now, I needed to understand the relationship between managers' performance against the 12 principles, and employee views of how managers performed and what impact that had on their engagement. Which of the 12 principles are most important to driving up discretionary effort? I wanted data-driven insights into what makes happier, healthier, more productive and purposeful teams.

My secret weapon was my son-in-law, Stefan Kaszubowski, who runs the special projects division of YouGov, a global online market research agency. Stefan and his team are passionate about the power of research to help leaders engage with their communities and communicate in ways that connect, persuade and create prospering societies. I put to him my quest, which I voiced as 'a mission to understand the relative importance of management behaviours and the extent to which employees feel respected and feel motivated'. I wanted to uncover the real drivers of discretionary effort, including the role of purpose.

'Stress-test my 12 principles', I said.

Stefan was nervous. What if his research disproved my work? The possibility never even crossed my mind. More than 40 years of work in communication was enough to tell me that these principles were sound. But I did now need the data to convince sceptical managers that these soft issues were important and could have a material effect on employee performance and therefore on their own ability to achieve their goals and ambitions.

Finally, Stefan agreed and he and his right-hand man, analyst Ben Mainwaring, set about interviewing more than 4,000 employees and managers. The first job was to unpack the 12 principles. You will quickly realize that the way I have articulated them in Chapter 3 is nuanced and can be interpreted in different ways. Each one requires some explanation. When surveying people, you have to be explicit and concise in order to be thorough, and to ensure that people not only understand the question, but can give a fair evaluation. Stefan and his team expanded the 12 principles to 20 very measurable behavioural questions.

Together, he and Ben decided that they would need to do a poll of managers, asking them to rate themselves against the 20 behaviours, and then conduct a separate poll of employees asking them to rate how important those behaviours were and then rate their own bosses' performance against each behaviour.

Here are the 20 questions they asked managers to evaluate themselves on (employees were asked the same questions, but they were also asked about how they saw their manager):

1 At work I really believe what I say.

2 At work I am honest.

3 At work I am sincere.

4 I am passionate about my work.

5 I care about my organization's values and mission.

6 At work I help others see where the organization is headed.

7 At work I make others feel like they contribute.

8 At work I show others how their work affects others.

9 At work I give constructive feedback.

10 I care about the people I manage.

11 I try to understand the needs of the people I manage.

12 I try to make the people I manage feel that their input and perspective is valued.

13 At work I consistently do what I say I'm going to do.

14 At work I demonstrate consistent principles.

15 I understand my weaknesses as a manager.

16 I care about my leadership skills.

17 I frequently talk with the people I manage about how we are doing as an organization.

18 I am effective at relating to other people in terms they understand.

19 I am effective at using body language.

20 I am an effective public speaker.

In addition, of course, there were a series of questions designed to understand the demographics of the survey sample, as well as seniority, industry sector and education. All respondents were also asked to rate which behaviours were most important in good managers.

YouGov interviewed 1,884 managers, comprising 134 CEOs or managing directors, 240 board level managers, 735 senior managers and 775 middle managers (66 per cent of the managers were male and 34 per cent were female; 28 per cent were over 55, 13 per cent were between 18 and 34, and 58 per cent were aged 35 to 54; of those interviewed, 53 per cent came from the private sector, 28 per cent from public sector organizations and 19 per cent from non-profit organizations).

YouGov then surveyed 2,121 employees, of whom 1,258 were employed in the private sector, 605 in public sector organizations, and 264 in the not-for-profit sector (these employees were evenly split male/female with 51 per cent of the survey sample aged between 35 and 54, while 24 per cent were 18 to 34 and 26 per cent were over 55).

The most important behaviours in a manager, according to research?

The critical place to start was to establish whether managers and employees agreed about the most important behaviours in a manager. If managers and employees could not agree on this, I would not have known where to begin. We posed the following questions: 'Which of the following would you say is most important in a manager? Which is the second most important? And which do you think is the third most important?'

The YouGov survey highlighted that the single most important attribute in a manager was *making employees feel important and appreciated*. Once again, here was research validating the view of neuroscientists. Make them feel worthy, and they will perform better, because they feel better.

YouGov designed the research to reveal the key drivers of discretionary effort. Analysis revealed four manager behaviours that have a particularly important relationship with discretionary effort. They are:

- communicating vision and purpose;
- helping employees feel like they contribute to the vision;
- valuing employee input and perspective;
- oratory skills.

Using the statistical technique of factor analysis YouGov identified five attribute clusters in the data: understanding and caring, being purpose-driven, showing organizational transparency, having sincerity and possessing speaking skills. The single most important cluster of attributes is understanding and caring, which includes:

- makes me feel I contribute;
- shows how work affects others;
- gives good feedback;
- cares about me;
- values my input and perspective;
- cares about leadership skills.

Feeling worthy – the top attribute

YouGov identified that 66 per cent of managers and 65 per cent of employees regarded making employees feel important and appreciated as the top attribute, by some way ahead of all other attributes. However, while managers and employees both know that being respected is important, all too often we see the exact opposite taking place. Managers either show disrespect to their employees, or allow employees to show disrespect to each other. This can have devastating consequences.

According to Christine Porath, associate professor at Georgetown University's McDonough School of Business in the United States, the opposite of respect – rudeness and disrespect – is rampant at work, and it is on the rise. Christine's research focuses on leadership, organizational culture and change. She focuses not only on the effects of bad behaviour, but also on how organizations can create a more positive environment where people can thrive. She shows how individuals and organizations benefit in terms of performance, creativity, well-being and health.

She says:

'Over the past 14 years we've polled thousands of workers about how they are treated on the job, and 98 per cent have reported experiencing uncivil behaviour.

The costs chip away at the bottom line. Nearly everybody who experiences workplace incivility responds in a negative way, in some cases overtly retaliating. Employees are less creative when they feel disrespected, and many get fed up and leave. About half deliberately decrease their effort or lower the quality of their work. And incivility damages customer relationships. Our research shows that people are less likely to buy from a company with an employee they perceive as rude, whether the rudeness is directed at them or at other employees. Witnessing just a single unpleasant interaction leads customers to generalize about other employees, the organization, and even the brand.'

Christine says that she and her research team have interviewed employees, managers, human resource (HR) executives, presidents and CEOs: 'We know two things for certain: incivility is expensive, and few organizations recognize or take action to curtail it.'

So, no surprise there then. Well, yes actually. If both managers and employees regard respectfulness as the most important attribute in a manager, why is there still such a large gap in perceptions about being respected at work? In our own YouGov survey, 73 per cent of managers felt they made their employees feel respected at work (a curious 4 per cent admitted they did little to respect their employees). However, only 40 per cent of employees said their bosses regularly made them feel respected.

Ouch. That is 60 per cent of employees feeling undervalued and underappreciated, a lot of the time. Imagine the level of negative neurotoxins at work in their brains! What effect would greater feelings of respect have on employee willingness to give of their discretionary effort? The YouGov research shows that if managers could move their performance here from poor to good (not outstanding, just good) the payback would be a 36 per cent jump in discretionary effort, according to the employees we surveyed.

A 36 per cent improvement in productivity, by simply showing more respect! Imagine the impact of that on productivity, costs, innovation, customer satisfaction, profitability?

The top eight behaviours of inspiring managers

What other management behaviours are important, then? Here is the list of the most important management attributes, as seen by both employees and managers:

1 making employees feel important and appreciated;

2 being honest, having sincerity;

3 demonstrating consistent principles;

4 listening carefully;

5 defining goals;

6 commitment to purpose;

7 understanding employee perspectives;

8 communicating customer expectations/experiences.

The YouGov survey found that all 20 of the attributes they tested were important. However, these top eight were viewed as the most important, and seen similarly by both managers and their employees.

If these are the most important attributes, how do managers rate their performance in these eight areas and how do employees rate their bosses? I have already reported that there is a significant gap in perception about whether employees are made to feel respected, but how do managers generally rate themselves on their honesty and sincerity?

Managers interviewed by YouGov either strongly or somewhat agreed – to the tune of 94 per cent – that they were honest at work, with 92 per cent saying they were sincere.

Employees, however, felt differently. Only 63 per cent agreed that the managers were honest, with 37 per cent having mixed views or disagreeing. Only 58 per cent of employees agreed that their bosses were sincere, with more than 40 per cent having mixed feelings or disagreeing.

While I have no doubt that the managers we surveyed genuinely believe they are honest and sincere, they should be worried about the sizeable perception gap. Trust really matters, and not only makes a difference to how leaders are perceived, but also to how teams behave. Low trust inhibits collaboration and creativity, and impacts negatively on performance. How would you be viewed? Do you know? If there is a perception gap between you and your team, what is causing it? Do you know? These things matter to your effectiveness as a leader.

Worryingly, the same perception gap emerged around the question of principles, with 90 per cent of managers saying they consistently did what they said they were going to do. Only 54 per cent of employees agreed. On the subject of demonstrating consistent principles (in other words, living the values), 91 per cent of managers said they did. Only 53 per cent of employees agreed.

Managers tend to overrate their performance

A significant finding of this research is that managers consistently overrate their performance on all of the attributes discussed above, often by quite some margin. Those on the receiving end, their followers, just don't see their managers' performance in the same way.

For example, employees believe there is much to be done on the subject of whether or not their bosses listen to them, and value their input and perspective. While 94 per cent of managers say they do this, only 60 per cent of employees agree. This could mean that 40 per cent of your team feels undervalued or disrespected, and (as we have seen) this could be inhibiting performance.

This is borne out by the fact that the biggest gap in perception in this survey emerges around managers' views that they care about the people they lead. While 93 per cent of managers say they do, only 52 per cent of employees agree. Worse, almost one quarter of employees actively disagree. This could be because employees just don't feel their bosses understand their needs. More than 9 out of 10 managers say they try to understand the needs of their team – but a significant number of them are failing. Only 48 per cent of employees say their managers understand them, with more than half having mixed feelings or actively disagreeing. If one of the prerequisites of high performance is that you make your team feel important and appreciated, a lot of bosses are failing in this regard. Are you one of them?

Two-thirds of employees say they regularly put in extra effort at work

What else do you have to do as a leader to encourage high levels of commitment and discretionary effort from employees? Let's start with looking at how managers and employees see the picture of whether or not they give discretionary effort.

YouGov cleverly found a way to isolate those employees who naturally take their enthusiasm, energy, commitment and extra effort from job to job. Employees carry something like 35 per cent of the discretionary effort from job to job, irrespective of how inspiring their leaders are. In our analysis, we were able to isolate this intrinsic component of discretionary effort and calculate how improvements in management behaviours would affect employee behaviours, above and beyond personal motivation levels.

When asked how often they put in extra initiative at work in their current position, 62 per cent of employees said they did so frequently. A further 28 per cent said sometimes and 11 per cent said rarely or never. These numbers were fairly consistent across the different age groups, with perhaps a slight and understandable tailing off in those aged over 55. Men were inclined to say they put in extra initiative more often than women did – with 27 per cent of men saying they very often did so, while only 21 per cent of women said the same.

This picture changed quite significantly when you looked at willingness to put in extra initiative depending on whether you were working in the private sector, the public sector or for a non-profit organization. Private sector workers, on average, said they put in extra effort 58 per cent of the time, while public sector workers said they did so 67 per cent of the time and non-profit workers said they did so 72 per cent of the time.

This commitment was also driven to some extent by the degree to which employees said they cared about their organization's values and mission. Only 47 per cent of private sector workers said they did, while 63 per cent of public sector workers and 72 per cent of non-profit workers said they cared, either very much or a good deal. With less than half of private sector workers saying they care about their organization's purpose, it is clear that managers have a huge job to do.

But, do managers agree that their employees put in high levels of extra effort? No. Only 41 per cent of managers said their employees regularly did so, and 46 per cent said their employees did so sometimes. On the other hand, these same managers said they themselves regularly showed extra initiative 69 per cent of the time.

I'm not really that surprised at the wide perception gap here – employees say they work hard and bosses say not hard enough. Bosses always want more – more effort, better results, more customers, more revenue – so it is not surprising they feel dissatisfied with the effort they see being put in. The danger is, this may cause them to fail to appreciate effort, and that can be hugely discouraging to employees, who then put in less effort next time, and so begins a vicious spiral. Appreciation matters, and even when teams have not quite delivered what you expected you have to appreciate first, then look to what can be improved.

The inspiration gap that creates the productivity gap

If this book is about how to be more inspiring, then how inspiring are you now? Do you know? We asked all managers to tell us whether they thought they were inspiring, and 73 per cent said they were extremely or somewhat inspiring (7 per cent extremely so, 66 per cent somewhat). There was a searingly honest 213 managers among the 1,884 that we interviewed who said that they were either somewhat uninspiring or actually very uninspiring.

Employees have a different view. Only 41 per cent surveyed agree their bosses are inspiring. Nearly 6 out of 10 of their bosses, they said, were either not inspiring or, worse, could be demotivating.

This inspiration gap, I believe, is one of the major causes of the productivity challenge we face – and is what I describe as the low-hanging fruit of performance improvement. Why? Because it is an area that I believe we should pay far greater attention to: how to help and train our managers to be more inspiring.

It doesn't take much to be more inspiring. Typically, when I talk to leaders about strategies for being more inspirational, their first instinct is to believe that they have to be more charismatic. Not so – being more inspiring is more about them (your staff) than you (manager.) You have to stop thinking about being inspiring, and start thinking about how to leave them feeling more inspired.

YouGov isolated the most important behaviours that managers need to demonstrate to be seen as more inspirational, motivating and caring. They include:

- showing that you care about your organization's values and purpose;
- helping employees to see where the organization is headed;
- making employees feel like they contribute to the purpose and goals;
- demonstrating that you understand employee needs;
- valuing the input and perspectives of your team;
- delivering on your promises;
- being effective at relating to people in terms they understand;
- speaking well in public.

As you see, the focus turns away from your charisma, to how you make employees *feel*. Yet, when I talk to leaders about who they see as inspirational, they often refer to famous leaders such as President John F Kennedy, Mahatma Gandhi, Winston Churchill, Mother Theresa, Nelson Mandela and other awe-inspiring leaders. They tell me that if they could be more like them, they would inspire their teams more.

Again, not so. It seems to me that, for the vast majority of us, trying to be like one of those leaders is a foolish pursuit. Instead, if we can focus more on others, and our impact on them, rather than on ourselves, we will be thinking in the right way. It doesn't take much to focus on how to deliver these behaviours, and the YouGov analysis shows that you can gain huge advantage by simply moving from being poor at them, to being good.

The secret to encouraging discretionary effort

The YouGov findings show that improving your performance to a good standard in all 20 behaviours listed above means that you are likely to be seen as 89 per cent more inspiring by your employees. You are likely to drive up their feelings of being respected by 65 per cent and improve their stated levels of motivation by 56 per cent. Most importantly you are likely to increase discretionary effort among your employees by 24 per cent, as reported by employees in the survey.

These are significant gains that can have a massive effect on engagement scores in your team. They can also have massive impact on your ability as a leader to deliver your own goals – whether that be to improve revenues or profitability, increase customer satisfaction, decrease accidents or decrease employee sick days.

Stefan Kaszubowski of YouGov says: 'These are statistically significant insights. Using the statistical technique of multiple regression, we have been able to understand which manager attributes are key drivers of employee engagement, including discretionary effort.'

Analyst Ben Mainwaring says: 'The survey shows that managers are a lot more effective when they are seen positively by their employees. However, it was clear that managers tended to think they performed better against these attributes than employees said they did, even though they both broadly agreed on what mattered most in a manager.'

However, some behaviours are more influential in obtaining extra effort from employees than others. Ben explains: 'This research reveals that managers who seem to understand their weaknesses and relate to other people effectively are well liked, but did not secure more discretionary effort. There are four management behaviours that have a uniquely important relationship to discretionary effort.'

The four most important management behaviours

Of the previous top eight behaviours, the most important are:

1 helping employees to understand the purpose and vision of the organization, and understand where it is headed;

2 making employees feel like they make a contribution to this;

3 being seen to value employee input and perspectives;

4 communication skills that enable managers to have good conversations and to be good when addressing large groups.

We live and work in a numbers-driven world. That is why I have spent time trying to find ways to quantify the benefits of making employees feel better, and what behaviours managers need to exhibit to achieve this. A good question for organizations and teams to ask is this: 'In order to make employees feel more inspired, more motivated, more respected and, as such, more likely to give of their discretionary effort, what should we, institutionally, be training our managers to do more of, and less of?'

As Christine Porath says:

'Feeling cared for by one's supervisor has a more significant impact on people's sense of trust and safety than any other behaviour by a leader. Employees who say they have more supportive supervisors are 1.3 times as likely to stay with the organization and are 67 per cent more engaged.

Employees who derive meaning and significance from their work (purpose) are more than three times as likely to stay with their organization   the highest single impact of any variable in our survey. These employees also report 1.7 times higher job satisfaction and are 1.4 times more engaged at work.'

When you feel worthy and respected, when you are committed to the team's purpose, when you know how what you do makes a difference to that purpose and the team's goals, when you trust the values of the team and live the culture yourself, and when you have regular conversations with your boss, you have a greater sense of purpose, and that powers your own levels of motivation and performance.

Next: how values contribute to a sense of purpose, and create value.

Key points from Chapter 4

1 Leaders rate themselves lowest on the ability to deliver purpose and values in their teams – and yet research shows that employees most want this.

2 YouGov's survey highlights that the single most important attribute in a manager is making employees feel important and appreciated. While managers and employees both know that being respected is important, all too often we see the exact opposite taking place.

▶

3 Employees believe there is much to be done on the subject of whether or not their bosses listen to them, and value their input and perspective. While 94 per cent of managers say they do this, only 60 per cent of employees agree; 4.7 per cent of managers surveyed said they were extremely inspiring, while a further 66 per cent said they were somewhat inspiring. Employees have a different view. Only 41 per cent agree their bosses are inspiring. The rest said their bosses were either not inspiring or were potentially demotivating.

4 There are four management behaviours that have a uniquely important relationship to interlocking discretionary effort. These are:
   – helping employees to understand the purpose and vision of the organization, and understand where it is headed;
   – making employees feel like they make a contribution to this;
   – valuing employee input and perspectives;
   – communication skills that enable managers to have good conversations and to be good when addressing large groups.

The value of values

05

How culture contributes to a sense of purpose and to better results

When leaders ensure that their people live the values of their organization, those values make a positive contribution to relationships, reputation and results. Commonly held values create trust – and that is the basis of prosperity. There can be no prosperity without trust, and trust comes from having the right values framework. But, take care with the values you select, to make sure they help you deliver the business plan, in the right way.

In the grip of a crisis, it is impossible to remember where the crisis manual is, let alone find time to read it.

Anyone who has experienced a real crisis – something that threatens the very existence of your organization – will know the mind-numbing reality of being caught by surprise, engulfed by global media, pressured to make instant and ill-informed decisions, bombarded by all sides for answers, all the while still trying to understand exactly what has happened.

In these circumstances, instead of reading the crisis manual, what do you do? You revert to your instincts and your values, and take action on what you think is right. Which might just get you into a whole heap of extra trouble.

Having had to handle crises in the chemicals, nuclear and airline industries when I worked for large organizations, and then, as a consultant, advise clients who were leaders of companies hit by a critical issue in retail, motor, food, IT and oil industries, I've had more than my fair share to deal with. Some of those companies had held regular crisis exercises and the best of them held realistic, sweaty-palmed simulations. But, when the real crisis came, nothing went to plan.

For companies that had never done these exercises, they were gripped by shock and took ages to organize themselves and respond. In that vacuum, the media frenzy and the reaction of hostile groups – either affected by the crisis or opposed to the business – deepened the hole they were in and caused more damage. Usually, however, it was their own behaviours that made matters worse.

Whether they were victims of a natural disaster, victims of criminals and fraud (increasingly, in today's world, hackers), guilty of organizational misdeed, or victims of a dreadful but unfortunate accident, very often what they did in response to the crisis caused a second and even worse issue for them.

They would sometimes take short-term, financially driven decisions that had a hugely negative effect on all of their key relationships and ultimately made their situations far worse and far more expensive. In those situations, their decisions and actions were influenced by the values they believed to be most important.

If they thought maintaining cash flow and share price was more important than maintaining relationships with all of their key stakeholders, they sometimes so badly damaged those relationships that they lost customers and cash flow, lost the trust of regulators and local communities, and lost the faith of their shareholders.

Warned by lawyers that an apology would be an admission of guilt, and therefore increase the liability, leaders stayed behind their office doors and refused to show their human side. Others refused to recall products that may cause damage. Others have done little to calm the nerves of spooked customers or shown little sympathy for the victims of their mishaps.

These were leaders and teams, I felt, who may have had a set of values posted on the walls, but who never truly believed them. Those who did believe their values, lived them every day in the organization and often acted out of a more ethical and moral base, and were more concerned about doing the right thing after a disaster, no matter what the cost. Although they took a short-term hit, they ensured the long-term survival of their businesses and often came back stronger than when they suffered their crisis.

Values are beliefs in action

I have always defined the values of an organization as its beliefs in action. Any organizational culture, really, is 'how we do things around here'. The key word is *do*. Values drive beliefs and beliefs drive behaviours. Those behaviours determine how well an organization performs. These behaviours are your culture.

Those values, therefore, if truly lived in an organization, can become a competitive edge that enables and drives all the right behaviours. As Dee Hock, the founder of Visa, says: 'Simple, clear purpose and principles give rise to complex, intelligent behaviour. Complex rules and regulations give rise to simple, stupid behaviour.'

This thought is echoed in a study of corporate ethics, which shows that being too obedient at work can turn off empathy and lead to poor decision making. Professor Roger Steare is a British corporate philosopher, speaker and author. Together with psychologist Pavlos Stamboulides, he conducts empirical research on moral character, judgement and behaviour. Together they designed MoralDNA, a psychometric tool that measures thinking preferences when making moral decisions. It is based on three ethical decision-making philosophies – the ethic of reason or logic, the ethic of care or empathy, and the ethic of obedience or compliance and the law.

Working with the Chartered Management Institute (CMI), Professor Steare surveyed a total of 2,500 CMI members across private, public and not-for-profit sectors. They found that managers use different decision-making processes at home than in the workplace, where they turn off their care and turn up the obedience. In other words, they become less ethical at work. He says:

> 'Large organizations are perceived as less ethical in their behaviour. Only 23 per cent of managers in large organizations – of more than 250 employees – give the organization top marks for ethical behaviour, compared to 59 per cent in organizations with fewer than 10 employees.
>
> It is clear that organizational cultures affect how individuals think and act in the workplace. Values and principles should drive management decision making. Avoid knee-jerk regulatory reactions to problems: too many rules lead to more, not fewer, ethical breakdowns.'

The CMI report found that stronger management ethics were linked to better organizational performance, and also helped to engage employees. Better ethics meant happier customers, and also paid off when managing risk.

Global surveys show values are valued

To explore how deeply values are embedded in organizations and to examine the role that values are playing, Booz Allen Hamilton, a US management consulting firm headquartered in Washington, and the Aspen Institute, a non-profit and non-partisan forum focused on values-based leadership and public policy, conducted a global study of corporations in 30 countries and five regions.

Senior executives of 365 companies were polled, almost one-third of whom were CEOs or board members. The purpose of the survey was to examine the way companies defined corporate values, to expand on research about the relationship of values to business performance, and to identify best practices for managing corporate values.

Here's what they found:

- *Ethical behaviour is a core component of company activities.* The survey found that 89 per cent of the global respondents possess written values statements, and that nearly three-quarters believe that both executives and employees are under significant pressure to demonstrate strong corporate values. Of the 89 per cent of companies that have a written corporate values statement, 90 per cent specify ethical conduct as a principle.

- *Most companies believe values influence two important strategic areas – relationships and reputation – but do not see the direct link to growth.* Of the companies that value commitment to customers, 80 per cent believe their principles reinforce such dedication. Substantial majorities also categorize employee retention and recruitment and corporate reputation as both important to their business strategy and strongly affected by values. However, few can prove that that these values directly affect earnings and revenue growth.

- *Most companies are not measuring their ROV – return on values.* In a business environment increasingly dominated by attention to definable returns on specific investments, most senior executives are surprisingly lax in attempting to quantify a return on values (ROV). Fewer than half say they have the ability to measure a direct link to revenue and earnings growth.

- *Top performers consciously connect values and operations.* Companies that report superior financial results emphasize – far more than their peers – such values as commitment to employees, drive to succeed and adaptability. They are also more successful in linking values to the way they run their companies.

- *Values practices vary significantly by region.* Asian and European companies are more likely than US firms to emphasize values related to the corporation's broader role in society, such as social and environmental responsibility.

- *The leader's tone really matters.* Of the respondents 85 per cent say their companies rely on explicit CEO support to reinforce values, and 77 per cent say such support is one of the 'most effective' practices for reinforcing the company's ability to act on its values. (This applies to leaders of divisions, of global companies, heads of countries of those firms, and leaders of every level.)

The Booz Allen Hamilton/Aspen Institute survey suggests that while the logic in relating values-based management to business performance has a strong following among executives around the world, the management practices and measurement techniques related to the values are works in progress.

This is a great pity. I believe it is because managers do not think about measuring values in the right way – by translating them into specific behaviours that can be observed and measured, allowing a better understanding of their role in value creation. The other problem is that companies do not think about which values to choose and use in the right way. Too often they choose values that are exactly the same as those of their rivals, generating little differentiation in behaviours and culture.

A recent report by Maitland, one of Europe's leading financial and corporate communications consultancies, found that only 17 of the FTSE 100 businesses in the UK do not declare a set of values on their website or in their annual report. Among the 83 who did, integrity, respect and innovation were the most commonly expressed values.

'It is interesting to note that so many of the more commonly expressed values relate to behaviour traits rather than strategic or operational characteristics such as flexibility, efficiency, speed and simplicity. These all feature in our research but tend to be found towards the lower end of the league table', commented Maitland.

The top 10 values in the Maitland survey were:

1 Integrity

2 Respect

3 Innovation

4 Safety

5 Transparency

6 Excellence

7 Team work

8 Honesty

9 Trust

10 Responsibility

The majority of the companies surveyed listed three to five values. Some expressed 16 or more. Perhaps it might be a bit difficult for staff to remember all of those?

These results raise, for me, an important question. Why do corporate value statements look so similar, when businesses are so different? Why is there such a level of sameness to the statements? An even bigger issue is the fact that while more and more companies openly express their values, it does not necessarily mean that they live them.

Enron, a US energy, commodities and services company in Houston, Texas, espoused the values of communication, respect, integrity and excellence. (Three of those values feature in the list of the most often expressed values of the FTSE 100 companies!) In 2001, it was revealed that its reported financial condition was sustained substantially by an institutionalized, systematic and cleverly planned accounting fraud, thus making it an example of wilful corporate fraud and corruption.

So, not only are some value statements bland and undifferentiating, some are as fraudulent as the leaders of the business. No wonder, then, that the majority of the public are looking for trustworthiness and reliability from big corporations. Corporate scandals of the past years have invoked profound scepticism about business ethics and conduct.

Four out of ten people believe business is unethical

For each of the past 12 years, the Institute of Business Ethics has asked the British public its view on business and ethics. In the latest survey, conducted at the end of 2015, almost 40 per cent of the British public still believed that British businesses were behaving unethically. It is not all bad news, however, as there has been a 6 per cent increase in the number of people now more likely to believe that companies are behaving more ethically than a decade ago.

Those aged 16 to 34 are the most positive in their perceptions of ethical business behaviour, with two-thirds of them believing that current business behaviour is, indeed, ethical. The issue that most worries members of the public today is corporate tax avoidance (34 per cent), with executive pay in second place at 25 per cent. This number has declined significantly over the past two years. Third on the list of worries is exploitative labour, at 20 per cent.

From the YouGov research mentioned in Chapter 4, it is clear that values that are not lived in an organization by every manager are hugely damaging to motivation and discretionary effort. Employees look to their bosses to be principled and honest, and to live a positive and moral set of values. When they do, performance improves.

For all these reasons, you can see why so many companies put integrity, honesty, responsibility and safety so high up on their lists. But, do these values truly differentiate their culture? Do they add competitive edge? Of course businesses need to have integrity, act ethnically and be honest. But these are licence-to-operate values, not differentiating values.

Values create more agile teams

Leaders today know they need to create more leaders, throughout their organizations, if they in turn are going to create more agile, responsive and faster companies. They need to give those leaders a framework for leading, a tight brief that enables decision making where it is needed, when it is needed, in the knowledge that those leaders will be able to use it to make the 'right' decisions.

To be able to make those decisions, people need to know what they are trying to achieve. What is the real purpose of their labours? They also need to know, exactly, what values and beliefs should be applied to those decisions And, finally, they need to know what the commercial goals are, what the picture of success is, in order to be able to make the right decisions.

Business in the Community (BITC) is a business-led charity with a membership of more than 850 companies, from large multinational household names to small local businesses and public sector organizations. BITC advises, supports and challenges its members to create a sustainable future for people and the planet and to improve business performance.

In guidelines to members, BITC says: 'A company's statement of values is a high-level statement that describes how the company behaves. It is not a mission statement that describes what task the company aims to fulfill. Corporate values are about what the company stands for and how its employees behave. They are about framing a role for the business that gives it a purpose beyond profit.'

Embedding values is not easy to do, but it brings dividends

The BITC says: 'It is not easy to do. For every one genuinely values-driven company there are many more where the corporate values statement simply exists as a poster on the chairperson's wall. The result of such circumstances is that employees in the call centres, and possibly even those working in the corporate centre, do not recognize the value statement as describing the actual values and behaviours in the workplace.'

BITC says that their research has shown that a key factor common to companies that have been enduringly great performers – at the top of the market for 100 years or more – was precisely a base of values that were strong enough to provide employees of the company with a common bond: a purpose beyond profit.

Getting it right, says BITC, can win all sorts of benefits:

- employees who are loyal to and supportive of the company, and more likely to stay if offered an equivalent position elsewhere;
- customers who are more likely to trust the company, because they see employees doing the right thing;
- enhanced relationships with investors, who may see that the company runs less risk of corporate scandals or controversies;
- good relationships with government and local communities, who begin to see the company as a good neighbour.

Paul Polman, global chief executive of Unilever, says that values build trust:

'I can visit my colleagues in any country of the world and I find that they may speak different languages and be working to different issues in their different countries, but within Unilever, they all have the same values. That creates trust, and trust enables us to work together – it helps us to build over the cracks that are in any system you design. And that is the basis of prosperity. So, there can be no prosperity without trust, and trust comes from having the right values framework.

You have to enable people to make decisions at the lowest possible level inside the company. I believe the best way to galvanize success in a company like Unilever is to be sure that decisions are being taken at the level where the knowledge is. That is a very important statement – that decisions need to be taken at the level of where the knowledge is. So as a CEO, as a leader, you always have to embed the decision making throughout the organization. It is not about rules and regulations – which stifle innovation – it is about having the right values and trust, which stimulate innovation.'

Values should be liberating and measured

In every interview I have ever conducted with CEOs, I asked the leaders to tell me what the values of their business were. Many admitted that their values could be common to almost any other organization, because often values represented the moral norms of the societies within which they operated.

Some companies had worked hard to use the values to differentiate themselves and say something about them that was unique. Nearly all of the leaders made sure that their purpose and values became part of the company's brand and were used as a source of competitive differentiation. The purpose and values were also used with suppliers and partners to ensure consistency everywhere on the value chain and ensure high standards.

Leaders were unanimous in their view that articulating values and purpose was one of the most important jobs of leadership. It was a conversation without end, on board and management agendas, discussed on roadshows and workshops. A shared sense of mission and values was inspiring, empowering and liberating and created enormous value in those companies that really brought them to life, they said.

Xerox CEO Anne Mulcahy has been widely quoted as saying that corporate values 'helped save Xerox during the worst crisis in our history', and that living the values has been one of Xerox's five performance objectives for the past several years. These values – which include customer satisfaction, quality and excellence, premium return on assets, use of technology for market leadership, valuing employees, and corporate citizenship – are far from words on a piece of paper. They are accompanied by specific objectives and hard measures.

About nine out of ten of the leaders I have interviewed say they believe that values create value and were increasing in importance in a transparent, radically connected world. They believe that these values help to create more collaboration in their businesses, improve their external image, reduce risk and even improve profitability.

Understand the different types of values

Values should encourage the right behaviours in an organization. They should ensure ethical behaviour, enable behaviours that help to deliver the plan, and enable people throughout the organization to make decisions on their own.

The problem is that depending on where you sit in the organization you are likely to opt for a different set of values. Managers will want behaviours that deliver high performance. Employees want behaviours that give them a great place to work. Marketers want behaviours that win and keep customers. Boards want ethical behaviours. Leaders want behaviours that deliver the future vision. All should be catered for.

This idea caused me to research the different categories of values used by many companies. I believe that anyone looking to refresh their values or establish new values for their teams or their businesses should think about these categories when devising the right value set for them.

Values should help the company to achieve its goals and deliver its purpose. Yet most organizations have what I would describe as a hodgepodge of values that do not fully empower employees and are exactly the same as most other companies, including competitors. When considering your values, think about what you are trying to achieve, and which behaviours you want to influence or engineer.

I believe there are six places to look for your core values. Here are the areas to think about:

- *Licence-to-operate values.*
  There are some values that every organization should adhere to. Honesty, integrity, respect, innovation – what business could survive if it didn't have these? That, I believe, is why so many of the FTSE 100 companies in the UK have exactly the same values. Everyone needs teamwork and collaboration. Everyone needs to be safe. I could go on and on. These are what I would describe as cleanliness values. Of course you must have them. Society expects these of you, but because of this, all companies have these and they do little to distinguish and differentiate.

- *Differentiating values.*
  These are values unique to your organization, which help to differentiate you in the marketplace. What is it about the way you do things that makes you different? How do you deliver unique offers to customers? What aspects of your brand are recognized and applauded by your consumers? These values need to be kept alive and leveraged constantly for you to maintain the promise of your brand in the marketplace.

- *Nice-place-to-work values.*
  Ask employees what matters to them, and you will find a whole set of values that ensure they work in a place that enables them to do their best, while also making them feel cared for and respected. You need these too.

- *High-performance values.*

  Talk to managers, and most of them describe a set of values around creating a high-performance culture. They want accountability, agility, ideas, commitment, innovation and more.

- *Current values.*

  As organizations grow and develop, a set of behaviours take root in that organization for all sorts of reasons. The founder might have had a personal set of values that became embedded as the organization grew. Successive leaders might have brought in their own beliefs and put in place operating processes driven by those beliefs. Whatever the reason, the organization will have a real set of values that manifest themselves as behaviours throughout the organization. These are the real and current values, not all of which are desirable and should be sustained. You have to truly understand what values live within the organization now and are brought to life in behaviours. Which are the behaviours that are undesirable and need to be stopped? Which behaviours happen only infrequently, but need to be made more commonplace? Which behaviours are critical to your success and must be maintained?

- *Future values.*

  Every team, every division, every company and every organization has a plan. Progress requires new and stretching goals, greater productivity, new products and services, new customers or new business from existing customers. To achieve these things will require new behaviours. If not, then what will enable the growth? And if they are new behaviours, what are the values that must underpin those behaviours? What beliefs need to be instilled in the business that will encourage the right behaviours throughout the organization? Too often, leadership teams fail to recognize that business plans require new behaviours, and those new behaviours may require new and different values that must be embedded.

- *Core values.*

  From all of these categories, the organization's core values should then be selected. These should become the deeply held beliefs that guide all of the company's actions, creating a moral compass that guides all decisions, at every level of the organization, always. Once decided on they should be sacrosanct, never compromised for convenience or short-term gain.

  As Paul Polman says, the core values should be the values that enable trust, collaboration and high performance.

Next: how purpose delivers value and how to measure it.

Key points from Chapter 5

1   Most corporate value statements look similar, in spite of the fact that businesses are so different. Why is there such a level of sameness to the statements?

2   About nine out of ten of the leaders I have interviewed say they believe that values create value and were increasing in importance in a transparent, radically connected world.

3   They were unanimous in the view that articulating values and purpose was one of the most important jobs of leadership – a conversation without end.

4   Most senior executives are surprisingly lax in attempting to quantify a return on values (ROV). Fewer than half say they have the ability to measure a direct link to revenue and earnings growth. This is because they do not look for the link between values and the behaviours that create value – and that CAN be measured.

5   Companies that report superior financial results emphasize such values – far more than their peers – as commitment to employees, drive to succeed and adaptability. They are also more successful in linking values to the way they run their companies.

6   Values should provide a licence to operate, be differentiating, create great places to work, enable high performance and, most of all, enable the business plan to be delivered.

Measuring the value of purpose

06

Meeting the needs of customers and, in so doing, creating long-term value for all stakeholders

Business success in the 21st century will be defined by more than just making a profit. Sustainable success will depend on how well organizations create value for a range of stakeholders, and on how well they report on that value creation. In the age of transparency, enabled by the internet, customers, employees, communities and shareholders will want to know exactly how well companies are delivering to their wider purpose.

It should take you about a minute and a half to read a full page of this book, if you do so at average reading speeds.

In that same time, almost 5 million posts will go up on Facebook. Google will have been searched 4.5 million times and more than 300 million e-mails will have been sent. About 600,000 tweets will have been posted on Twitter and 83,000 photos will have been uploaded to Instagram. Almost 70 million WhatsApp messages will have been sent. And around 600 hours of video will have been uploaded to YouTube. (Assuming you were prepared to watch all of those videos, and assuming you had really, really dedicated yourself to the task, it would take you 52 days, working 12 hours a day, just to watch what was uploaded while you read this page!)

All of that happens in just a minute and a half of online activity. People are sharing information and insights, news and views, gossip and trivia, in staggering numbers. And it will only grow. This is the reality of this digital world. Technology has enabled people all over the globe to become better connected, better informed and much more empowered. Instantly.

Changing the way business thinks and acts

As a result of the digital world people are emboldened, and in a globalized economy this better connected, more informed public is changing forever the way that businesses think and act.

PricewaterhouseCoopers (trading as PwC) is the largest professional services network in the world and one of the big four auditors, along with Deloitte, Ernst & Young (EY) and KPMG. For 19 years, PwC has been interviewing CEOs around the world to find out their views on leadership, the global economy and the big issues they are facing. Every year, PwC announces the results at Davos. In 2016 PwC interviewed 1,409 CEOs in 83 countries.

Introducing the survey, Dennis Nally, chairman of PwC International Ltd, said it was not lost on CEOs that a great many of these technologically empowered citizens were also their customers or potential customers:

'CEOs must navigate a world that is being dramatically shaped by other megatrends such as increasing urbanization, climate change and rapid demographic and social shifts. Faced with these changes, CEOs tell us that customers will increasingly judge companies based on how they help greater society and how they live up to their own values. Notably, nearly one-quarter of CEOs said their company has changed its sense of purpose in the last three years to take into account the broader impact it has on society.'

Dennis said that to successfully address the expectations of a super-connected and technologically smart society, companies were looking to technology (of course) for answers. PwC's research suggested that CEOs would be focusing on three priorities for the foreseeable future. The first is improving their technology, because technology is central to innovation – and CEOs of companies that are 'digital natives' find it easier to track changing consumer expectations and innovate with agility, and engage better with investors.

Second, CEOs recognize the wider stakeholder expectations of their business, particularly the customer. Reshaping companies built on profit alone into ones where profit and purpose combine is not going to happen quickly or easily, but it is a transformation that is already starting and that businesses need to keep pace with. 'We asked CEOs whether business success in the 21st century will be redefined by more than just financial profit and 76 per cent of them agreed; 69 per cent of CEOs indicate that they have adjusted their organization's purpose to include the broader impact on society', said Dennis.

The third priority that CEOs are focusing on is in line with the second – reporting and communicating broader measures of success. 'In a digitally driven world, where theoretically every part of business can be measured, CEOs have not yet mastered how to measure the long-term success that comes from being a trusted company and good corporate citizen', says Dennis. 'Over time, technology, once again, will no doubt help CEOs effectively to measure how better products and services, combined with soft drivers such as transparent relationships with customers, employees and greater society, can future-proof their companies in this uncertain world.'

Intangible assets – the real drivers of success

The soft drivers that Dennis Nally refers to are also often referred to as intangible assets. These are the assets of companies that cannot physically be seen or touched – things like reputation, relationships and trust. Even though they are fantastically difficult to measure and manage, they are worth staggering amounts of money.

Tangible assets are physical assets such as land, vehicles, equipment, machinery, furniture, inventory, stock, bonds and cash. These assets devalue the more they are used and are at constant risk of being damaged or stolen.

Intangible assets are non-physical, and include everything from goodwill to trademarks, internet domain names, reputation, relationships, and even company culture. These increase in value the more they are used. They add to a company's possible future worth. But they are also based on sentiment – and bad news can have a dramatic impact on sentiment and cause huge volatility in share prices.

The World Bank is an international financial institution that provides loans to developing countries for capital programmes. It is a component of the World Bank group, which is part of the United Nations system. The World Bank's official goal is the reduction of poverty. However, according to its articles of agreement, all its decisions must be guided by a commitment to the promotion of foreign investment and international trade, and to the facilitation of capital investment.

This is one reason why the World Bank keeps data on the market capitalization of listed companies around the world. It says that the total value of all listed companies, in its latest audit in 2014, amounted to US$66.5 trillion. That is up from US$50 trillion in 2010.

The United States could boast US$26 trillion of value from its listed companies, while Japanese listed companies were worth US$4.3 trillion and Indian companies were worth US$1.5 trillion. Companies in the United Kingdom were valued at US$3.183 trillion.

US$53 trillion of value from things you cannot see

Speak to the global accounting institutions and they will tell you that up to 80 per cent of that value is made up of intangible assets. That means that more than US$53 trillion of value on stock markets is made up of things you cannot see! Five years ago it was thought to be around 60 per cent. A decade ago, it was thought to be 20 per cent – with 80 per cent of the value of listed companies in its tangible assets.

This is a massive turnaround. It explains why stock markets are so volatile. When investors panic about things that might affect the companies they invest in, they worry about whether that company will be able to give them a return on their investment. The only way those companies can give a return on investment is if they grow. And whether they grow or not depends on the state of their intangible assets more than anything else. So a huge amount of value that is expressed in current share prices has to do with the concept of 'future worth'.

Intangible assets enable growth. If you don't have the right people in the right culture, if you don't have the right reputation, if you're a company that is not trusted, growing will be somewhat difficult. So employee attitudes, reputation and relationships are all intangible assets.

Intangible assets are *the* key value drivers in our economy. If you could measure them, and they could be made more transparent, investors would have a better understanding of a company's ability to grow and deliver worth in the future. The trouble is, it is notoriously difficult to measure intangible assets. Any sensible person would recognize the enormous value of top management quality and experience, combined with an ability to execute on strategy, combined with a company culture that has the ability to constantly solve problems, all driven by positive and loyal employees. But how do you measure it?

Current reporting models for these intangible assets are inadequate, built for a time when tangible assets were more than 80 per cent of the value of a company. Most companies are very well managed – for the traditional tangible assets they have. But if 80 per cent of their value is in intangibles, and therefore any future value is critically dependent on those intangibles, how can you properly manage what you cannot properly measure?

A great deal has changed since the current reporting model was designed. Trends such as globalization, growing policy activity by governments around the world in response to financial, governance and other crises, heightened expectations of transparency and accountability and environmental concerns, require new standards of reporting.

The type of information needed to assess the past, current and future performance of companies is now much wider than what is provided by existing reporting models. There are huge interdependencies between strategy, governance, operations, financial and non-financial performance that need to be made much clearer in order to demonstrate an organization's ability to create value now and for the future.

Non-financial issues can have a dramatic effect on performance. Take for instance, the issue of trust.

Trust is an intangible asset of enormous worth

Leaders everywhere recognize that they are being challenged by the shifting attitudes of people around the world. People's attitudes have grown more negative to business in general, but big business in particular. This is leading to mistrust in capitalism.

Building trust is hard. Members of the public seldom have all the information required to make a well-informed judgement, are quick to judge and often make naive assumptions that give rise to the flames of mistrust. Fuelled by the media, and fanned by social media, illogical and negative conclusions spread the blaze, particularly among young people. These young people are going to be future buyers, decision makers, or government officials who can change regulations. And, of course, they will be voters.

As I have reported in previous chapters, the 2015 Edelman Trust Barometer, which surveys 33,000 respondents in 28 countries, shows that all too few people trust business. Only about half the people surveyed do. And only 18 per cent trust business leaders.

The major reason for this decline in trust is that the majority of people believe that business *fails to contribute to the greater good*. At the same time

81 per cent agree that companies can take specific actions that both increase profits and improve the economic and social conditions in the communities where they operate.

'Trust Across America' is a global collaborative initiative designed to help enhance trustworthy behaviour in organizations. Its mission is to unite organizations under the common cause of furthering organizational trust. Every year it tracks the performance of the most trustworthy public companies in the United States.

'The results are nothing short of staggering', says Trust Across America. 'Trustworthy companies in the United States have produced an 82.9 per cent return over the past five years versus the average return of 42.2 per cent of the S&P index.'(The Standard and Poor's 500, often abbreviated as the S&P 500, or just the S&P, is a US stock-market index based on the market capitalization of 500 large companies having common stock listed on the New York Stock Exchange or NASDAQ.)

There are many reasons why trustworthy companies perform almost twice as well as other companies on the S&P, says Trust Across America:

- High levels of trust can attract new customers and help to retain existing ones, creating more revenue.
- Trust prevents burdensome and costly regulations, savings that improve efficiency.
- Trust makes employees more disposed towards joining a company and then more committed to delivering high-quality work, improving productivity.
- It encourages business partners to be more willing to collaborate, increasing innovation.
- All of this makes shareholders more willing to invest their money and creates a virtuous circle of success.

Trust is money. It enhances cash flow and improves capital value and can be worth billions of dollars to organizations. Interesting. So how do you best influence trust?

Purpose delivers trust, and higher growth rates

Global research shows that companies who want to be trusted need to be clear about their sense of purpose, show how they serve a purpose wider than profit, engage well with customers and employees as well as other stakeholders, produce high-quality products and services and be willing to collaborate in solving social challenges.

The International Institute for Management Development (IMD) is a business school based in Lausanne, Switzerland. It is one of the world's premier business and management institutions. Working with Burson-Marsteller, a global public relations and communications firm, the IMD recently conducted an in-depth study looking at the relevance of corporate purpose among more than 20 leading global companies based in Europe.

The IMD report said that European companies express their purpose either in terms of balancing the interests of stakeholders or through customer-focused messages. Customer-driven statements of purpose tended to be more specific and credible, they said, since they provided organizations with a clear sense of fundamental priorities by establishing the focus on a single constituency that carried high level of legitimacy – the customer.

The report said that, among large European companies, effectively communicating corporate purpose was more positively associated with higher financial performance than company size: 'Our research showed that strong and well-communicated corporate purpose could impact financial performance by up to 17 per cent. Today, companies that are successful at communicating their purpose are likely to be high performers – in the future, companies who do not have a purpose may not survive.'

As I reported in Chapter 2, the EY Beacon Institute, an organization dedicated to transforming business, recently teamed with Harvard Business Review Analytics Services, to talk to global executives about the impact that purpose has upon their ability to grow, innovate and transform. Valerie Keller, global lead for the EY Beacon Institute, reported that they found a very high level of consensus among executives that not only does purpose matter, but that companies who clearly articulated their purpose enjoyed higher growth rates and higher levels of success in transformation and innovation initiatives.

The EY Beacon Institute study found that companies that prioritized purpose performed much better than those that did not. However, only a minority of companies used purpose as a driver of strategy and decision making: 'As our survey findings showed, this was due not only to external issues, such as short-term pressures from investors, but to internal issues such as insufficient leadership commitment and misaligned performance metrics.'

And yet, the same executives believe that corporate purpose went beyond delivering financial results, to enabling the creation of more value for customers, positive impacts for society as well as greater financial returns for shareholders. Why? Because purpose-driven companies generated greater employee satisfaction, greater customer advocacy and higher-quality products and services.

Their conclusion? Purpose is being underleveraged by business today. Why? Many of the executives surveyed said that the biggest barrier to being purpose driven was a lack of meaningful metrics to capture and track long-term value creation.

If purpose is about creating value for all, how do you best track long-term value creation?

To understand more about how best to measure and track long-term value creation, I spoke to Charles Tilly, who was then the chief executive of the Chartered Institute of Management Accountants (CIMA).

CIMA is the largest management accounting body in the world, with more than 227,000 members and students in 179 countries. It is based in the UK and offers training and qualification in management accountancy and related subjects, and is focused on accountants working in industry. It provides ongoing support and training for its members.

Charles Tilly says that for most of his time in the accounting profession, business focused on profit first, and customer second:

> 'That sentiment has changed dramatically and the focus today is mostly on what we need to do for the customer. If we can get that right, and create value, then we will create a profit. The question is really about the wider purpose of business. I think it is primarily to meet the needs of its customers and in so doing create value over the long term for all of its stakeholders.
>
> If a company is going to be there for the long term then it has to act as a good corporate citizen in terms of looking after the world's resources and making sure that it has all the resources it needs to do business for the long term. The long-term success of business is good for communities and good for the world.'

However, he warns:

> 'It is all very well saying that but you very quickly have to get into the measurement game to fully understand the wider value that business brings. The first challenge we have is that 80 per cent of the market value of the

business is virtual and not tangible. Only 20 per cent can be seen on the balance sheet and it is extraordinary how long it has taken for the accounting profession to wake up to this change. I think we can be quite seriously criticized but I am also delighted to say that CIMA was one of the first to recognize this challenge and call for a review of the corporate reporting system.

The old reporting system was broken and only relevant to the 20 per cent of tangible assets. Together with the American Institute of Certified Professional Accountants (AICPA), we have been working to find better ways of measuring non-financial assets.'

Your value-creation story = competitive edge

If your purpose is to create value from customers, and in doing so create value for all, being able to measure how successfully you are delivering your purpose – and report on this to shareholders and stakeholders – will suddenly become a huge competitive edge. As we saw in Chapter 2, shareholders and investors are calling on business to report better on how they create value, and how they build the intangible assets that enable long-term future growth.

Leaders at all levels of companies, entrepreneurs setting up businesses, public sector leaders – all will have to start better articulating this value creation story. 'If you think about it, reporting is critical in explaining how a business creates value', says Charles Tilly. 'Being able to excel in telling your value creation story will be an increasing source of competitive advantage. You need to have a framework that tells the whole story of how you create value if you want to win trust and secure reputation.'

In July 2014 CIMA conducted a survey of its members in conjunction with AICPA, and spoke with more than 350 senior executives in the United States, Africa, Asia-Pacific and Europe:

- 94 per cent believed that it was important to be able effectively to create value throughout the corporate reporting process.

- Only 26 per cent felt that their current reporting met the information needs of investors and other external stakeholders.

- The majority believed that their current focus for strategic planning was too short – they believed they should use a horizon of five years and over rather than the current two- to three-year strategic planning horizon.

The vast majority were positive about the benefits of bringing together financial and non-financial information, with very few feeling that there were no benefits.

Charles says:

> 'This research enabled us to get together with the AICPA to really drive the management accounting agenda. A very important part of that agenda is providing businesses with non-financial metrics. The key issue is that business leaders have all the financial and non-financial metrics they need to run their businesses in a more integrated way. To do that they need more integrated financial reporting.
>
> Only then will they be able to tell a compelling story about how they create long-term value and so contribute to the greater good, not only in pure business terms, but also for society at large. If you want to be trusted then you have to be transparent and fully show the customer why they should trust you, and do the same for employees, governments, communities around you, and also for investors. When the accountants are able to pull all of this information together they can enable better decision making throughout the organizations they serve.'

Integrated reporting helps to account for purpose

This is how Charles Tilly describes integrated reporting. First of all, it has to explain how an organization creates value over time. Value is not created by or within an organization alone, as it is heavily influenced by the external environment and created through relationships with a variety of stakeholders. It is also dependent on a variety of resources. A fully transparent report must provide insight about the resources and the relationships used and affected by the organization. Those resources include financial, manufactured, intellectual, human, social and relationship, and natural resources. The report should explain how the organization interacts with all of those 'capitals' to create value in the short, medium and long term. For the purpose of integrated reporting the capitals are categorized and described as follows:

- *Financial capital*: the money that is available to the organization for use in the production of goods or the provision of services, obtained through financing such as debt equity grants or generated through operations or investments.

- *Manufactured capital*: manufactured physical objects available to an organization for use in the production of goods or services, including buildings and equipment.

- *Intellectual capital*: these are knowledge-based intangibles including patents, copyrights, software and licences, as well as organizational capital such as knowledge, systems processes and protocols.

- *Human capital*: these are the competencies, capabilities, experience and motivations of people working for a business, including their alignment to the organization's purpose and values, their ability to implement the organization's strategy, and their loyalties and motivations for improving processes, goods and services.

- *Social and relationship capital*: this includes the relationships with groups of external stakeholders, including customers and other networks, especially with regard to those stakeholders' willingness to trust and engage with the organization. It also includes intangibles associated with the brand and reputation that an organization has developed. Most important is the organization's social licence to operate.

- *Natural capital*: this includes all renewable and non-renewable environmental resources that support the past, current and future prosperity of an organization. It includes air, water, land, minerals and forests, biodiversity and ecosystem health.

An integrated report must show the business model of the organization, how it draws on the various capitals as inputs and, through its business activities, converts them to outputs (products, services, by-products and waste). These activities and outputs lead to outcomes in terms of effects on the six capitals. Companies using integrated reports would have to report on the outcomes (both positive and negative) for the six capitals, as well as identify risks and opportunities relevant to the organization and its business model. Its strategy would have to identify how it intended to mitigate or manage these risks and maximize opportunities. All of this would be based on setting up measurement and monitoring systems to provide information for decision making and monitoring of its performance.

Says Charles: 'It is clear that investors think such reporting would be more helpful for the analysis of company performance. So it would not only better meet the needs of investment professionals, but I believe also encourage more cohesive decision making within companies to support longer-term value creation.'

Enter the International Integrated Reporting Council (IIRC), a growing global coalition of regulators, investors, companies, standard setters, accounting bodies and accountants, and NGOs. This coalition is promoting communication about value creation as the next step in the evolution of corporate reporting. The IIRC's mission is to establish integrated reporting and thinking within mainstream business practice as the norm in the public and private sectors. By doing so, it wants to align capital allocation and corporate behaviour to wider goals of financial stability and sustainable development through the cycle of integrated reporting and thinking.

Having helped to create and market test an international integrated reporting framework, explained above by Charles Tilly, the IIRC now wants to achieve what it describes as a meaningful shift towards early adoption of the framework.

Integrated reporting enables better decisions

The IIRC was launched in 2010 by His Royal Highness the Prince of Wales, and its CEO is Paul Druckman. Charles Tilly sits on the IIRC council and chairs its technical task force.

Paul Druckman says there were over 90 businesses in the pilot programme for integrated reporting, including Unilever, Coca-Cola, Microsoft, China Light and Power, Hyundai and HSBC. It has also set up an investor network, made up of over 30 investor organizations, in order to help shape the framework by providing an investor's perspective on the shortfalls in current corporate reporting.

Says Paul Druckman:

'The modern corporate is increasingly seen as having a wider purpose in society beyond delivering value to shareholders. As the board's governance role expands accordingly, so IR is increasingly being used as a tool to understand and communicate value creation in its broadest context.

Why would a company not want to find a better way to communicate with everyone how they create value, so that they can build a deeper understanding and a richer dialogue with investors and other stakeholders? Businesses are the engines of value creation and it is through their capabilities that many of the challenges we face as a global society will be addressed. If businesses are not making and seen to be making a positive contribution to the societies of which they are part, then they will lose trust and value as a result.'

Integrated reporting (IR) is gaining traction internationally. Already there are about 1,000 companies that are adopting some IR principles into their reporting practice. These principles are as valid for small to medium-size enterprises as they are for large global corporates.

The message is clear: companies that want to be trusted and be able to deliver over the long term need to be clear about their purpose; measure and then communicate how they serve a purpose wider than profit; engage fully and transparently with customers, employees and other stakeholders; and show a willingness to collaborate in solving social challenges. But they can do none of this unless they produce high-quality products or services that are needed and wanted by customers.

First, create a customer, then create value. By doing all of this, they will be far more likely to attract investors who are willing to take a long-term view and help them to deliver sustainable success.

Next: stories from the front line – how leaders have used purpose, values and stretching goals to enable success.

Key points from Chapter 6

1 Globally, CEOs recognize that customers will increasingly judge companies based on their wider purpose – how they help greater society and how they live up to their own values – but they have not yet mastered how to measure the long-term success that comes from being a trusted company and good corporate citizen.

2 The total value of all listed companies around the world amounts to US$66.5 trillion. Up to 80 per cent of that value is made up of intangible assets. This means that more than US$53 trillion of value on stock markets is made up of things you cannot see!

3 Employee engagement, reputation and relationships are all intangible assets. Purpose influences all these assets, which are *the* key value drivers in our economy.

4 Current reporting models for these intangible assets are inadequate, built for a time when tangible assets were more than 80 per cent of the value of a company.

▶

5   Business leaders need all the relevant financial and non-financial metrics to run their businesses in a more integrated way. To do that they need more integrated financial reporting. Only then will they be able to tell a compelling story about how they create long-term value and deliver their wider purpose.

6   Integrated reporting is gaining traction internationally. Already there are about 1,000 large corporates, as well as small and medium-size companies, that are adopting IR principles into their reporting practice.

PART TWO
People with purpose: how leaders use purpose in their own organizations

From surviving to thriving   07

The importance of a long-term vision

A long-term vision gives employees a sense of security and this has a powerful impact on their engagement. If you want your people to have a greater sense of purpose, you must give them an audacious goal 10–20 years away – so audacious it gives them a sense of urgency today. If you want to transform the world, you better get started right away.

All too often, I hear business leaders complain that they cannot take a long-term view because of the short-term pressure for quarterly profit growth that comes from their investors. These powerful forces of short-termism negatively impact on corporate behaviours, they say, and stop leaders from investing in long-term growth. At worst, these forces also lead to scandal, pollution and poverty.

Many blame the meltdown of the world's global financial institutions, which in turn, in 2007–08 led to one of the toughest and longest recessions we have ever known, on exactly this – short-termism and greed.

Some of the leaders I have spoken with say that you have to resist these forces and try to attract to you investors who want to share a long-term view of the future. To do so, you have to be bold and you have to be assertive and you have to have a powerful story about how you will create long-term value.

Many is the time I have worked with leaders who have taken their company private, and the relief they express at having investors who are not driven by the quarterly reporting cycle is palpable. They still need to provide a return on the investment, but at least they have the time to do so without materially affecting the future of their organization.

It would be easy to think that this drive for short-term profits is indeed the need of all investors, but I have found many, as I reported in Chapter 2, who advocate a different view.

Recently, the world's biggest investor published an open letter to US and European business leaders, in which he appealed for longer-term thinking, wiser investing for future growth, and more transparency in corporate reporting on the real drivers of growth. This long-term thinker is Laurence D Fink, the chairman and chief executive of BlackRock, a global investment management corporation founded in 1988 and based in New York City. With more than US$4.5 trillion of assets under management, it is by far the world's largest investor.

Larry Fink, as he is known, says that this short-termism is not only a problem in business but also in politics. Investing in long-term growth is an issue of paramount importance for BlackRock's clients, he says, most of whom are saving for retirement as well as other long-term goals. In fact, he says, it is also paramount for the entire global economy.

Business is not investing for long-term growth

In Larry Fink's open letter to US and European business leaders, he wrote:

'While we have heard strong support from corporate leaders for taking such a long-term view, many companies continue to engage in practices that may undermine their ability to invest for the future. Dividends paid out by S&P 500 companies in 2015 amounted to the highest proportion of their earnings since 2009. As of the end of the third quarter of 2015, buybacks were up 27 per cent over 12 months. We certainly support returning excess cash to shareholders, but not at the expense of value-creating investment.

We are asking that every CEO lay out for shareholders each year a strategic framework for long-term value creation. Additionally, because boards have a critical role to play in strategic planning, we believe CEOs should explicitly affirm that their boards have reviewed those plans. BlackRock's corporate governance team, in their engagement with companies, will be looking for this framework and board review.'

Fink believes that annual shareholder letters and other communications to shareholders are too often backwards looking and do not do enough to articulate management's vision and plans for the future. This perspective on the future, however, is what investors and all stakeholders truly need, including, for example, how the company is navigating the competitive landscape, how it is innovating, how it is adapting to technological disruption or geopolitical events, where it is investing and how it is developing its talent. As part of this effort, companies should work to develop financial metrics, suitable for each company and industry, which support a framework for long-term growth. Components of long-term compensation should be linked to these metrics, he suggests.

Fink explains that one reason for investors' short-term horizons is that companies have not sufficiently educated them about the ecosystems they are operating in, what their competitive threats are and how technology and other innovations are impacting their businesses. Without clearly articulated plans, companies risk losing the faith of long-term investors.

'With clearly communicated and understood long-term plans in place, quarterly earnings reports would be transformed from an instrument of incessant short-termism into a building block of long-term behaviour. They would serve as a useful "electrocardiogram" for companies, providing information on how companies are performing against their long-term plan for value creation', wrote Fink.

Fink did not stop there. He said that in the United States and other countries, politicians often defined long term as the next election cycle. This attitude was eroding the economic foundations of countries, which needed instead public officials who adopted policies that supported long-term value creation.

Get value from shareholders, not just for them

One of the most interesting talks I ever attended was by Paul Polman, global CEO of consumer products company Unilever, when he gave the annual Marketing Society lecture in 2012. He said that leaders had to turn around their thinking and seek to get value *from* shareholders not just create value *for* them.

He felt that consumers have never been further ahead of business leaders, and were adopting new ways faster than business could. They had never been more connected and never felt more powerful and were demanding change faster than business or government could deliver it. It was they who defined markets or killed markets, it was they who set ethical standards, and it was they who were shouting for change. Consumers would choose brands and companies that contributed to, not just took from, society. What built trust in the past would not build trust in the future. It was clear, he thought, that you needed both performance and purpose in business today.

Success, said Paul, would depend on business being more open, more transparent and creating *shared purpose*.

This resonates with all the research I have done, with report after report showing that a sense of shared purpose with customers and society was what made employees most proud. Doing something that was important and worthwhile – and was seen as such by external audiences – was central to their sense of engagement and motivation, especially when leaders could show how an employee's individual efforts contributed to that purpose.

But this is not enough. It is no good doing something good if you feel you will not be able to do it for very long. All the better if you can combine your purpose with a scary long-term goal, which implies both a long-term future and being able to do more good.

From surviving to thriving

A long-term vision gives employees a sense of security and, as neuroscience shows, has a powerful and positive effect on their creativity, their willingness to collaborate and their willingness to go the extra mile. When they are under threat, these employees exhibit negative behaviours that compound the problems of their organization, even though they are wholly understandable and very human reactions. A long-term vision is part and parcel of giving people a greater sense of purpose, and needs to work in tandem with a compelling purpose statement, strong values and stretching goals.

Among the 30 leaders who I interviewed for this book, there were six who were notable for having to come in and rescue the organizations they led. It was clear in every case that these leaders developed and executed survival plans, while always being anxious to move as quickly as possible to a state where employees in the company would no longer feel threatened, and would be moving towards a more secure and long-term future.

'Surviving is one thing, but thriving is another', says Natalie Douglas, CEO of Healthcare at Home, one of Europe's leading providers of clinical homecare and speciality pharmacy. When her organization suffered a catastrophic breakdown in IT, resulting in an inability to provide vital medicines to patients at home, Natalie first engineered a turnaround, but as soon as practically possible, articulated and communicated a more uplifting long-term vision to her employees.

This was expressed as: 'To provide inspirational health care in the home for millions worldwide.' Natalie and her leadership team talked not only about the vision, but also about the strategic goals they needed to deliver to achieve their long-term aspiration, and spirits within the organization quickly lifted. Natalie said that one particular piece of feedback summarized for her the feedback she received from hundreds of members of staff when she articulated a long-term vision: 'Thank goodness the business is going to survive. We love what we do, it really matters, and it's so good to have a plan that we all can believe in.' Since then the business has gone from strength to strength.

The same was true for Andrew Swaffield, CEO of Monarch Airlines Group, the UK's leading independent travel company. He recalls having to rescue his company from the very precipice of bankruptcy, which had been a matter of mere hours away. In order to do this, he had had to ask for significant sacrifices from staff in the group, which included salary reductions, pension reductions and the loss of many staff through a redundancy programme.

It really mattered, he said, that staff were given an uplifting vision of the future as soon as was practically possible. They needed to know that their sacrifices had not been in vain and that they were all striving for something worthwhile.

Andrew set the company's long-term vision as: 'to be Europe's most recommended airline group'. He knew this would take a long time to achieve, but he knew everyone would want to help him achieve it. The goal was also measurable and possible – not out of reach.

Debbie Hewitt is non-executive chairperson of Moss Bros, one of the UK's leading menswear stores with more than 150 stores and global ambitions. When Debbie arrived, the company was in need of a radical turnaround in order to survive. Faced with such a crucial focus, inspiring and empowering people was not first on her agenda. But, as soon as the turnaround was bearing positive fruit, the leadership team turned its attention to articulating a long-term future and an inspiring purpose.

While their long-term vision is to become the number one men's suit specialist, more important was to inspire staff to provide brilliant service to customers everywhere. They did this by saying that their purpose was: 'To make men feel amazing.' This purpose statement was chosen to help drive behaviours on the shop floor, and resonated with the DNA of staff. Their vision was an aspirational target, a future measure of how well they could deliver their purpose.

Moss Bros is currently reporting significant improvements in revenues and profits.

Vision and purpose work together

Another example came from Craig Kreeger, CEO of Virgin Atlantic, the British-based airline. He was recruited to help turn around the business while being careful not to destroy its brand and service ethos:

'Very quickly I realized that turning the business around would not take very long. I made it clear to staff that this was a two-year recovery plan, that we would be profitable again reasonably quickly and would soon be having to think about our long-term future. I wanted them to be clear that fixing the airline was a short-term focus.

Having fixed the business, it wasn't long before we had to turn our attention to planning for a longer-term future. We needed to move from thinking about surviving to thinking about thriving. There had been an amazing amount of pride in the fact that the airline still existed after 30 years, but my view was that this was the wrong source of pride. I wanted people to stop being proud of surviving and start being proud of winning.'

Craig and his team quickly set a plan to win, and now describe their ambition as: 'To be the airline most loved by customers. We will achieve this by being uniquely Virgin Atlantic.'

Key to that long-term future was finding a purpose statement that resonated with staff and gave them a focus for all decision making. It had to express the culture of the organization, which was all about empowered individuals providing a great service to each and every customer. 'After much discussion, we agreed on this as our mission statement: 'To embrace the human spirit and let it fly'. The long-term vision and the purpose statement had to work hand in glove.

Craig said: 'To me a purpose statement is more than just a set of words. We make sure that all the decisions we make, particularly around our customer proposition and how we deal with our people, are consistent with our overarching purpose.'

On virtually every metric, from passenger satisfaction, to revenues and profitability, Virgin Atlantic is once again making positive strides.

Sustainability versus thrivability

All of the leaders I interviewed were keen to create an environment in which their people felt that they as individuals, and the companies they represented, were thriving. Simply being able to sustain themselves was not enough. To be able to create an environment in which they, their customers, their suppliers, their shareholders and the communities in which they operated were all thriving was a far better concept.

Yet, the majority of company purpose statements today talk about creating sustainable long-term success, even if, as Larry Fink says, they then do not present plans and insights that convince shareholders of this. The word sustainable, however, is still a defensive word, one that does not quite capture what I hear so many leaders and employees saying – that they want to do something important that helps people to thrive.

Here is how the dictionary defines the word sustainable:

sustainable: able to be maintained at a certain rate or level.

These and many other leaders I have spoken with give rise to an important thought, which is this: aiming for sustainable long-term success is perhaps not inspiring enough?

The word 'thrive' induces a more positive state of mind than the word 'sustain' and, if used more widely, could give rise to more positive and beneficial behaviours. Here is what the dictionary has to say about the word thrive:

to grow vigorously: flourish;
to gain in wealth or possessions: prosper.

If we want to create a world in which the predicted 9 billion people who will live in it in 2050 can thrive, business needs to play its part in working towards a thriving society and a thriving planet. It could very well be the difference between simply surviving – or thriving. Thinking about sustainability only means thinking about minimizing impact, and will never mobilize organizations and people to the breakthrough thinking that will deliver a thriving planet.

One such centre of thinking is The ThriveAbility Foundation, a UK registered charity whose mission is to support the development of a ThriveAbility Index that enables decision makers in both business and civil society, as well as investors, to design and select investments and business models that will deliver a green, inclusive economy by 2050. The role of the ThriveAbility Foundation is to enable key decision makers to maximize the 'thrival' of every single one of the key stakeholders in and around their organization. They too encourage business leaders to think long term and to take actions now that will build a more prosperous future.

Create an audacious 10- to 30-year vision

Professor Mark Taylor is dean of Warwick Business School, an academic department of the University of Warwick. It is one of the most prestigious and highly selective business schools in the world. Due to the school's historical international outlook, its alumni hold leadership positions in corporate, government and academic institutions around the globe. Speaking on the subject of long-term vision, Professor Taylor said an effective vision needed to be: 'Out of reach but not out of sight.'

You should be able to visualize your organization achieving this vision but it should not be possible to reach out and take hold of the vision straight away. If it could be achieved in the next year, or even five years, it is not really a vision, he says. A vision should be a future-oriented goal that is exciting, inspiring, motivating and more than a little stretching. If you cannot picture or imagine your organization achieving its vision, no matter how hard you try, it is likely that this 'out of sight vision' is either the wrong one for your organization, or does not fit with your organization's passions, purpose, values and beliefs – or it is so overambitious as to be unachievable.

'Out of reach but not out of sight' is also a great way to describe what management consultant and world-famous author Jim Collins describes as a 'Big Hairy Audacious Goal' (BHAG), pronounced BEEhag. With fellow author Jerry Porras, Collins wrote in his best-selling book *Built to Last* that a BHAG encouraged companies to define visionary goals that are more strategic and emotionally compelling. He said that many businesses set goals that described what they wanted to achieve over the coming days, months or years. These goals helped to align employees of businesses to work together more effectively, but were often very tactical, not very compelling, and failed to act as a clear catalyst for team spirit.

BHAGs needed to be audacious 10- to 30-year goals that were clear and compelling and had a clear finish line. They could either be qualitative, such as Ford Motor Company's vision to 'democratize the automobile', or quantitative, such as Walmart's vision in 1990 to become a US$125 billion company by the year 2000, which it not only achieved but exceeded.

The power of the BHAG is that it gets you out of thinking too small, says Collins. A great BHAG changes the time frame and simultaneously creates a sense of urgency. It is a real paradox. It is clear that you will not deliver a BHAG in three years, nor five years. It is likely to take at least a decade, maybe three decades, he says. Because it is so big and so audacious, it actually creates a sense of urgency, even though it is long term. If you want to transform the world, you had better get started today. The only way you can achieve something that big is with an absolutely obsessed, monomaniacal, overwhelming intensity and focus that starts today and goes on tomorrow and the next day and the next day and the next day for 365 days and then for 3,650 days – that's how you do it. And it is a brilliant way to inspire a sense of purpose in people.

Also, says Collins, one of the roles of the BHAG is that you cannot achieve it if, in the process, you don't build a great company, a great organization. Another feature of a long-term goal is that it is most likely to outlast the tenure of the current leader. People will be loyal to the goal, if not the leader. The leader's role is to act as a steward of the business, improving all the time its ability to achieve the long-term vision. In other words, to improve the chances of the business thriving.

The difference between a long-term vision and purpose

Most companies will have both a long-term vision statement (what they want to achieve) and a purpose statement (why they exist).

Monarch Airline Group has its own version of a BHAG, which it refers to as its True North. It wants to be 'Europe's most recommended airline group', a goal it will take a decade or more to deliver, but which is very measurable. Its purpose, however, is far more emotional, and is articulated as: 'To show we care'. This purpose goes to the heart of what people in the group feel is one of their key values – that they are there to win the praise, loyalty and advocacy of passengers on every trip. It is something they do every day en route to their BHAG.

Dame Louise Makin is CEO of BTG plc, an international specialist health-care company that is developing and commercializing products targeting critical care, cancer and other disorders. BTG is a fast-growing business, headquartered in London and employing over 1,200 people world-wide. It operates in three discrete business segments: interventional medicine (oncology, vascular and pulmonology products), specialty pharmaceuticals (antidote products) and licensing (royalties from licensed assets).

Dame Louise took over as CEO in 2004. It is ironic that, while BTG's products help physicians to perform minimally invasive procedures, Dame Louise had to perform major surgery on the business, reducing it to just 57 people by 2008, but with a secure revenue stream from patents and a world of possibilities. With smallness, BTG had agility and it had royalties it could use to invest. It also had curiosity and an openness to opportunities in health care that would enable it to build a competitive position. The leadership team at that stage did not know exactly where it was going to go, but knew that if it wanted to succeed it was going to have to be fit for purpose.

'We wanted to do meaningful things and build a company that was respected by our mates in the pub. To be meaningful, we realized that we are going to have to be big. Being big by itself wasn't a get-out-of-bed vision, but we wanted a really stretching goal that told people we were going to take big steps because we had a big ambition', said Louise. 'Our goal was then and still is to get into the FTSE 100 [a share index of the 100 companies listed on the London stock exchange that have the highest market capitalization]. Given that our market capitalization was probably around £350 million at the time, getting to the then £2 billion threshold to enter the FTSE 100 was a sizeable goal.' The FTSE 100 threshold is a rising index, and is even higher today.

But size alone is not compelling enough for staff, says Dame Louise. 'More important is to be truly meaningful for all our stakeholders – patients, customers, the health-care system, employees and investors. We came from nothing and we want to make sure that what we do in this world is really meaningful', she says. 'Our core purpose is to advance the treatment of underserved patients. This means identifying unmet medical needs, acquiring and developing innovative products, manufacturing those products to the highest standards and selling them directly or commercializing through partnerships. This is what gets our people out of bed every day', she says. Whether or not BTG gets into the FTSE 100 (their long-term goal) is simply a measure of how well they deliver their purpose.

When you achieve your long-term vision, set another one

Merlin Entertainments is a company built on fun – and more than 60 million guests a year choose to spend time in one of more than 100 global attractions owned by Merlin and spread across 23 countries and four continents. These include some of the best-known names in global leisure, including Sea Life, Madame Tussauds, The Dungeons and Legoland, as well as icons such as the Coca-Cola London Eye, Sydney Tower Eye, Blackpool Tower and also Alton Towers Resort.

Nick Varney is CEO of Merlin Entertainments, a position he has held since 1999. Prior to that he was managing director of Vardon Attractions. He has over 22 years of experience in the visitor attractions industry. He says:

'The whole concept of the business we are in is about removing people from their everyday humdrum, sometimes troubled lives, and putting them into an alternative magical reality. As a company we grew from 400 employees in 1999, to the 24,000 we have today. We all share the same purpose, which is to deliver memorable experiences.

The idea that we are creating these magical experiences for people is what gets us out of bed every day, and it is that shared purpose that has driven the growth of the business. However, our purpose is very different to our long-term vision. Back in 1999, we said that our BHAG was to become a top-10 global player in the visitor entertainment business. It seemed impossible at the time, but we are now number two in the world. Our current BHAG is to become number one, and that means one day overtaking Disney. They don't get much bigger than The Mouse. If we are so passionate about our business why shouldn't we seek to be the biggest and the best at it?'

Another stretching goal that Nick sets his sights on is for Merlin to be recognized as one of the great companies of the world, up there with Google or Amazon. 'We have this focus on being a business that excels in every area of what it does, and want to be recognized as one of the world's best businesses', he says.

A qualitative long-term vision

Anthony Thomson is a serial entrepreneur. He is co-founder and chairman of the Financial Services Forum, a member-based community for senior financial services executives. He is co-founder of MoneySpinners, an organization that sets up an annual cycle ride for financial services executives to raise money for good causes. He is founder and former chairman of Metro Bank, at its launch the first high-street bank to launch in the UK in more than 150 years. He is also founder and chairman of Atom Bank, which aims to be the world's first digital-only bank.

Atom Bank is a new digital banking system, authorized by the Prudential Regulation Authority (PRA) and regulated by the Financial Conduct Authority (FCA). They offer an app-based experience, using leading technology. Atom Bank is based in the UK and does not have any branches. Instead, customers can do all their banking on their mobile phone, 24/7.

It claims that it will offer the first real alternative to traditional high-street banks.

When Anthony launched Metro Bank, he did so on the basis of an insight that said that people wanted value from the banks. 'Banks perceived this to mean prices, but if you delved into the data, it said that customers cared about service and convenience and transparency, as well as consistency of delivery. That was the basis for Metro Bank', he explains:

> 'Spool forwards to the current day and you see the most seismic shift in consumer data that I've seen in 30 years. It was the move from traditional branch-based banking, to digital, and mobile in particular. It was clear to me from this data that this was the future.
>
> I believe passionately that the purpose of business is to give customers a better product or a better service or a better experience. If you manage your business well, it will make a profit as a by-product of doing this. I think that one of the great malaises in business today and with banks in particular is that they have lost sight of this idea and they think their business is just to make money for shareholders.
>
> So in setting up Atom Bank we defined our purpose as: to change banking for good. By that, we mean to change it permanently and to change it for the better. However, if you want a vision to cause people to take in a sharp breath or give a nervous giggle, it has to be really bold. So the vision we have come up with is to be the world's first telepathic bank. This means two things to us. First, it means making sure that we are at the forefront of technology to enable truly telepathic ways of controlling your devices and therefore controlling your banking. This may or may not be achieved in my lifetime. It also means, however, using data analytics to know more about what people need from us than they know themselves, and therefore be able to predict their every need.
>
> Most people will only look at their banking needs once a week, whereas we will be spending 24 hours a day, seven days a week analysing data and building the ability to predict what people want. This is why we now say that Atom Bank is established in the future. Indeed the conceit of our name, Atom, is that we will never be more than an atom away from a customer.'

Changing the world

Another company with a qualitative long-term vision is Cisco Systems, a US technology company headquartered in California. It designs, manufactures and sells internet networking equipment. At a prosaic level, it provides routers and switches, security and surveillance systems, voice and conferencing systems, Wi-Fi access points and network storage systems.

More simply put, Cisco designs and sells broad lines of products, provides services and delivers integrated solutions to develop and connect networks around the world, thus helping to build the internet. Over the last 30+ years, it has been the world's leader in connecting people, things and technologies – to each other and to the internet. The company employs 70,000 people in over 400 offices worldwide. The name Cisco is derived from the city name San Francisco, and its logo is intended to depict the two towers of the Golden Gate Bridge.

Phil Smith is the chairman for Cisco in the UK and Ireland. He has a 30-year track record in the information and communications technology industry. He leads around 5,500 Cisco people in the UK and Ireland. He is also the chairman of Innovate UK and chairman of The Tech Partnership. He sits on the board of the Business Disability Forum, the Foundation for Science and Technology (FST) and the National Centre for Universities and Business (NCUB). He is also the co-chair of the Future Technologies and Infrastructure Working Group for the Information Economy Council. In December 2013, Phil was hailed by *Computer Weekly* as the fifth most influential person in UK IT.

He says:

'At Cisco, more than five years ago we saw the impact that connecting people, processes, data and things would have on organizations and countries. Today, across the board, our customers' top priority is to use technology to drive growth and productivity, manage risk and gain competitive advantage.

In this digital world, data, and the insights it provides, is our customers' most strategic asset. It is increasingly distributed across every part of their organization and ecosystem. Their ability to secure, aggregate, automate and analyse the data, at speed, will ultimately define their success.

As Cisco marked its thirtieth anniversary year in 2015, we witnessed the inflection point in the next wave of the internet. This next wave will have five to ten times the impact of the first. As 50 billion devices come online and connect over the next few years, the network and Cisco have never been more relevant or more strategic. Our vision is to change the way the world works, lives, plays and learns. That is a big, bold vision, and is about changing the world for the better.'

Phil explains further:

'If you are a technology company, which provides stuff that typically sits inside cupboards in data centres and wiring closets and so on, you could just set yourself up and say we are going to be the best providers of plumbing, essentially. But, in fact, Cisco has a massive aspiration to change the world. What we mean by this is that we not only put wiring into hospitals, but by doing so we actually change the way staff in that hospital behave, because better care for patients matters to everyone and we can enable that to happen.

This is how we encourage people throughout the organization to think – how can we improve the performance of our customers through the products and services we can provide? It is not about saying how we can get people to do more things with computers, it is about how we can make computers and connectivity make it easier for people to do things, by speeding up and simplifying all the other time-absorbing stuff they have to do.'

Having been launched in December 1984, Cisco Systems now generates revenues of US$49 billion per annum, and has a market capitalization of more than US$130 billion. It is in the top 20 most valuable brands in the world.

Leaders need to hold up a long-term vision for a variety of positive, value-creating reasons. First, it gives investors and stakeholders a clear reason to support the business, for the long term, and, when well articulated, helps to avoid short-term, excessive profit-taking behaviours that destroy value. Second, it gives employees a greater sense of purpose, and more security. This, in turn, helps them to feel better and perform better. When leaders think about creating a purpose framework, it should encompass a long-term stretch goal, a compelling purpose statement and, as we shall see, values that create the right culture. It should also have goals that everyone can relate to. It is this combination that helps to engender a greater sense of purpose in people, which drives all the right behaviours, and enables high performance.

Next: why your purpose statement should focus on customers.

Key points from Chapter 7

1 Short-term business thinking is eroding the economic foundations of countries. Business leaders must think and plan and communicate a long-term vision, which creates shared purpose with all of their stakeholders.

2 Neuroscience proves that a long-term vision helps employees to perform better.

3 Leaders should think about creating thriving businesses and communities, rather than ones that have a 'sustainable' future. The word 'thriving' is more evocative and can help drive all the right behaviours.

4 A long-term vision can be either qualitative or quantitative. Either way it should be so big and bold that it creates a sense of urgency and even greater purpose in the business.

5 It should describe how you are going to change the world for the better, and be so audacious that it creates a sense of urgency in the organization today – 'if we want to have this massive impact, then we have to be the best we can be, starting today'.

Authentic purpose

08

Start with the customer to truly engage with people inside and outside your organization

Defining common purpose is a key task of leadership. Purpose stays constant while strategies and practices constantly adapt in a changing world. Research shows that leaders who focus their purpose on making customers' lives better are more likely to inspire truly customer-centric staff, who work hard to keep those customers coming back, thus outperforming competitors. Only by meeting the needs of customers can you fulfil the wider purpose of creating value for all stakeholders.

For more than four years now I have been asking business leaders – well over 150 – to tell me what they think is the purpose of business. As you might imagine, I hear a wide variety of views. Their answers tend to cluster around one of four groups: shareholder purpose, customer purpose, social purpose or higher purpose.

A significant number still subscribe to the view of *shareholder purpose*, developed in 1970 by economist Milton Friedman, from the Chicago School of Economics. He said that the purpose of business was maximizing profit for shareholders. Leading politicians of the time, including US President Ronald Reagan and British Prime Minister Margaret Thatcher, supported Friedman's thinking, which centred on the notion that one could find the solution to many problems in free markets by focusing simply and only on making money.

Indeed, when you look at the current purpose statements of many companies, they still say exactly this. Some may now acknowledge the need to create value for all stakeholders, but their primary purpose remains the same: to maximize value for shareholders. One could argue that Jack Welch, the former CEO of General Electric (GE), was the poster boy for that purpose. During his tenure at GE, from 1981 to 2001, it is reported that the value of the company rose 4,000 per cent. When he retired from GE, it is said he received a severance payment of US$417 million, the largest such payment in history, and a large part of his estimated net worth of more than US$700 million. It is surprising to learn, therefore, that Jack Welch is quoted as saying 'shareholder value is the dumbest idea in the world'. Why? Because, he said, it should be a result, not a goal.

Other than profit, what kind of purpose?

Other leaders cluster on the idea of *customer purpose*. They tell me that they believe in the definition created by Peter Drucker, an American management consultant and author whose writings have profoundly influenced many businesses. He has often been described as the founder of modern management. He said: 'If you want to know what a business is, we have to start with its purpose. And the purpose must lie outside the business itself. In fact it must lie in society, since a business enterprise is an organ of society. There is only one valid definition of business purpose: to create a customer. The customer is a foundation of the business and keeps it in existence. The customer alone gives employment. And it is to supply the customer that society entrusts wealth-producing resources to the business enterprise.'

As Charles Tilly, immediate past CEO of the Chartered Institute of Management Accountants, says: the purpose of business 'is primarily to meet the needs of its customers and in so doing create value over the long term for all of its stakeholders'. His view bridges the gap between those who focus on the customer, and those who talk about the need of business to have a wider purpose.

These leaders talk about the idea of *social purpose* (or stakeholder purpose) and say that the purpose of business is to create value for all stakeholders, including customers, employees, suppliers, local communities as well as the people with all the money to lend. If you do that well, while ensuring that you also protect the environment, then money and profits follow. These leaders talk about the triple bottom line – people, planet and profit.

The fourth group of leaders say that every business should be motivated by what they described as a *higher purpose* – in which the purpose of business is to find solutions to human needs. They say that doctors and nurses make money, but their purpose is to heal. Pilots make money, but their purpose is to fly. Architects make money, but their desire is to build. It is a myth that business people only want to make money, they say. They are inspired to find solutions for human problems, ranging from the prosaic, such as providing soft toilet paper for delicate bottoms, to the more profound, such as curing cancer. These people argue that business is about creating prosperity, and that prosperity should be measured by the rate at which new solutions to human problems become available. Customers will follow, and profits will follow that.

Every business is based on an idea about how to solve a problem. Being able to convert great ideas into products and services that fulfil fast-changing human needs better and faster than anyone else is what defines successful businesses. They say that, if only people could see business as society's problem solvers, rather than simply as vehicles for creating shareholder returns, it would make life easier. It would enable them to better balance the interests of multiple stakeholders and also shift the emphasis towards long-term investment – few human problems can be solved in just a few months.

This discussion on purpose has been going on for decades. In my research on the meaning of corporate purpose, I quickly came across Chester Barnard, an American business executive and the author of pioneering work in management theory. His landmark book, *The Functions of the Executive*, was published in 1938. In it, he said that a company comes together only when three things occur concurrently: there are people 1) who communicate with each other; 2) who have a task or action to complete; and 3) who all have a common purpose. He described the task of defining common purpose as a core task of leadership. It was only this that would encourage cooperation, as individuals would normally act uncooperatively unless there was an objective that united them.

Jim Collins and Jerry Porras, the authors of *Built to Last: Successful habits of visionary companies* (1994), say that companies that enjoy enduring success have a core purpose and core values that remain fixed, while their strategies and practices endlessly adapt to a changing world. They say that a great vision framework provides two key things – core ideology (purpose and values) with an envisioned future (bold stretch goals vividly described). Purpose does not describe the organization's output or outcomes, nor its target customers – it captures the soul of the organization. A core part of core purpose is to guide and inspire, providing an overriding reason for existing – a shared sense of 'why do we exist?'

Mission is different to purpose

When you discuss purpose with leaders they often interpose the word 'mission' with purpose: I think this is a mistake. I believe a company's mission statement is different to a purpose. A mission describes what business the organization is in (or what it is not in).

To my mind, the ideal example of a mission statement comes from the Airbus Group, whose chief executive Tom Enders is divesting parts of the business based on a simple thought: 'We make it fly.' The company, a European-based multinational aerospace and defence corporation, head-quartered in Toulouse, is planning to sell off those parts of the business that do not design, make and sell things that fly, and will concentrate its vast operations on aeronautical solutions, whether it be commercial aircraft, satellites, helicopters, missiles, gliders or drones. In this context, 'We make it fly' is a simple but highly effective mission statement.

A business mission for a global accounting firm might be: 'We provide audit and assurance, tax and consulting services to customers worldwide.' The mission statement is simply a factual presentation of what the business does, and who it sells to. Such statements are rarely inspirational, mainly because they don't capture the thought of how the business improves people's lives – a key motivator for employees, as we have seen in previous chapters. To me, this is the essence of a good purpose statement – one that captures the customers, rather than explaining what the company does. You need both a purpose statement and a mission statement!

Companies with a customer purpose outperform

Jim Stengel, former global head of marketing for Procter & Gamble, is author of the bestselling book *Grow* (2011), for which he conducted an unprecedented, 10-year growth study utilizing Millward Brown Optimor's global database of more than 50,000 brands, and additional research. (Millward Brown is a British multinational market research firm focused on advertising effectiveness, media and brand equity research.)

What Jim found was key: brands that centred their businesses on the ideal of improving people's lives resonated more with consumers – and outperformed their category competitors. An investment in the top 50 businesses in the growth study – 'The Stengel 50' – would have been 400 per cent more profitable than an investment in the S&P 500 over that same 10 years.

Why? Because top-performing brands are built on ideals, he says – higher-order purposes that transcend products and services and provide a shared goal of improving people's lives.

According to Jim, a higher-order purpose or brand ideal is a business's essential reason for being – the higher-order benefit it brings to the world. By enhancing consumer/customer centricity, top brands are more likely to build purchase intent, driving business growth. A higher purpose of improving people's lives is the only sustainable way to recruit, unite and inspire all the people a business touches, from employees to customers, he argues. It must have a meaningful connection with customers or consumers, set the business apart from competitors, and help drive up brand equity, and by so doing drive up purchasing intent.

The 50 brands that rose to the top of Stengel's studies come from a wide variety of industries and countries. They included companies such as Amazon, Coca-Cola, Google, Hugo Boss, Jack Daniels, Mercedes-Benz, Red Bull, Samsung, Starbucks and Visa. Despite the huge variety and sectors these businesses occupied, Stengel found that the ideals that drive these brands could be grouped into one of just five fields of what he calls 'fundamental human values' that improve people's lives by:

- eliciting joy: activating experiences of happiness, wonder and limitless possibility;
- enabling connection: enhancing the ability to connect with one another and the world in meaningful ways;
- inspiring exploration: helping people to explore new horizons and new experiences;
- evoking pride: giving people increased confidence, strength, security and vitality;
- impacting society: affecting society broadly, including by challenging the status quo.

The best purpose statements that I have seen take customer focus to a new level, not just because they resonate with customers and emphasize the importance of serving those customers (and understanding their needs), but because they put managers and employees into customers' shoes. The neuroscientists I met said that such statements were powerful because they showed 'we are doing something for someone else', and connected with both the heart and the head.

Create value for customers to create value for all

Creating value for customers is the only way to create value for shareholders and other stakeholders. Shareholder value is an outcome, says Jack Welch, and it should be blindingly obvious to everyone that no company can be a force for good for all of its stakeholders unless it makes a profit. Making good profits enables you to do good. Serving customers better than your competitors do helps to keep your business in existence, give employment, hire suppliers and provide value to local communities.

In a world of connected consumers, whose publicly stated views on brands are far more powerful than any direct advertising a brand might do, resonance is everything. How you make them feel is critical to your success. That is why I hear more and more leaders becoming obsessive about customer centricity, and ensuring that their purpose reflects this.

But what is customer centricity? To me, it means knowing exactly who the customer is, what their needs are and what they are trying to do. If every person in the organization knows and understands this, it shifts the emphasis from an inside-out focus to an outside-in one. It can help to make you more human, because everyone in the organization thinks of the customer as a human, thus developing far greater empathy and respect for customers. Being able to do that brings huge dividends. By bringing the customer to life in these ways, organizations stand a better chance of driving greater engagement inside and outside the organization, and improving trust and reputation.

Customers want to be respected

In 2014, Good Relations, part of Chime Communications (a global sport, entertainment and communications business) conducted research with more than 12,000 consumers in the UK to find out which brands they really loved, and why. As relationships with customers are, in particular, such a valuable asset, Good Relations asked themselves if they could create a way to truly understand the nature of relationships with customers, studying and contrasting the best- and the worst-performing brands to understand the key drivers of quality relationships today. They created 'Triple G', a ground-breaking study that measured how good a business is in the eyes of the UK public. Where a Triple A rating in the City of London is used by the investment community as an aggregator of an organization's 'hard capital' or financial performance, the Triple G rating scores a company's 'soft capital'. Soft capital does not appear on a company's balance sheet, but reflects how 'good' a company is, as seen by the public – a true indicator of a company's sustainability and future performance.

Relationships are a consequence of 'what you do, how you engage with people, and then what they say about you', which in turn determines your reputation. Good Relations, using Chime's Insight and Engagement research division, asked consumers to score each brand on those three elements.

They asked the 12,000 consumers about 120 brands and focused on:

- good actions: 'what the business does when no one else is looking';
- good engagement: how well the business communicated and listened to their consumers;
- good recommendations: how strongly respondents were prepared to recommend the brand to friends, family and colleagues.

Brands that scored highly on all three dimensions included John Lewis Partnership, Amazon, Waitrose, Samsung, Asda, Kellogg's, Cadbury, Virgin Atlantic and Johnson & Johnson. Out of the 120 brands tested, just 16 were awarded the Triple G rating for good actions, good engagement and good recommendations.

An emotional bond is your Teflon layer

The research proved that creating an emotional connection with people offers a huge competitive advantage to brands. The Triple G research showed that brands that do this effectively show they share a customer's values, generating a sense of closeness and real empathy. Today, consumers want to look behind the image and seek more substantial ways of choosing who to align with. Brands that create great relationships of respect with their customers create a Teflon-like ability to withstand uncomfortable scrutiny.

The research also showed that you need to give respect to get respect. Surprisingly, companies do not do this enough. Brands that performed well in the Triple G survey all showed respect and care for their customers in everything they did and said. And brands that achieved the highest Triple G ratings did this really well. They managed to convey that they really care, and created a mutual relationship that worked effectively for both parties.

Sectors and companies that either mindfully or inadvertently disrespected customers set up a cycle of destructive disrespect, creating high numbers of detractors, who we all know are more active than happy customers. Close analysis of more than 50,000 verbatim comments from the 12,000 consumers researched, showed that the three key lessons of the highest-rated brands were quality, respect and relevance.

First and foremost, a great product or service was the foundation for a great relationship. If it answered consumer needs better than anyone else, the brand was already at an advantage. Second, those brands that demonstrated active care and attention that went beyond expectations, and showed they respected their consumers, were able to capitalize on a good product and service and cement the relationship for the long term. Finally, those brands that did both the above well, and also constantly showed their compelling relevancy to their audiences, whether it was through products that answered needs or through being a force for good, had the highest rating of all.

Deliver the promise and respect the customer

One company that lost the respect of consumers, because consumers felt they were not respected by the company, was parcel delivery business Yodel.

To win back customers, Yodel had to find a common purpose that directed every action towards a consumer focus. After much debate, they expressed it as 'take delivery personally'. This was the one thought that everyone who worked for Yodel (the majority of the workforce are not directly employed) had to understand and commit to.

They had to remember that a parcel was personal to every recipient and they had to take personal responsibility for delivering it successfully. How well they did this was rigorously measured and the results were transparently shown to Yodel's retail clients, who were co-opted as partners in the business improvement programme. Their purpose – taking deliveries personally – had an implicit customer benefit in it that was a major catalyst in improving the business.

Yodel has an estimated market share of 8 per cent, making it one of the largest independent UK parcel carriers. On a busy day it delivers up to

1 million packages. It was formed by the 2010 acquisition of the UK domestic business of DHL by Home Delivery Network. The combined business was rebranded as Yodel in May 2010. Yodel is the short form of 'YOur DELivery. The company is privately owned by the billionaire Barclay brothers, Sir David Barclay and Sir Frederick Barclay.

In 2011, Yodel attracted some very negative publicity when newspapers reported, somewhat inaccurately, on how many parcels Yodel staff were delivering late for Christmas. These media reports were subsequently retracted but were followed up by the BBC's *Watchdog* consumer programme, which broadcast a highly critical segment about Yodel's parcel delivery service. In January 2014, Yodel was voted as the worst delivery service in the UK for the second consecutive year, in a poll by MoneySaving Expert.com of 9,000 people.

I was able to interview executive chairman Dick Stead. 'It was clear', he said, 'that we had a lot of work to do and a lot of difficult decisions to make about the business.'

Brought in by the Barclay brothers to develop a strategy to transform Yodel into a profitable UK parcel carrier, with industry-leading customer centricity, Dick could see that some stark choices had to be made. 'We were not located in the right properties, our IT was not up to scratch and we had a highly disengaged workforce, many of whom told us they were ashamed to admit who they worked for when down at the local pub. Looking at the state of the business it was clear we could either decide to close it, sell it, or bite the bullet and invest and grow it for a long-term future. I am glad to say that the Barclay brothers completely backed the plan to grow it, because they could see the size of the opportunity as online shopping continued to grow.'

Yodel delivers 150 million parcels a year to every postcode across the UK. It has a relationship with 85 per cent of the country's top retailers, and partners with courier services in the Republic of Ireland and the Channel Isles.

Because of earlier problems with deliveries, Yodel had a poor reputation online, mainly because social media has a long-lasting footprint with messages that can be searched and found years after any mishaps. In addition, there was a constant stream of critical social media commentary from customers complaining about Yodel service.

More than a parcel

'The first thing to do was get everyone in the organization to realize that we were delivering so much more than a parcel. It's an item that could mean the world to someone – or even change their world in an instant. That's what we needed to appreciate more, to understand the importance of our work and what those parcels meant to our customers', says Dick. 'Before we could impress that emotional concept in all of our minds, we faced a dilemma. If we were going to recover and become the service with the best reputation in the industry, we had to make a simple but critical decision. Who, really, was the customer?'

Was it the retailers, who contracted Yodel to deliver their parcels? Or was it the consumer who, although not directly paying, was the person who most felt the benefits or frustrations of the parcel service? The dilemma Yodel faced was that retailers obviously wanted to keep their costs down and the delivery service cheap, while the customer wanted quality. Says Dick:

> 'We decided that our reputation was going to be determined by the people who received the parcels, so it was on them that we had to focus all of our efforts and strategy. It was on them we had to focus our purpose. This meant finding ways to collect more data on their experience, and understand where some of our real problems lay. If we could improve our reputation, and develop fame for being a quality service, it would enable us to lift our prices. This would enable us to secure a long-term future for the business. Yodel had had years of loss-making so it was imperative that it found ways to get back into profit.'

Yodel initiated an innovative and industry-leading customer opinion programme called 'Have Your Say' to listen to the views of literally more than 1 million customers each and every day to gain real-time understanding of their delivery experience. Through this feedback the leadership team are able to quickly identify and reward best practice in Yodel, to correct issues as they occur, and work with clients to develop service improvements and innovations to meet consumer needs. Says Dick:

> 'From this we quickly determined that about one-third of complaints we received were valid and we needed to take action to fix the problems causing them. About one-third of the complaints lacked any record of purchase and we had to find ways to better identify genuine customers who really had received our service. The final one-third of complaints had to do with many customers who had received their items, but for various reasons were looking to get discounts or refunds from the retailers. The best way to do that, it seemed, was to falsely claim problems with the delivery.'

Consumers will decide reputation

To turn the business around Yodel articulated and then launched a new vision and values. They expressed their ambition as: *to have the best reputation in the country*. Dick explains:

'It was simple but hugely effective. It is our view that consumers will eventually decide what parcel carrier is used and not the retailer. So we have to pin everything to the reputation.

We told our people that our strategy was *to build a sustainable business, and that we would do this by delivering a great customer experience at a great price*. To do that, each and every person in the organization had *to take delivery personally*. This is the common purpose throughout Yodel now.'

Yodel made it clear to everyone that it had four strategic priorities, all focused on the customer. These were:

- deliver customers' parcels to them on time;
- deliver the parcels in great condition;
- always show customers a great attitude;
- keep customers informed about their deliveries.

'This transparency and data enables us to do a lot more than simply fix problems quickly. It is transparent, and a powerful driver of performance improvement', Dick says.

Has the change programme been successful? So far, so good, says Dick: 'Clearly there are still improvements to be made and we will accelerate activities, which have already seen our customer satisfaction score increase, so we can get to where we want to be – the best in the industry.' Happily, Yodel is now also heading back to profit, after five years of losses. The company is still often criticized by consumers for poor service, but steadfastly stays committed to improving service.

Making customer care your purpose

Ford Retail Group, operating as Trust Ford, operates at over 65 sites in the UK and sells more than 100,000 vehicles per annum. With more than 3,000 staff, the total turnover of the group exceeds £1.5 billion a year. It sells new and used cars, as well as commercial and motability vehicles.

The chairman of the group is Steve Hood, who has had a long career in the motor industry. He says: 'We took a long time to settle on our purpose, and not without considerable debate. Our purpose is '*to drive the standard in customer care*':

> 'About 50 of our trading locations are full service dealerships, with sales, service, parts, and many of them with body shops as well. We operate in a very competitive marketplace and thankfully we've got a good product range with Ford. But to do well we have to wrap around that very good service from very good people who are highly engaged and who care about our customers and care about our brand.
>
> We've only recently articulated our purpose, as part of an exercise when we considered how to sustain our growth and profitability. We had a huge debate about whether or not our purpose was to make a profit for our shareholder. The overwhelming view was that profit was not sustainable without good customer satisfaction and only that would drive loyalty, which would drive a sustainable business.'

Consumers buy in to your values

Steve says that, increasingly, customers in the automotive industry do not feel trapped by local franchise dealerships. They will drive further than ever to buy and to service if they feel it worthwhile, so having a franchise in your town is no longer the guarantee of getting a customer that it once was:

> 'This is because the modern consumer is buying into your values and your purpose. They make decisions based on whether they trust you and whether they think you care about them. To earn that trust everyone in the organization has to understand what our purpose means and why it is so important.
>
> For example, it's really easy to identify with customer needs in smart showrooms with shiny new cars, but for the person managing parts in a warehouse it's not quite so obvious how important they are to the customer. So we try to bring this to life for every employee and will explain to that parts person that if they don't get the right part on the right van at the right time to the right dealership, then someone who owns the car is going to be badly let down. It means the customer cannot collect their children from school and do something that is really important to them. If we fail them on that we will lose their trust, lose their business and possibly lose money.'

Steve says that you have got your purpose wrong if you cannot articulate it in a way that works on the parts warehouse floor, in a service workshop or in a showroom. It has to be versatile and applicable to everyone: 'It's all about relevance – to the employee and to the customer. If it's not relevant to every job role and every layer of the organization, if you can't talk about it with them and you can't articulate it clearly and simply, then I think your purpose is wrong. It has to be able to drive every conversation you have and help you to steer every decision you make.'

Steve describes Trust Ford's ambition as *being the envy of competitors*. To do this, the company aims to be recognized as the benchmark in all of their operations, and openly commits to growing and retaining the best people who can share in the company's success. Their ambition is directly linked to their purpose. So are their values.

'Our values have to help us achieve our purpose and we call these our principles. They are about honesty and integrity, always, respecting and caring for everyone, having a positive attitude to make things happen and enjoying what we do.' However, points out Steve, it is pointless having the right words on paper if those words don't change behaviours:

> 'Without your purpose and your principles being made clear to everyone, with everyone engaged in them, you could find yourself with hundreds of different agendas in operation in your business. Some people will be in your business because they like the customer service element. Some will be there because they like cars and some simply will be there to earn money. You would then have such a fragmented set of viewpoints and objectives that the customer is very unlikely to get a consistent experience and you are very unlikely to stand for something worthwhile in their view.'

Use language that resonates with customers

Knowing what is important to your customer means knowing the language to use to resonate with them. Taking an outside-in view will help you to formulate better a purpose that really does resonate. Many leadership teams make the mistake of formulating a purpose that is inside-out driven and fails to engage external audiences at all.

Ian McCaig is chief executive of First Utility, a fast-growing independent supplier of gas and electricity in the UK, now challenging the big six energy suppliers in Britain, which include British Gas, EDF Energy, Scottish Power, npower, SSE and E.ON UK. The company was launched in 2008 as a spin-out from First Telecom. By the end of 2015, First Utility had doubled customer numbers in three of the previous four years, to attain a market share of 2 per cent and become ranked as the seventh largest supplier in the UK.

McCaig, who was previously CEO of last minute.com, an online travel and leisure retailer, joined First Utility because he believed that 'UK consumers should be able to protect themselves now and in the future from ever increasing energy costs.' He said:

> 'First Utility was the only company to be challenging the status quo, the only company saying that its mission was to help its customers consume less and spend less on energy. One of the ways we do this is to apply customer facing technology to help people to understand their energy consumption better, and then figure out ways to use less.
>
> By being very customer focused, and listening to customers, we understood that consumers didn't like the idea of using less energy. That put them in a state of mind where they thought they had to make compromises. They thought they were going to have to give up some comforts. However, we soon found out that if we suggested that by adjusting our messaging to suggesting we could help our customer waste less, this was a much more engaging and accessible and positive way to express our purpose. And it was well received.
>
> In our customers' minds, the thought of using less meant that it was going to hurt. By moving away from this language, First Utility was able to identify with and create common cause with millions of households in the UK. People were joining us not only because we are efficient and good at what we do, but because we are able to engage them in ideas, initiatives, technologies, tools that will help them to get to a place where they are more in control and therefore can make decisions to waste less.'

Ian argues that his company's positioning is different to the big six precisely because First Utility took an outside-in view: 'It's all about how one sees one's purpose and how one speaks to one's purpose. Almost without exception all of the executives I've met from big energy companies started their lives working on infrastructure, building power stations, building networks to provide distribution. They see the world from the power station out, rather than seeing the world from the customer in.'

You have to resonate with employees, too

You cannot articulate a purpose that resonates with customers but fails to excite employees. Employees need to feel excited by the purpose, because it does good for others and makes them feel worthy. A purpose that is explicitly about serving shareholders can turn people off. Some leaders learn this the hard way.

Old Mutual plc is an international investment, savings, insurance and banking group. At the end of 2015, the group had more than 16 million customers and about £304 billion of assets under management. Within this empire resides Old Mutual Wealth, itself a leading global wealth management business, operating primarily in the long-term savings and investment market. The CEO of Old Mutual Wealth is Paul Feeney, who joined in January 2012 to transform the company from being an investment platform business to become the UK's leading wealth and investment management enterprise.

He says that one of the biggest issues facing many countries is an inability to pay pensions, which is causing a looming retirement time bomb. Whether people save enough so that they can retire on a comfortable nest egg, is crucial. When one in five people are retiring below the poverty line, you have a cause that can help you focus everyone in the company on making a significant difference in people's lives, he says. 'You have to make an emotional connection with your people so that they put their heart and soul into the job. If you get that wrong you can really damage your business.'

Paul says that he himself had a rude awakening on the subject of communicating strategy to his people in a way that grabbed them emotionally and resonated with them in ways that powered their performance: 'I had developed a strategy that pleased our investors, and which I said was about building a leading, vertically integrated wealth management business with strong asset management at the core. When I took it to our own people I had a real light-bulb moment that was seminal and for which I'm still truly grateful.'

Paul says the moment came when he travelled to Old Mutual Wealth's Southampton offices, 'where a couple of thousand people are housed to do administration for the UK business'. He was giving his usual speech about 'building a modern vertically integrated wealth management business with strong asset management at the core, blah blah blah.'

When he had finished talking to his huge audience, he realized he was in trouble when there was only a smattering of applause. Embarrassed and puzzled he left the podium and was then approached by one of his local managers, who bravely asked him whether he had a moment to spare and whether he would accompany her to see something she wanted to show him. He agreed and was led down to the underground car park, where she asked him to describe what he saw.

'I was puzzled but attempted to do as she asked. I said I could see a lot of cars, a skip full of rubbish, lots of cement and so on. She said "Okay, fine, but now come with me to the top floor", where she again asked me to describe what I could see through the large windows', explained Paul.

Now he described a whole new vista – from the local harbour through to the New Forest in the distance, as well as the surrounding buildings and the skip of rubbish he had seen from the basement:

'She said, "Yes, same view, different perspective."

She explained to me that the top floor was the view that I had, but that the basement was the view that staff had. They could see some of what I could see but I had a much broader perspective and I wasn't conveying it very well. The penny dropped and I knew I had to go back to the drawing board.

I've now told the story a number of times in our business and I'm really grateful that she helped me to understand that I just wasn't communicating in a way that was resonating with people. After much heartache, I realized that I was describing a business strategy not a purpose. I had to go back to the core of what I was trying to do, which was enabling positive futures for our customers, and securing the future prosperity of millions of people in this country.

We're going to do this by investing the money for them with the best asset management and the best investment management services available so that we can create real solutions for real people.'

Paul says it was only by connecting with the hearts of his employees that they were able to transform the business so quickly and so effectively: 'That was key to driving up our engagement levels even during a period of significant change.'

Paul has to be one of the few CEOs I've ever met who has written a poem for his people and widely publicized it as part of the process of explaining the organization's purpose. Sitting on the beach one holiday he wrote a poem called 'The Changemakers'. It reads:

> Here's to the changemakers
> to the courageous and the scorned
> to those who guard our children's future
> who stand apart and make a call
> who built their lives with their own hands
> and now help their children build a better one
> to the ones who ask 'why not?'
> And never accept 'because'
> who strive to succeed, to contribute,

at times just to survive.
But always share their lot.

To the responsible ones
whose values make them wealthy
irrespective of the value of their wealth
their word is their bond
and they expect no less in return.

These are the people we build our company for
who invest for the future
to build a better world.

'Clearly I'm not a good poet but I wanted to find a way – a very personal way – to explain to people how we wanted to position our company. I wanted to explain that we were determined to make a difference for people who want to make a difference with their investments, with their money and with their time. I wanted to explain in simple language to all of our staff that it was with these kinds of customers that we wanted to resonate', said Paul.

So what kind of value has Paul and his team created in his transformation programme? As we were going to press with this book there were reports in the media about potential plans by Old Mutual plc to break up its £9 billion business. With over £300 million of profit in 2015, Paul's business is now worth several billion pounds.

Give your customers an authentic experience

Not only should your purpose resonate with both customers and employees, it should also strive to capture the authenticity of your organization. When you do this, you are able to differentiate through your purpose.

Sir Rocco Forte is chairman of Rocco Forte Hotels. At present, his company operates in key European destinations such as London, Edinburgh, Brussels, Florence, Rome, Munich, Frankfurt, Berlin and St Petersburg. In 2009 Rocco Forte Hotels launched Verdura, the company's first resort on the island of Sicily.

Sir Rocco, a veteran of the hotel industry, says his hotels are today unique, unfussy and aim to reflect the spirit of the cities they are in:

'Our purpose is to bring the best of our cities to our guests, and through inside knowledge, shape guests' experience of them. To do this, our values are about being generous, open and genuine in spirit, with our guests and with one another.

When I get complimentary letters back from guests who have used our hotels, they invariably speak about the people more than they speak about anything else. Authenticity is crucial, and we strive to be authentic to the city we are in, and authentic as individuals.'

Be authentic to your purpose

Sir Rocco says that how his staff interact with guests is so crucial that they are being given special training in communication to help them interact with them in a natural way. 'It gets a bit irritating when you arrive at a hotel to be asked by every one of the staff how your flight was. You start wondering whether they knew something about the flight that you didn't. Being natural is about getting away from that, and being natural allows you to deliver authenticity.'

Rocco Forte Hotels employs around 2,500 people in 11 hotels, and huge effort is made to train staff in English. 'If you can speak English, you can communicate with 90 per cent of our customers', says Sir Rocco:

'Most of the big international chains of hotels try to replicate the same hotel wherever they go. I think that's a shame. It robs you of the authentic experience of different cities when you feel like you're staying in the same place all the time. That's why we decided to make our hotels individual to each city.

Each hotel needs to have its own personality, be authentic to the city and reflect that it's part of a family business with family values. Our training programmes reflect those values and every employee who is inducted into the company is taught about the history of the company, the history of the family, the history of the hotel they are working in, and will be given special training about the city they work in as well.'

Sir Rocco says that he is fanatical about the guest experience. 'If your purpose and your promise is to give guests a unique experience, ensuring high standards and genuine warmth means that I always show up in these hotels and then show that I care greatly about the details – from the way the table is laid, the decoration on the table, the way a menu looks and is prepared, how people treat your guests and, especially, how they handle customer complaints. You have to be the guardian of your purpose as a leader.'

Staying true to your purpose over decades

In a world of constant change, you have to keep changing your goals, strategies and practices. But you seldom have to change your purpose. If well articulated, it can be the one constant that keeps people focused when everything else is changing.

The Peabody Trust is over 150 years old. Founded in 1862, it is one of London's oldest and largest housing associations, with around 27,000 properties. It is also a charity and an urban regeneration agency. The trust was founded by London-based American banker George Peabody. While staying in London, he developed a fondness for the city and was determined to make a charitable gift to benefit it. After considering various schemes, he settled on establishing a model dwellings company. His mission was to ameliorate the conditions of the poor and needy in London, and provide them with comfort and happiness.

Peabody's current CEO is Stephen Howlett, formerly chief executive of the social housing organization Amicus Group, which became Amicus Horizon Group in 2006. The Peabody Trust provides rented housing for people who are unable to afford to rent or buy in the open market; it provides supported housing and care for those who need additional support; low-cost home ownership, particularly shared ownership; and community regeneration activities such as the provision of learning opportunities and access to training and accreditation. Stephen says:

> 'You can imagine how much change we've had to go through in 152 years. When I joined we had 300 or 400 homes in our development pipeline. Today it is 8,000, more than at any time in the history of Peabody.
>
> While we are constantly inspired by the legacy of George Peabody, we have had to consider how we can be constant to our purpose but current in the way we deliver it. For example, there was a time when we would get 80 per cent of the cost of a new home provided by a government grant. We are now down to 10 per cent so we've had to become a far more commercially driven operation to ensure that we can get the funding to carry out our social purpose. If all our properties were empty and we were able to sell them, we would have more than £10 billion worth of homes on our books. This is what enables us to get finance from banks to enable us to carry out our purpose and broaden the scale of our ambition. Nevertheless, we are constantly thinking about ensuring that we stay true to the original purpose.'

Reconsider how you articulate your purpose

Stephen says that he and his leadership team had recently to reconsider the way they talked about their purpose. They discovered that the idea of tackling poverty in London was alienating for many of the 80,000 residents in their homes, who didn't necessarily feel they were in poverty. 'They saw poverty as people in Africa, and in some ways the way we talked about our purpose was stigmatizing, and quite a negative mission, so we changed it and turned it around. We now say that we're here to make London a city of opportunity for all, by providing for as many people as possible a good home, a real sense of purpose, and a strong feeling of belonging.'

To Stephen and his staff, a good home means a place that is safe, warm, clean and well maintained, so that it evokes personal pride. A real sense of purpose means regular endeavour, whether that is work, learning, caring for others or personal development: 'Doing something that people look forward to because it makes them feel valued.' Finally, a strong feeling of belonging, they believe, grows from active involvement in the neighbourhood and the spirit of togetherness and friendliness that goes along with that (in other words, helping people to feel worthy, by giving them purpose and community):

> 'We involved all our staff in developing the new purpose statement and everyone was keen to maintain the original spirit of George Peabody's mission. Our 1,100 staff still have a great affection for Mr Peabody, and when we introduced a new IT system a few years ago they decided that we should call it "George". So it was crucial that we stayed true to the original intent.
>
> People can embrace constant change far more easily if they feel you are staying constant to your purpose.'

What makes a corporate purpose authentic?

An authentic purpose guides every decision a team, division, department or company makes, and is central to developing strategy. It is key to guiding and motivating employees, and should enable consistent communication internally and externally. Purpose comes first, and is not a marketing slogan or a communications tool. In a radically connected and transparent world, if your purpose is not authentic you will be found out very quickly.

Jeremy Galbraith is CEO for Europe, Middle East and Africa for Burson-Marsteller, one of the world's leading public relations and communications firms. It operates in 110 countries across six continents. Since 2008 Burson-Marsteller has been working on corporate purpose with the International Institute for Management Development (IMD), a Swiss-based executive education business school. Jeremy says that authentic purpose is really all about leadership: 'Effective leaders who are both convinced and convincing set the purpose agenda and ensure that an organization stays its course and embeds and lives its purpose over the long term.'

Perception, he says, is often reality because it is built on awareness and knowledge about a company gained through experience, as well as communication. Leaders who ensure that everyone in the organization effectively walks its talk are essential: 'A truly authentic corporate purpose is one where there is full alignment between a company's perceived purpose and the strategic decisions and actions that it takes.'

How people perceive you is your reputation. As we have heard many times in this book so far, today's leaders are highly aware of how valuable the intangible asset of reputation really is. Having a good reputation is high on their agenda. However, I believe many people have the wrong way of thinking about reputation. They think reputation is the end goal. I believe it is the starting place.

How your customers, investors, employees and regulators view you, and what they want from you in return for their trust and support, is where executives need to start in planning their purpose and their strategy. A good reputation is also achieved by understanding what matters, and what the company needs to do to deliver on stakeholder expectations.

Understanding stakeholder perceptions is the input to strategy development, if you are to secure a relationship of trust with customers and all other groups of people on whom you depend for success. Communicating an authentic purpose enables you to talk with those groups about what you stand for, what you believe is important, and what you are trying to do to improve their lives. It is a far better place to build a relationship from, rather than making it clear that all you want to do is take their money.

Success from staying ruthlessly true to your purpose

The Cambridge Satchel Company was founded in 2008 by Julie Dean and her mother Frieda Thomas, in Cambridge. It was a way to pay school fees for Julie's children. From humble beginnings on top of a kitchen table, Julie's vision was simple: to revive the traditional British leather satchel – an iconic bag that had all but disappeared.

When she started the company, Julie was determined that she would produce all products in Britain, and make sure they were made with care and expertise by skilled craftspeople. To enable this, she founded her own workshop in Leicester.

She started the business with just £600 but, with her mother, has built the business to be now worth more than £50 million, and has achieved recognition from the British government as an export success story. From making just a few satchels per day, she now exports to more than 120 countries. Hers is the seventh fastest-growing company in the UK in the fast-track league tables.

Julie is fiercely committed to preserving British manufacturing and, in spite of enormous pressure to satisfy demand with an overseas production model, she has ensured that each stage in producing every bag takes place on British soil.

'I think that a satchel is a British bag, I think that British manufacturing is brilliant and I think it is fundamentally wrong not to care where your product is made. This belief came from my father, who always was adamant that there is nothing better than British manufacturing', says Julie.

Julie, who grew up at a time when the mines were being closed and is highly conscious of what unemployment does to towns, regards it as a real privilege to be able to create jobs. She now has more than 150 people working in her company, and their devotion to the purpose of producing authentic British satchels, she says, is admirable.

Julie believes her Cambridge satchels have become a truly inspirational global brand because she has stayed rigidly true to her purpose – to make authentic British satchels, which have enormous appeal with customers. 'No matter how big we grow I'm going to ensure that the spirit of this brand is there right the way through everything and every market we might enter', she says.

As Julie has shown, and as the other CEOs in this chapter have said, it is essential that your core purpose must be focused on your customer. Ideally, it should be expressed as a benefit to them. Your wider purpose, to create value for all your stakeholders, is better placed in your vision statement – either your long-term or near-term vision. Employees will then take pride from the purpose, and align with the good you do for the people you serve, helping you to create value for all.

Next: how leaders fashion culture so that it enables the purpose to be delivered.

Key points from Chapter 8

1 The most successful companies all have a customer purpose – one that centres on the ideal of improving people's lives. This resonates more with consumers and employees and helps companies to outperform their competitors.

2 The purpose has to be made personal to every individual in the company, and enable them to see how they are improving lives outside the business. Relevance is everything.

3 Leaders who transparently measure performance against the purpose, using customer metrics, enable individuals throughout the company to take action and responsibility for delivering the purpose.

4 Leaders are guardians of the purpose and have to be ruthless about ensuring that teams deliver it.

5 Take care to express your customer purpose as a benefit those customers value. Your social or higher purpose is best expressed in your long-term vision or your ambition statement.

Culture is your competitive edge

09

How leaders align purpose and values to create winning teams

Organizations with a winning culture have given people a shared purpose, shared values and shared goals. Those organizations with rich, healthy cultures achieve income growth seven times higher than those with less well-defined cultures. As a result of their strong cultures, those companies are also better at attracting the talent that enables them to keep generating growth and value. Leaders must choose their values with care, and use them to drive conversations everywhere about not only their purpose and goals, but also the way in which they will be achieved.

Leaders who pay attention to culture achieve superior results. They know that purpose, values and goals combine to create value, and that middle managers are key to culture. They manage simultaneously to create both a high-performance culture, while also ensuring their people have a great place to work. They do it by articulating a set of values that they live by, and then making sure their managers and people live and breathe those values too. In this chapter, we learn from CEOs who have focused on culture to enable success.

'Even after 12 years at the helm, it is the culture of this organization that keeps me awake at night', says Dame Louise Makin, CEO of BTG (first described in Chapter 7). BTG employs 1,200 people worldwide and is a specialist health-care company:

> 'Our company has changed significantly over recent years as we have grown organically and through acquisition. I honestly believe that the absolute key to our success is the quality of our people and the way we conduct our business. Everything we do is guided by our values, which we long ago designed to underpin and foster a culture that would enable us to grow fast and be a meaningful company.'

At the very outset of their journey, Louise said her team set an ambition to be in the top 100 FTSE companies, which she said was code for an intent to take big steps and grow fast. It wasn't a 'get out of bed' purpose, she explains, but it was all about being bold enough to say the company was going to be a lot bigger and a lot more meaningful than it was when they had just 200 people. Louise says:

> 'If we were going to grow fast then we were going to have to make an awful lot of decisions about people. To do this we set our values really early and every step of the way we have made sure that we have had, at our core, integrity, teamwork, accountability, delivery, openness and continuous learning as our values. I always say them in that order. Integrity is about being a human being. Teamwork, accountability and delivery are all about being a company and team. But, actually, our values of openness and continuous learning are what differentiate us. Openness is code for very robust and challenging conversations around one framework and one framework only – and that is what is best for BTG, not what is best for divisions or individuals.'

Dame Louise explains that you can only truly have robust debate if you have one agenda. That robust debate enables you to make better decisions and be more agile, but you cannot do that if there is a suspicion that other people are trying to achieve conflicting aims.

Values statements should be provocative

Dame Louise pulls from her handbag a battered and tattered leaflet, which carries the BTG values as well as 14 statements about 'Our DNA'. These, she says, are deliberately in discordant language to be provocative and emotional, and rich in meaning. Her personal favourite is: 'We speak up, in the open, and with respect. We listen to others and expect to be heard. We assume goodwill.' She says it is amazing how transformational that thought is – to assume goodwill.

Another is: 'We are on top of things. We see, hear and feel our customers, our competitors and our environment.' As a keen sailor Louise always asks of her managers whether they get it, whether they're on it, and whether they've got their heads out. These are terms from racing sailing. By do they get it, she means do managers live the values and work as a team. By are they on it, she means managers restlessly working every angle:

'When you race on a sailing boat the wind is microscopically changing all the time so you don't just set your sails. You are constantly on it all the time, shifting your weight, moving just microscopically, with a ruthless, restless performance drive.

However, you don't win sailing races by just going fast. You will win by reading and reacting and making – better than anyone else – judgements about the macro external environment: looking at a wind shift over there, a tide moving faster over here, a boat about to move there. So you also have to have the capability to have your head out, and be reading the environment and be prepared to make a judgement. That's about bandwidth and having the capability to be ahead of the curve.'

Other statements in the BTG DNA leaflet include:

- We never give up in adversity. We do give up fast when we are on the wrong path.
- Patients come first, customer second; then comes BTG and our place in the org chart afterwards.
- We don't compromise with the truth, ethics or integrity.
- We don't accept the status quo. If it's too comfortable, it may not be bold enough, so it may not be good enough.
- We share ideas and learning without borders. There are no organization chart restrictions for communication and collaboration.
- Working here makes us better human beings. Dreams are welcome. Fun is the bonus.

Says Louise:

'We were very considered in a choice of language to describe our DNA. We wanted the statements to speak to people in emotional terms that made it very clear what we expected of people.

It is the job of all managers in BTG when they on-board newcomers to ensure that they quickly understand and live all of our values and act in a way that is consistent with our DNA. Our culture has been absolutely crucial to our success and we make sure that we lose people quickly if they don't fit. Often that is not a reflection on whether they are talented people, it's just that they don't fit our culture and we won't compromise on that.'

BTG has given their values real force by articulating them in powerful, emotive language that makes the meaning crystal clear to staff. Too often, leaders use words without sufficient explanation to have meaning, and that cannot truly drive culture.

Middle managers bring the culture to life, or kill it

Killian Hurley is chief executive at Mount Anvil, a specialist residential-led property developer in central London. Its purpose is to create homes and communities where people love to live. Together with joint venture partners, Mount Anvil has created more than 5,000 London homes, and is planning to build another 2,500 homes, worth more than £1 billion, by 2020. It has been one of the *Sunday Times* 100 best small companies to work for, for 10 consecutive years. It has also been rated by the British Safety Council as the number one company in the UK for health and safety, for two consecutive years.

Killian is the co-founder and majority shareholder of Mount Anvil, and has worked in the London property market since 1988. Under his leadership, the company has seen an almost tenfold growth over the past 10 years.

He says: 'One of our core values is to relentlessly strive to do the right thing. That means when we are hiring people, one of the qualities we are looking for is decency. It's in our job specification. What it means is that we want people who, when faced with tough choices, will do the right thing, whether it be health and safety, negotiating with the customer, dealing with the customer's complaint or whatever else might come up. We absolutely know that the right thing to do is the best thing to do. In the long term it's the most profitable thing to do as well.'

Killian, although hugely respectful and mindful of customers, says that as far as he is concerned customers don't come first. His people do. If he can't get the culture right, then he will never satisfy customers and never achieve the company's ambitious growth targets.

Mount Anvil works at any one time with at least 1,000 subcontractors on their sites. Collaborating with suppliers is crucial to success. 'This can only be done if you value the value of respect. When it comes to health and safety, respecting people and their right to come to work and go home safely is key. The British Safety Council audits our sites and has given us the highest score ever for health and safety – 99.93 per cent. This is because of the high standards in our processes, our management, our communication and, in particular, our culture.'

People drive the numbers, numbers don't drive people

Killian says he is acutely aware that people drive the numbers and numbers don't drive the people. 'We want to be central London's most respected developer. Not the most profitable, not the biggest, the most respected. That word carries an awful lot of obligation with it, and being decent and giving respect are critical to being the most respected. I'd like to think that as a leadership team we're probably not motivated primarily by money. But it's also true that the more we try to be the most respected developer, creating homes and communities in which people want to live, the better our results.'

Killian says that one of the most rewarding aspects of his work is the amount of repeat and referral business that Mount Anvil gets: 'That's a killer statistic that gives us a lot of pride. When you see people buying a second flat or a third flat or their uncle or aunt or a friend of theirs comes in to buy a flat, that's what gets us out of bed. That's when we know our culture is paying dividends.'

Both Killian Hurley and Dame Louise, though, point to one very significant fact – it is your managers who either enable or kill the values you want lived in the organization, so you must concentrate your efforts there. Employees, no matter how willing or keen, will not be able to live and breathe your values if your managers don't. No matter how much the top team lives the values, if your middle managers are not doing so as well, consistently, then culture breaks down and fragments and competitive edge is lost.

Unfortunately, this happens more than you might realize, unless you are obsessed with culture. The research done for me by YouGov, featured in Chapter 4, showed that employees thought that 'demonstrating consistent principles' was the third most important attribute in a manager. Showing a commitment to the organization's purpose was the sixth most important. When asked whether they believed their managers actually cared about the values and purpose of their organization, only 64 per cent of employees agreed (82 per cent of managers said they did). And on the subject of whether their managers demonstrated consistent principles, only 53 per cent of employees agreed, compared with 91 per cent of managers who said they did. Worse, almost one-quarter of employees disagreed.

It is in this gap that culture breaks down, and it is here that employees become cynical about the values that the leadership team says they want lived in their team or organization. Unless all managers are consistent and live the values in all their actions and words, it will be impossible to deliver the strong culture that can be such a competitive edge.

Beware of barriers that prevent people from living the values

Too often, leaders accidentally put things in the way of employees and prevent them living the values. When you remove the barriers, and encourage the values, you can transform performance. This is amply demonstrated in the story of Odeon and UCI Cinemas, led by Paul Donovan, chief executive.

Not many bosses can put themselves up on the screens of 240 cinemas in seven countries, any time they like – but Paul can. And he does, regularly. Why? He does it to inspire the 9,000 staff of Odeon and UCI Cinema Group, a leading European cinema operator.

At the group's 240 cinemas, there are 2,200 screens. In 2015, the group welcomed 83 million visitors to watch films and events on those screens. This was a big improvement on the year before, which had been a very bad year for cinema. It was this experience that led Paul on his quest to better motivate his staff and create a far stronger culture. He wanted to be less reliant on the movies coming out of Hollywood, and more reliant on his own people to create a thriving business.

It was a bad year in 2014 because there were fewer than normal blockbuster hits. In a year of all too few blockbusters, it seemed, people just weren't going to the cinema any more. Rising ticket and popcorn prices, so many more video-streaming options from newcomers on the block such as Netflix and Amazon Video, as well as better-quality TV and a move to binge-watching box sets, meant it was just too easy to stay at home.

Engaging staff crucial to turnaround

Odeon and UCI Cinemas is owned by Terra Firma, the private equity firm founded by financier Guy Hands. Several times Terra Firma came to the brink of selling the group but each time pulled back, believing that they could make more money from the sale if they waited. But first, they had to improve the performance of the group. For this, Guy Hands brought in

Paul Donovan, previously CEO of Eircom Group, Ireland's largest telecommunications company. Prior to that he was the CEO for emerging markets for the Vodafone group, where he had been responsible for the group's transformation programme, 'One Vodafone'.

Says Paul: 'Terra Firma had owned the cinema group for around a decade, which is an extraordinarily long time for a private equity company to hold a property. My brief was to build business that was attractive to prospective purchasers because it was capable of creating long-term value.'

Odeon and UCI has cinemas in the UK and Ireland, Spain, Portugal, Germany, Austria and Italy. All of those were markets hard hit by the recession, and competition came from not only video sources, but any place that could offer reasonably priced entertainment for people, including restaurants, clubs, theatres and others.

In the UK, people visit the cinema on average 2.6 times a year. In Europe it is 1.5 times a year. This was Odeon and UCI's opportunity, says Paul – with a combination of good content, good marketing and a good customer experience, there was no reason that the category wasn't capable of developing strongly. Paul knew that the following years would present a much better slate of films, so content seemed to be less of a challenge.

The first thing to do was to clean up the estate. This meant getting rid of some poor-performing venues, investing in new technology, including bigger IMAX screens, cutting-edge digital screening and sound, more comfortable seats and better catering, including a wider range of food and beverages.

The next thing was to get better at marketing. This is being done by segmenting customers better and getting even more data for better insights. By harnessing social media and putting more focus on building relationships with audiences, intensified marketing helps to attract people to the cinema by keeping them more aware of entertainment they might enjoy.

'Our strategy is driving change across the group, offering guests great reasons to come to our cinemas, ensuring that they have a terrific time, and want to visit us again soon', said Paul. 'We are first and foremost a hospitality business and our strategy is to differentiate ourselves from our competitors by using innovative and best-in-class processes and technologies to deliver a great experience for every guest.'

Excite staff to excite customers

The biggest challenge for Paul and his team was his staff. 'An engagement survey conducted the year I arrived showed that our employees lacked any sense of shared vision, had no sense of common culture, and had very little faith in their leadership. Engagement was in the lower quartile when compared with peers, and had been exactly the same for five years. Little had been done to inspire our 9,000 people', he said. 'If we wanted to show them we cared, we were doing a bad job. And we actually put barriers in their way when we asked them to live our values.'

Paul explained:

'For example, we had a policy that wouldn't allow our employees to see any new film for the first two weeks. When customers came in and asked about movies, staff just shrugged. They couldn't say anything.

A visit to the cinema should be exciting, and we want our staff to make it so for cinemagoers. Now we enable our staff to see the films on the day they come out. Equally we have technology that allows us to broadcast to every single one of our cinemas in real time and so we can produce employee communication where our staff sit down in the cinema and we – the leaders of the organization – appear on the big screen. We can tell them everything that is going on and, in particular, add more depth and breadth to their understanding of the product.

We can get our film buyers in to talk about the films, talk about the director and give them more background to the movies. With this knowledge, they can engage with our visitors more and help them to enjoy the experience.

This was just one of many things we did to inspire staff to live our values. And when we came across poor managers who were not consistent with those values, we got rid of them. It was the only way to improve the culture.'

Odeon's management then drew up a new purpose statement: creating inspiring experiences for every guest.

It is essential to bring vision and values to life

'For all of our senior leaders and general managers, we launched a training programme called 'Lead to Succeed', which helped them to understand more about how to be more motivating and engaging. We insist that they go and work in the cinemas and be more visible. We have been hiring managers for the right attitude, and we ask them to hire friendly people keen to be good to our visitors. We give them rigorous training, enabling them personally to develop in a wide variety of ways', Paul says.

For all of these people, Paul's team has now created a very clear vision and values, which they ensure everyone knows and understands:

'We want our staff to be film fanatics, committed to delivering excellence.
This means our values are about *teamwork*, in an *informal and empowering environment*, which will allow their *passion* to shine through.

To enable this to work we launched it to our top 150 leaders, with a series of workshops on how they could bring the vision and values to life in their cinemas, and how they could interpret strategy for every single member of staff. Our new purpose statement has been critical in engaging all our staff.'

Paul and his team have put a huge effort into helping his people to understand and deliver their purpose. At every cinema, staff were invited to find ways to better live the values – from dress-up days to special events for customers. An 'advent' calendar of 29 windows was designed and sent to every cinema. Each window contained a discussion topic and task around the refreshed purpose and values. Staff were encouraged to film and photograph what they were doing to better live their values, and share those actions across all cinemas.

Says Paul: 'This unlocked incredible energy across the 250 cinemas, as people could see what their colleagues were doing across the organization, and how they were better aligned to our common purpose and values. This made our vision and values tangible enough for everyone to participate in the process and feel the experience. Everything was focused on our guests, and as we've done this more and more, our results improved too.'

In an environment where investment funds for capital expenditure were constrained, changing culture was crucial. As Odeon did this, guest satisfaction levels improved, market share increased and business results improved. 'We had to really bring it to life for people, and help them to see the difference and feel different about themselves, which was so crucial to giving our guests a better experience', said Paul.

By campaigning so hard to bring the values to life, rather than just putting words on a poster, Odeon and UCI managers have been rewarded with a huge leap in employee engagement, significantly higher than other companies trying to change culture. 'Motivation levels have almost doubled, belief in the leadership and strategy have leapt up, and staff say the culture and climate has improved significantly too', says Paul.

In its most recent financial results before going to press, Odeon & UCI Cinemas Group announced its best results for six years, and the growth of customers to its cinemas outstripped the average market growth by almost one-third! In July 2016, it was announced that Odeon & UCI Cinemas Group had been bought by AMC Entertainment, a US chain owned by Chinese conglomerate Dalian Wanda, in a deal worth £921 million (US$1.21 billion). Dalian Wanda, the world's biggest movie theatre operator, is led by China's richest man, Wang Jianlin. Odeon & UCI Cinemas will continue to be based in London and will operate as a subsidiary of AMC.

If you have the wrong values, change them

Merlin Entertainments is the world's second-largest operator of visitor attractions. The company runs 110 attractions in 23 countries spanning four continents, including resort theme parks and iconic attractions such as Sea Life, Madame Tussauds and Legoland Parks.

Nick Varney, Merlin's chief executive, says that one of his major preoccupations is the company's culture:

> 'We grew from 400 employees in 1999 to 27,000 today and a large part of that transformative growth has been from acquisitions. Every time you bring in groups of people from another company you have to ensure they integrate into a common culture. This starts with you as the leader. I've been in this business since 1990 and I love everything I do in the business and I'm sure it shows. At the core of everything is the fact that everyone in our business is equally passionate about what we do, is passionate about our brands and so we have been able to maintain an authentic culture throughout our growth.
>
> We talk a lot about what a Merlin person is and we are very clear that first and foremost it is someone who absolutely loves the business, gives everything to it, likes working as a team and doesn't shirk responsibility. The people who don't last are the ones who come in and look to blame others for mistakes, so we have a strong culture of people doing what they say and all clearly focused on delivering memorable experiences to our visitors.'

After one particularly big acquisition, the Merlin leadership team tried to create a set of values that were common to both Merlin and the newly acquired business. Nick said:

> 'We ended up with something that just didn't quite fit the culture – it felt very corporate and imposed from above and it took a really good HR director to tell us that the values written down were not the values we exuded on a daily basis. We scrapped them and focused on articulating the values that had developed organically rather than trying to force-fit values that you could read in a textbook.
>
> We're all very clear that it's all about delivering memories to people that will last way beyond their visit, and stay with them for weeks, months or even years. We are very fortunate to be in a business that can deliver something like that and it's the very worst thing for us when we sometimes mess it up.'

He adds:

> 'Given our ambition to continue to grow rapidly, expanding across four continents, the challenge that preoccupies me morning, noon and night is all about our people and our culture. I always tell people to be true to

themselves, and only to work here if they feel really proud about the business, because that sense of pride in the good things we do is right at the heart of our passion and enthusiasm. The whole concept of the business we are in is about removing people from their everyday humdrum, sometimes troubled lives, and putting them into an alternative magical reality. We have to keep all our people passionately involved in delivering that purpose, safely.'

Leaders may desire certain values to be lived, and even live those values consistently themselves, but they have constantly to check that their values are being lived all the way to the front line.

To understand culture, put your leaders in the front line

On an average day in London, there are more than 30 million journeys undertaken on the Transport for London (TfL) network.

TfL is the city's integrated transport authority, responsible for most aspects of the transport system in Greater London. The body is organized in three main directorates:

- London Underground, the capital's underground rail network;
- London Rail, including Docklands Light Railway and London trams;
- Surface Transport, including London buses, London river services, London's congestion charge, London streets and the Public Carriage Office, responsible for licensing the famous black cabs and other private-hire vehicles.

At the time of writing there are 8.6 million people living in London, with more living there than ever before. The city's population is set to reach 10 million by 2030, and because new transport systems take so long to plan and implement, a major feature of TfL's activities is planning the future.

Vernon Everitt is managing director of Customers, Communication and Technology for TfL. He is responsible for TfL's customer and technology/data strategies and their delivery. This includes accountability for fares and payment operations, contact centres, customer information, employee engagement, marketing and customer insight, media relations, public affairs, travel demand management and all core and operational technology.

He focuses on how TfL can use technology and open data to deliver better journeys on public transport and the road network, and enable TfL's employees to provide better customer service. Says Vernon: 'Our organization emanated from a heavy engineering culture. As a leadership team, we have focused on the fact that we are one huge retail customer service organization that delivers through transport. We directly employ 30,000 people, with another 50,000 employees in the bus companies, and we have another 60,000 people we are involved with throughout our supply chain.

Draw a direct line from the job to the purpose

'We are concentrating on engaging with our whole workforce', says Vernon Everitt. 'With many different disciplines and at all different levels – in a way that recognizes our changing environment and does so with passion and pride. You can draw such a direct line between what we do every day and making a world-leading city work, so that London remains an engine room of the economy and is a national asset driving housing, jobs and growth and wealth.'

Vernon says that developing the culture of the organization has been all about trying to see life through the eyes of the customer, and learning to think about what TfL is doing through that prism. 'We truly made a huge leap when we all united to make the Olympic Games in 2012 one of the most extraordinary events in the city's history, where we saw visitor numbers to London going through the roof. We all united behind a common purpose with real passion; failure simply wasn't an option. Having that sort of common purpose galvanized us to look at customer service in a different light.'

The TfL purpose is to 'keep London moving, working and growing and make life in London better'. Its ambition is to be a customer-focused and commercially driven organization that keeps transport affordable to the millions who rely on it every day. Says Vernon: 'We know that we exist to serve London and we are committed to the thought that every journey matters, no small commitment when you consider that there are 30 million such journeys every day.

This promise that every journey matters means every member of the team needs to understand that they have to live this promise, conveying to every passenger that their individual journey matters, says Vernon. 'We've taken some lessons from world-class retailers and service providers in looking at our customer strategy and approach, and we know that your reputation is defined by how well you respond when things go wrong.'

Vernon says that the TfL leadership team has spent a lot of time listening to employees, who interface with customers every day and who have a great deal to say about how to improve customer service:

'One thing that used to bother our people was that they had to tell customers to ring business-rate numbers when they had complaints or queries. When we changed to low-rate numbers, based on that feedback, it encouraged our staff to offer the service to customers. It was a simple but incredibly powerful action that took a lot of heat out of the organization, and there are hundreds of those sorts of things that we've done since. It's all about showing our people that we are intent on removing the things that frustrate our customers and that means engaging properly and proactively with the people who know best – and that's our front-line staff.'

Understand the employee experience to improve customer experience

To do this, TfL has initiated for leaders a 'front-line experience', where all the senior leadership have to spend at least two weeks of the year out in the field, acting as a revenue inspector on the Tube, or on the bus service, or mopping the decks at one of the piers where the river boats turn up. 'It's only by doing this, by standing shoulder to shoulder with staff, that we can truly understand their experience and help them deliver a better service.'

Vernon says that culture is often defined by the type of environment you give people. 'The technology means that we have been able to bring staff out from behind inaccessible glass screens at stations and make them available when customers need them most in the public areas. That's a big improvement for customers and drives a different culture. And we are developing customer focus, equipping people with the technology and information they need to do what we're asking them to do.'

Developing a customer-focused culture is all about alignment – alignment of your functions, alignment of your purpose and values, aligning your technology to enable people to deliver, and alignment of all of the leaders in the organization, Vernon explains: 'Everyone needs to be true to that.'

Leaders must always be aware of the impact of the values they choose – especially when it comes to impact on customers. For example, a call centre that chooses to value the speed of call handling, which makes obvious commercial sense, could be repelling customers, who want to take as long as is needed to sort a problem. An employee incentivized on speed might behave in ways that make the customer feel disrespected and angry, and this then could actually be commercially very damaging.

Your values bond customers to the brand

Steve Hood, chairman and chief executive of Trust Ford, the dedicated Ford dealer group, says: 'Managers come and go, so if you can embed your values in everything your employees do, you can create a differentiator for your brand. The modern consumer is big on values and will make decisions based on how they see you behaving, not just on the quality of the product you deliver.'

Although Trust Ford sells more than 100,000 vehicles a year, Steve knows that unless he can get his customers truly engaged with his brand, and not just the cars they buy, his chances of growing the business are vastly more difficult. 'Your culture is hugely important, both for attracting the right employees and winning and keeping customers. If you don't have engaged employees living your values you'll never retain your customers.'

David Statham, managing director of Southeastern, a British railway company serving the south-east of England, fully agrees: 'Your values bond people to the brand, so the values you choose and live are crucial to your success.'

Southeastern is operated by Govia, a joint venture between leading transport operators Go-Ahead and Keolis, and has been running the train service between London and Kent and parts of East Sussex since 2006 – one of the busiest networks in the country. It also runs the UK's first domestic high-speed service with Javelin trains. Built by Hitachi in Japan, they run at speeds of 140 mph.

More than 4,000 employees in Southeastern enable 640,000 passengers to travel every weekday, serving 178 stations, including Charing Cross, Victoria, Blackfriars and St Pancras in London. This amounts to almost 200 million passenger journeys a year.

'Happier customers give us long-term security', says David. 'If we want our franchise renewed in 2018, then ensuring that we have high passenger satisfaction scores is the name of the game.'

In 2013, due to infrastructure challenges caused by landslips and other problems, Southeastern suffered closures on parts of its network for eight weeks. Consequently they delivered their worst ever passenger satisfaction scores, down from 84 per cent to 72 per cent – a massive drop. David says: 'As a leadership team our biggest single challenge is to regain the trust and confidence of our passengers, because it is that reputation that will enable us to regain the franchise, bid for other businesses in the future, grow our revenue and motivate our staff.'

Part of the challenge for the company is to rebuild the infrastructure that they operate on, something that in some cases has not been done since the Victorian era. 'This presents a dual challenge', says David. 'We are building a railway for the future while coping with a growth in passenger numbers – something like 40 per cent growth since we have owned the franchise in 2006. We've put out more than 200 extra services a day in that time.'

With all of these challenges, David and his team have been rethinking the purpose and values of Southeastern. The old purpose statement ('Working together to bring people together') was not seen as inspiring. 'When our people are on the trains or on the platforms, having to make decisions in sometimes stressful circumstances, you can't make rules for every single circumstance. You have to provide a framework that enables people to make these decisions every single day. You can only do that by instilling in them a sense of purpose and a set of values that liberate them to make the right decisions.'

As a result, Southeastern have expressed their purpose as 'delivering the best ever passenger experience to our customers'. David says that this was a result of talking to staff to find out what truly got them out of bed in the morning. Their three-year ambition is to achieve 85 per cent satisfaction rates higher than ever.

'You've got to make your purpose and values personal', says David. 'The people who travel on our networks are our colleagues, members of our families, our friends, our neighbours. So it's all about looking after people we know and ensuring that every member of staff recognizes that they can make a difference. Whether it's the smiling ticket inspector, the person in finance making sure our supplier bills are paid, all the contractors who clean our stations – everyone has an opportunity to make a difference.'

This is why, in the Southeastern values statement, they say: 'Put simply, passengers are everything to us. What matters to them, matters to us. Our values help us to do the right thing by our passengers.' David explains: 'We will only get to our satisfaction targets if our passengers know that our values and our purpose are centred on them.'

A strong set of values empowers and energizes people

Organizations that create more leaders are more agile. To create more leaders, you need to empower more people to be able to make decisions without always going up and down the management chain. When leaders provide a resonating purpose and clear principles, they enable people everywhere to make the decisions that need to be made, at speed, confident that they are 'the decision the leader would have made', which is how leaders have a presence even when they are not around.

This is exemplified by the chair of clothing business Moss Bros. In 2010, Moss Bros Group Plc was in dire straits. The group owned several brands and fascias including Moss, Moss Bros Hire, Savoy Taylors Guild and Cecil Gee. It was a listed business on the London Stock Exchange but in 2010 it was running out of cash, it had been making losses for a number of years, and its 165-year heritage had become something of a millstone. Instead of modernizing its old fashion stores, it ploughed resources into developing a new brand and ventured down several strategic cul-de-sacs. This all resulted in a further drain on cash, a loss of brand equity and an unpromising future.

In April 2010, Debbie Hewitt MBE was appointed non-executive chairperson to work with newly appointed CEO Brian Brick to turn the business around. When I met her for our interview in 2015, Debbie was 'full on'. As one of Britain's busiest businesswomen, a mother of seven-year-old twins, and with a busy and successful husband and homes in two locations, life was hectic.

She had started her career with Marks & Spencer, later joining Lex Service plc, where she sold used cars while studying for an MBA at Bath University. Later she became operations director at the RAC (a well-known UK consumer brand providing roadside assistance and general motoring insurance, and a Lex subsidiary) and soon became its managing director.

After the RAC, Debbie started a portfolio career and is now chairperson of The Restaurant Group plc, operator of the Frankie & Benny's and Chiquito brands, and non-executive director at NCC plc and Redrow plc as well as holding non-executive roles in private companies White Stuff, Visa UK and Domestic & General. She is extremely thoughtful about how best to inspire people.

How to be present even when you are absent

Says Debbie: 'As a leader I am obsessed with the idea of how you are present when you are not present. What I mean is, how do you lead in a way that enables your people everywhere to make decisions, even if you're not there, because they know exactly what the mission is, what your values are, and what decision really matters to the success of the company. As a company gets bigger it is so important that everyone carries that leadership mantle and feels empowered to deliver it.'

But when you are faced with a turnaround, inspiring and empowering people is not the first thing on your agenda. Survival is. The first job was to get Moss Bros's cash under control and get oxygen into the business. The company had 4,500 colleagues and many of them were going through real hardship to carry out their jobs. That hardly put them in a state to provide brilliant service.

In the early days of the turnaround, the executive team of Moss Bros had to make a lot of tough decisions and be brutally honest with people:

'We had to spell out the problems and engage them in helping us to fix them. The Executive were very conscious that we couldn't turn our attention to our vision and values until things were stabilized. Thinking about a long-term future and an inspiring purpose when you are in the midst of a crisis – and possibly about to hand the keys to the banks – is shallow and jars with people. It simply would not motivate them while they are thinking they might not get paid next week.

However, once we began to see progress, we could then turn to thinking about how we could once again, grow the business. Our CEO, Brian Brick, and his team had done an amazing job of turning the business around and giving it the opportunity of a much brighter future. At this stage we needed to engage the commitment of the front-line teams.

With a lot of consultation, we were soon very clear about what our mission statement should be. The previous one was to be the UK's number one formal-wear specialist. It didn't engage or energize our people. It wasn't emotional and it wasn't the reason people came to work every day. When we thought about our emotional purpose it was something very different. We need to describe it with more emotional language. After many iterations, the team opted for the mission, *making men feel amazing*.

We really do feel that this translates well into behaviours on the shop floor. I might put a really expensive suit on you but if it doesn't make you look good then it isn't going to make you feel amazing, even though I want to sell it to you. It absolutely gets our values over.'

The group's strategy is to be *the number one men's suit specialist* through creating a multichannel menswear business focused on its target customer groups.

Make staff feel amazing to make customers feel amazing

While there were a lot of operational issues to sort out, including investing in new products, refurbishing stores, training and developing people and modernizing the Moss Bros image, at the heart of the company's recovery has been the motivation and ethic of its people. 'We knew that unless we could make them feel amazing they would never make our customers feel amazing', says Debbie:

'Not only did we need to give them better training and development and working conditions, but we also had to rebuild our culture. It took us a little longer, including hiring a new human resources (HR) director, to put in place the right values, but with the appointment of a new HR director we have brought momentum to this. We discussed the fact that we needed to "live our values" before we "laminated them". I encouraged Brian and his team to focus on behaviours first. You can't successfully grow a business, unless you engage the hearts and minds of your people and that is done through the leadership behaviours of the top team.'

These are the Moss Bros values:

1 *Customer for life*: we care deeply about understanding and anticipating what the customer wants, wherever and whenever they shop. We are motivated by doing the right thing, for tomorrow as much as for today. We offer unrivalled personal service... a surprise and pleasure in today's world.

2 *Winning teams*: whether in-store, at head office or at the distribution centre we work together, doing what we say we will do and finding win-win solutions that deliver the best results for the business. We believe in the power of teamwork, developing relationships based on trust and respect for each other.

3 *Passionate experts*: with our understanding of men's tailoring and our pride in our product, we style our customers; inspiring them to look great and feel amazing. Customers have confidence in us; we know what we're talking about. This expertise, passion and enthusiasm is why customers keep coming back to us... and why our business is growing.

4 *Proud to sell*: we celebrate every sale and get a buzz from success, it's what gets us out of bed in the morning. We delight customers by making shopping a great experience: inspiring, uncomplicated and easy. We don't give up easily, working hard to get a great result for the customer and the business.

These values work hand in glove with the purpose – to make men feel amazing; and together, the hard strategy work and cultural revival have had a remarkable effect on the morale and behaviours of Moss Bros staff. In the latest annual results available before going to press, Moss Bros Group plc were reporting significant improvement in revenues and profits, with two successive years of profits to encourage shareholders. Financial analysts at various stockbroking firms are now recommending that Moss Bros Group plc shares be bought by investors. Many predict these shares will outperform and deliver significant returns to investors.

You have a culture in your organization, whether you try to engineer it or not. It is in your agendas, it is in what you pay attention to, or don't pay attention to, it is in your behaviours, in how you treat people, and how you treat customers, at every touch point. So don't let your culture develop at random, and become a poor culture, which costs you money and customers, as well as causing a high churn rate among your own people. It makes sense to pay attention to culture, as shown by an 11-year study by Harvard Business School professor and author John Kotter. He found that those organizations with rich, healthy cultures achieved income growth seven times higher than those with less well-defined cultures. Those same companies were also better at attracting the talent that would keep them generating value.

In a high-performing culture, people have a great sense of individual and collective purpose. To deliver that, you have to use purpose, values and goals in the right way.

Next: the purpose framework.

Key points from Chapter 9

1 Think carefully about your values, ensuring that they reflect the DNA of your organization. Ensure they enable you to achieve your goals.

2 Put your leaders and managers on the front line so that they can understand the culture and what changes to culture are necessary.

3 There must be a close link between your purpose and your values, which should enable everyone in the organization to make decisions based on knowing what you would do if you were not in the room.

4 Use your purpose and values to create a single agenda that drives discussions everywhere – around not only what to do, but how to do it.

5 Spend more time ensuring that middle managers live the values, for it is they who kill the culture if not.

6 Values matter to employees, and they look to managers to deliver those values consistently – a worrying gap exists in survey work about whether employees think their managers do believe in and deliver the values consistently.

7 Watch out for policies that prevent employees from living the values. Nothing kills engagement and motivation faster.

8 Your values bond customers to the brand, so make sure there is consistency between your internal culture and external expectations.

A framework for success 10

How leaders create alignment by putting purpose, values, vision and goals on a single page

To transform performance, everyone must be aligned to the purpose, values and goals of your organization. When articulated and communicated well, a purpose framework can help to direct, align and inspire the right actions on the part of large numbers of people. Without this, change programmes quickly dissolve into a list of confusing, competing and contradicting projects that absorb time and money and take you nowhere at all.

Most organizations are packed with people who have the potential to do great things. It is my belief that leaders are not harnessing that potential well enough, and that is one of the reasons we have a productivity challenge.

The best leaders have incredible faith in the energy, creativity and passion of their people. They *know* that those people can help them to achieve the impossible. That belief and passion translates itself to their followers, who become inspired to achieve more than they thought was possible. It is a virtuous circle. But it is not enough. The trick to achieving successful change is unleashing all that energy and creativity in an aligned way.

To do that, you have to have an inspiring purpose that resonates with people and makes them want to get out of bed every day to come to work. You have to have a powerful vision of success that excites your team. You have to have the right culture to ensure all that energy, creativity and passion is put to your purpose in the right way. And you have to have a set of strategic priorities that everyone in the organization understands, because every one of them has a set of tasks aligned to achieving those strategic priorities, which in turn helps to achieve the vision. It is this alignment between vision, values, purpose and goals that creates an aligned and agile organization.

Being a visionary manager or leader is a great thing, but the ability to translate that vision in a meaningful way to employees is equally vital. Unfortunately, all the research I have seen points to a significant gap in leadership effectiveness in this particular area. In the YouGov survey that I mentioned in previous chapters, where the international online market research company conducted two quantitative opinion polls (among 1,884 managers and 2,121 employees), this gap was starkly evident.

When managers were asked whether they helped their people to see where the organization was headed, 80 per cent said they did. Only 4 per cent disagreed. However, when employees were asked the same question, only 47 per cent agreed. Almost one-third disagreed, which means that more than half are unconvinced. As leaders, we need to do a better job of setting and sharing goals.

Employees want to contribute to strategic goals

Understanding goals is one thing, but feeling that you can do something about them is even more important. The YouGov research showed that it was critical to motivation that employees felt they were making a contribution to your organization's goals. So, how well are managers doing this? Not brilliantly. In this research, while 93 per cent of managers said they made their staff feel they were contributing to goals, only 60 per cent of employees agreed, and more than 20 per cent actively disagreed.

Highly motivated people tend to give of their discretionary effort to their employers. This is the level of effort one is capable of bringing to a task, versus the effort required only to get by. A significant factor behind employee willingness to deliver discretionary effort is how much employees feel committed to their organization's goals. In the YouGov research, 72 per cent of the employees in not-for-profit organizations said they cared about their goals, and 72 per cent said they regularly put in extra effort. In public sector organizations, 63 per cent of employees said they cared about their goals, and 67 per cent said they gave extra effort. Among private sector employees, only 47 per cent said they cared, and 58 per cent regularly gave extra effort. This, to me, was a clear correlation between caring about the goals and being prepared to go the extra mile to achieve them.

According to research by Deloitte, the global accounting firm, organizations that make it easy for employees to set clear goals are four times more likely to score in the top 25 per cent of business outcomes. The research also found a major impact on business outcomes when employees felt vested in their goals and senior leaders created an environment of accountability for goal achievement. Similarly, organizations that have employees revise or review their goals quarterly (or more frequently) were 3.5 times more likely to score in the top 25 per cent of business outcomes as well. The YouGov research also found that employees whose leaders regularly reviewed their goals and outcomes were more motivated. Levels of motivation dropped away the more infrequent those reviews were.

Success only comes from alignment

So, success depends on ensuring that employees have an understanding of and a commitment to corporate goals, and an ability to set their own goals to align with those corporate goals. These must be regularly reviewed.

Why? Because if you want to lead your team or your division or your company to success, it means delivering change across the entire organization you lead. If you are going to change something then everyone in the organization needs to be on board, and committed for the long term. Whether those people are on board or not is to do with how successfully your vision, values, purpose and goals have been articulated and communicated. More importantly it is about how well people have been able to develop their own goals and align them to the corporate goals, so that they have a direct line of sight between what they do every day and the big hairy audacious goal you have set the organization.

Unfortunately, it is clear that leaders simply do not spend enough time articulating the strategic initiatives that are so key to people understanding how they relate to the vision. Not only that, but they seldom ensure there is a process that encourages employees to develop their own goals – the tactics that ensure everything anyone in the company works on is mapped to one of the strategic initiatives. These strategic priorities also help to form your core culture – when everyone is aligned to a common set of goals, that does as much to encourage a winning culture as a strong purpose and a compelling set of values.

All too often, I have seen client companies listing hundreds of projects that 'need' to be completed. When you delve into these, you find that the leadership team has not identified, defined or actively managed those projects for maximum strategic impact. Without that discipline from the top, dozens of those projects remain unfinished, go over budget or are even shelved – without ever having made any real impact on the organization's vision and key goals. What a waste of time and effort! Worse, some of these projects can divert you from your mission, and prevent you from achieving your goals.

How Monarch Airlines came back from the brink by aligning the company

There is nothing quite like a big crisis to focus the mind and reduce the number of unnecessary projects in an organization.

One such crisis recently befell the Monarch Group, the UK's leading independent travel group. The majority of the group's revenues comes from Monarch Airlines, a European scheduled leisure airline flying almost 7 million passengers a year to 39 destinations on the Mediterranean and the Canary Isles. It also has Monarch aircraft engineering, a maintenance and repair operation, which not only services the airline's own aircraft but third-party customers as well. The group's tour operations comprise Monarch Holidays (formerly Cosmos Holidays) and Avro.

Group CEO Andrew Swaffield recalls that when he joined Monarch he did not fully appreciate the trouble it was in: 'I didn't do enough due diligence and assumed that because the airline had been owned for 47 years by a billionaire Swiss family, its future was assured. Not so. At the time I joined, I was employed as managing director. I discovered fairly quickly that the group was in trouble and was set to make yet another loss.'

Andrew had enjoyed a stellar career up to this point. He had joined from Avios Group Ltd, where he was managing director for seven years from 2006. He had enjoyed over 25 years' management experience in travel, aviation and airline loyalty gained with Thomas Cook and British Airways, where he headed leisure sales in the UK and Ireland, as well as running its travel agency and tour-operating subsidiaries. Nothing, however, had prepared him for the monumental task that now lay ahead.

'To my horror, the business I had joined was not sustainable and the billionaire Swiss Mantegazza family had decided that enough was enough. My executive chairman Iain Rawlinson headed for the exit, and in this maelstrom of change the owners asked me to take it over as CEO. They also said they didn't want to own it any more and gave me three months to find new owners', said Andrew.

In order to find new owners the group had to restructure because it was clear the business was going to lose money for years to come. It had a massive pension deficit, a huge cost base that it could not sustain, too many aircraft, too complex an operation and too many employees. 'Unless we radically changed things no investor was going to be interested. I was appointed CEO on 28 July and we completed the sale to new owners Greybull Capital on 24 October. That was the most tumultuous period of my career – 80 hours a week every week', said Andrew.

A noble brand deserved a second chance

'I had to admit that I did contemplate leaving prior to accepting the CEO role', says Andrew. 'But there was something noble about the Monarch brand. It had an outstanding reputation with a discerning customer base and every employee I met had customer care deep in their heart. Even though we were staring into the abyss, I felt that everyone there deserved another chance.'

There are 86 airlines in Europe and half of them have a bad cost base, explained Andrew. Most of those will have to make the same tough decisions that he was about to make. Having a low cost base was crucial. Says Andrew:

> 'Along the way to recovery, working with my management team, we had to get the pilots, cabin crew and engineers to agree to a 30–35 per cent pay cut, new terms and conditions and a cap on their pensions.
>
> We had to persuade aircraft lessors to take back the long-haul planes we no longer wanted. We had to make redundant more than 700 staff, cutting back to just 2,800 people. We had to cut unprofitable routes. We had to develop a convincing business plan for the next seven years that would make sense to hard-nosed investors, and also negotiate and plan for a new fleet of aircraft to start arriving in 2018. This was good news for Boeing as we ordered 30 new generation 737s, which would give us much greater operational efficiency.'

On 24 October the Monarch group signed the deal with Greybull Capital, a European family investment firm, who paid a nominal sum for the business. The key was their agreement to provide £125 million of funding into the firm for a 90 per cent stake. The remaining 10 per cent went to the pension protection fund, as a consequence of them taking on the pension deficit.

While all this was happening, Andrew decided that he wanted staff to be treated in the same way that he would like to have been treated – and that meant telling them the truth and involving them as much as possible in finding solutions. 'I had to confide we were going bust and unless we had their help we would not survive. We took a huge chance doing this but they respected the confidentiality and worked with us to reduce our cost base', said Andrew. 'We then shared our 100-day plan and later our seven-year plan with them, the same plan that had convinced our investors, and which showed them we had a future. This, however, was purely a financial plan and – after the pain of all the restructuring – it soon became obvious that we needed to address our vision and our values and goals to align the whole business to our growth strategy.'

Were personal sacrifices worth it?

One of the hardest parts in a turnaround is often getting the necessary cultural change, getting staff to come with you to understand why you have to do it. That part was fairly clear-cut. But now staff were looking at Andrew and his leadership team and asking whether there was a future and whether their personal sacrifices were going to be worth it in the long run. People were quick to tell Andrew that the values they had up on the walls were not the values they had in the business and that people were hugely cynical about the previous vision and values. Look where those had got them! Andrew says:

> 'We spent a huge amount of time thinking about how best to articulate a long-term vision, our business plan, our values and our purpose. We went back to rethinking the brand and how we expressed it.
>
> It was a root and branch exercise. We knew that we would not convince people to behave in the way we now needed on the basis of a set of numbers and profit targets. We needed a much more emotionally driven approach that would speak to their hearts and resonate with them. We also knew that this had to be rooted in some clear strategic priorities that everyone in the business was going to be involved in delivering, a new set of values that would help us to achieve our goals, and a brand positioning that resonated with our staff and built on the pride they had in being a Monarch employee. We addressed all of this in what we call our True North framework.
>
> We set our long-term vision: *to be Europe's most recommended airline group*. We knew this would take us a long time to achieve, but we knew everyone would want to help us achieve it and we also knew that it was a goal that was measurable and possible.'

Andrew and his team then defined the group's purpose as: *to show we care*.

The vision and purpose were not easy words to find and define. The leadership team consulted widely to arrive at them, including with their shareholders, and were careful to make sure that they resonated with the DNA of the organization. Key to enabling everyone in the organization to see how they could play a part in achieving the long-term vision, was defining medium-term goals and making clear the key things they would all have to work together to achieve if they were to deliver the plan.

They defined their medium-term vision as: *double passengers and double margin.*

To get to this, Monarch set six strategic goals:

- build a strong balance sheet and competitive cost base;
- increase overall passengers while maintaining core customer loyalty;
- develop profitable all-year-round flying schedule;
- successfully introduce the new fleet;
- gain highest European airline net promoter score;
- become the best European travel company to work for.

'Each of these goals had a series of tasks, showing how we were going to achieve them, and effectively outlining our strategy to every single member of staff', explained Andrew.

The company then also articulated four key behaviour values that would be crucial to its success. These were:

- winning the praise, loyalty and advocacy of customers on every trip;
- being driven to improve our performance;
- supporting each other and working as a team;
- being agile and efficient in everything we do.

Strategy on a page

Each of the above four values, Andrew says, has four or five supporting behaviours to make clear what they mean in every case:

'It was only being this detailed that would help us to move to the culture that we needed to drive our long-term success. All of this is now on one page in what we call our True North Framework and is, therefore, more cohesive and demonstrates both the emotional and rational sides of our story. The first stage of roll-out of the True North was to engage employees by asking for feedback, creating specific feedback channels, e-mail addresses, cross-sectional focus groups, sending surveys, talking to and creating intranet forums, and inviting people to share their views. And employees did, in bucket loads.'

Next was to show the framework to Monarch's top 100 managers and challenge them to really try to pick holes in it. They ran a special workshop to tease out potential issues of applying the framework, collected all the feedback and then applied it. Says Andrew: 'We asked our managers to nominate members of their team who already lived the values, perhaps without knowing it, and nominate them to become our True North ambassadors. Those who accepted the nomination became an empowered working group. These ambassadors were then used as a sounding board and feedback loop before any activity was planned, and were given sneak peeks of communication before it was sent and before employee engagement budget was spent – a really good way to run ideas past the people of Monarch.' The result of collating all this feedback and applying it to the roll-out plan led to managers feeling that the framework directly reflected what their teams had said – it is a lot easier to get team members wanting to apply a framework when the words are those they have inputted and suggested.

In summary, Andrew says: 'We know that some things will not change overnight. Our True North is a long-term commitment and we hope that employees feel engaged, prepared and connected to our vision and our values. In 2014 we were bereft of strategic direction, staring into the abyss – 12 months on, we are heading in the right direction.'

(On 7 December 2015 Monarch issued the following press release: *Monarch, a leading independent UK leisure airline group, has returned strongly to profit in its first full year of trading under new ownership. The group expects underlying earnings for the year to 31 October 2015 to be in excess of £40 million before interest and tax (EBIT). That represents a turnaround of £130 million compared to the losses suffered in the previous year.*)

A framework for success

The Monarch airlines leadership team has created a framework within which Monarch's long-term goal, short-term business plan (or three-year ambition), strategic goals, purpose and values all reside on a single page. The beauty of this is that it enables every employee to see how what they do contributes to the success of the organization. This framework allows them to check whether they are behaving consistently with the values of the organization, whether what they are doing contributes to the key strategic initiatives, and whether decisions they need to make will help advance the company to its long-term goal.

It is what Dame Fiona Reynolds, formerly chief executive of the National Trust, called a 'Framework for Freedom'. She said this was a framework that gave leaders freedom because it was empowering and enabled anyone to make a decision and know from this framework the right thing to do.

By articulating six strategic priorities, Monarch made clear what the company would focus on to help close the gap between its current reality and where it needed to be to achieve its long-term goals. It provided the leadership with a framework to review all of its current projects, define the expected impact on the mission and then focus on the few projects that would cause the most needed changes. These strategic priorities were not 'business as usual' initiatives, they were designed specifically to help achieve Monarch's BHAG (big hairy audacious goal). This now enables the leadership team to focus on the few things that will truly drive the execution of the company strategy, and also enable them to drive up employee engagement by giving employees the power to set their own goals, which then create far greater alignment.

Whenever I run workshops with leadership teams, at the end of what are normally quite intensive sessions to create a shared vision, we take stock of the major gaps between their vision and the reality of where they are now. The shared vision inevitably gives them a greater capacity to debate and discuss the strategic priorities they need to focus on, as well as the key measures of success that will enable them to track progress to the goals. Having studied the vision frameworks of all of the leaders I interviewed for this book, as well as dozens of others that I have been able to find online on company websites, it is clear that they all follow a similar structure.

They outline a core purpose (their reason to exist), which feeds the big hairy audacious goal that they want to achieve over the next decade or more. This BHAG is measurable, but hugely stretching, and will be the organization's North Star for years to come. Every decision will be taken in the context of this guiding light, and will be the company's True North. While this True North is likely only to be achieved in a decade or more, most of these organizations also outline a strategic vision of success, usually for the term of their business plan – in other words, over the next three years or so. Both the True North and the strategic vision will be a measure of success in implementing the core purpose.

Strategic initiatives link to employee goals

No more than five or six strategic initiatives will then be described in order to focus efforts for the next two to three years on achieving the strategic vision. These will be highly visible initiatives that all employees will understand and contribute to in some way. They will contribute at every level of the organization by developing their own aligned goals – the tactics that enable the delivery of the plan. All of these activities will be guided by a set of core values – the beliefs that drive the behaviours that define the way the company delivers its goals.

Some companies then go on to describe their mission, an explanation of what they actually do, and combine that with a brand slogan that makes an external promise to customers. A few of these companies are also articulating an employee value proposition, a statement of intent that describes what employees can expect to get by working in the company.

Earlier in this book I described the Purpose-in-Life scale developed by psychologists James Crumbaugh and Leonard Maholick, in 1964. This is still widely used by psychologists today. Crumbaugh and Maholick said that a person's Purpose-in-Life scale is based on three dimensions:

- believing that life DOES have a purpose;
- upholding a personal value system;
- having the motivation to achieve future goals and overcome future challenges.

Purpose. Values. Goals. The same structure is being used by most companies today.

How a new purpose vision and values framework turned around a critical health-care business

One of the often cited benefits of a True North, or vision and values framework, is how it empowers people to make decisions. Tough decisions should be meat and drink to leaders. We expect our leaders to bring order to chaos, to fight ambiguity and to provide us with clarity and direction. We expect them to make decisions, all the time. And we expect them to make the right decisions, all the time.

As we know, that is not always possible. Many leaders I know have sometimes, somewhat flippantly, joked that they don't worry about making decisions because they only have to be right 51 per cent of the time. But that is not true. Making good decisions in difficult situations is extraordinarily challenging. The nightmare that all leaders live with is making that one bad decision that could kill the business. Trouble is, how do you know which one carries that deadly threat?

This was the story at Healthcare at Home, one of Europe's leading providers of clinical home care and speciality pharmacy. One bad decision brought the company to its knees, and caused hardship and stress to thousands of patients who were, as a result, unable to get their vital medications.

Set up in 1992 with the aim of enhancing the way in which care was provided for patients at home, the company has provided clinical care to 1.4 million patients over the past 24 years. With 1,500 staff, Healthcare at Home currently serves more than 150,000 patients each year. It provides nurse-led patient support, pharmacy and distribution of medicine and has operating companies in the UK, Germany, Austria and Switzerland. The patients they serve have rare, or acute and long-term conditions. In 2013 Healthcare at Home took over almost 3,000 patients from another drug delivery company, Medco Health Solutions, which pulled out of the UK market. This put huge stress on the business.

A logistics nightmare hurts patients

Core to Healthcare at Home is warehousing and logistics. In order to help with their growth plans, the leadership team decided in 2014 to move from an in-house-operated delivery service to using an outside company. Management believed that the move would improve their service, but some of the new IT systems failed almost as soon as the subcontractor took over the operation. This failure of IT caused a logistics nightmare and left patients with life-threatening conditions frightened about their ability to get hold of their drugs. (Healthcare at Home dispenses, delivers and often, through nurses, administers prescriptions to patients who are suffering from serious illnesses such as cancer, haemophilia, HIV and multiple sclerosis, or who are receiving fertility treatment or drugs following organ transplants.)

Under normal conditions, the company received 3,000 calls per day from patients requesting delivery-time updates. The IT failure led to more than 10,000 calls a day from patients suffering from no-shows, wrong contents and repeated delays and prevarication. Into this chaos stepped Natalie Douglas, called in by the company's private equity owners, Vitruvian Partners. Healthcare at Home is a business with a reported turnover of £1 billion per annum with pre-tax profits of £15 million a year. Vitruvian Partners were anxious that their investment was about to bleed to death.

Natalie took over as CEO, off the back of a long history in the pharmaceutical industry. She was the former chief executive of Idis, a company that specializes in providing medicine to patients with unmet needs. She also served on the boards of companies such as Shield Therapeutics and had 20 years' experience in the pharmaceuticals and health-care sector. This is her account of events:

> 'Our customers – the National Health Service and the pharmaceutical industry – were alarmed at what was happening and so too were investors. We were being investigated by the pharmacy watchdog, and we were appearing on the front pages of newspapers – and not in a good way. We were overwhelmed with patient complaints and the business was in meltdown. Of our 1,500 people, 60 per cent of them are clinicians and the majority of those are nurses. We are a caring business and it was enormously distressing to everyone in the company that we were failing to help the people we truly cared most about – the patients.
>
> The whole building was practically on fire. People were very distressed and quite probably many were clinically stressed. We were experiencing a high staff turnover rate. People were often crying and there was lots of emotion around. People were exhausted trying to do everything they could to solve the problems. By the time I walked in it had been going on for weeks.'

Conversations were key to recovery

'The first thing I did was to hold as many one-on-one conversations as I could with key people throughout the organization. This was enormously important as I demonstrated first that I was prepared to listen and, second, that I respected their views. Third, I wanted them to know that we were going to fix the problem and quickly. The most important thing about leading people through that crisis was to respect them and listen to them. It became very clear that the bad decision had been made in spite of views from front-line people that it was not going to work – so you can imagine how sceptical people were about whether or not management was truly going to listen this time.

While trying to show as much empathy as I could, and that I cared about the business as much as they did, we also had to fix the problem. It was clear that we not only had to fix the problem really quickly in order to survive, but that we also had to move rapidly to a more positive story about a long-term future in order to re-engage people and keep them with us.

It took us 12 weeks to get the business back to normal, and that took focus and application and clear direction around the most important things to deliver. We cut down the number of key performance indicators from 300 to just seven in order to provide that focus. By demonstrating that I had listened to them, and by incorporating their ideas into the plan, we managed to engage people in a magnificent turnaround. I saw some amazing and inspirational examples of leadership throughout the team as we fixed not only a broken business but also a lot of broken people.

A very significant moment came when we took the decision to reverse the idea that we could outsource our warehousing and logistics. Instead, we would keep our warehouses and keep our core competence close to heart. We would not make people redundant at those warehouses – in fact we would expand our capabilities in this area. To do all this we had the complete support of our investors. The business soon stabilized. Surviving is one thing, thriving is another, so we also needed a long-term plan. By the end of that year we had a strategy in place to take us to 2020. By January 2015 we had rolled it out to the whole company.

People needed to know that we had a long-term future and that all of their efforts had been worthwhile. We had three sessions of 500 people each and I stood in the middle of everyone and took them through our plan. Other members of the executive leadership team were dotted around the room, and once we had explained the vision, people were able to ask any question they wanted – anything.

It was the first time the leadership team had stood up and talked about where the business was going to go and what everyone needed to do to help it grow. One of the main reasons that these sessions were so inspiring was because we talked about the reason we come to work every day. We talked about our patients, not as patients but as the people we serve and whose care we hold in our hands.'

Why people get out of bed in the morning

'Our purpose statement now says: "Inspired by their stories, their courage and resilience, we take pride in the role we play and the responsibility we hold in our hands in caring for people. We shall continue to innovate and improve in order to provide the supreme care, service and attention the people we care for and our partners deserve."

We concentrated on the reason that people get out of bed in the morning. Our staff know that no one enjoys going to hospital and that their patients find it stressful, inconvenient and probably a little scary too. They know that patients are in such a better place when highly qualified clinical teams can spend quality time with them at their home, providing personalized care and the support they need. With no travel, no waiting times and less stress, those patients have all the little worries removed so that they can focus on what really matters.

It was important to focus on this passion and use that to show people how, as an organization, we were doing so much good. By growing, we could do even more good in more places, delivering our services around the world. The point about growth for our employees was not about making more profit, it was about doing more good in more places. Making money would satisfy our shareholders who would continue to invest in us and that would enable us to grow.

So we also focused on giving people an idea of our direction of travel, our vision of long-term success, which we now express as: 'To deliver inspirational health care in the home for millions worldwide.' This will be our guiding light for years to come.

But to get there we have to have a medium-term plan, which we describe as our mission. This we articulate as: "By 2020 to be caring for 2 million people, delivering health care in homes across the world." This is a much more specific target and will only be achieved if we deliver our four strategic objectives, which involve:

- developing our pharmaceuticals pipeline;

- serving a greater number of patients across all market segments;

- creating a gold-standard organization for home-care solutions that is scalable and operationally efficient;

- building a clinically and data-driven company that is patient-focused.

These strategic objectives are underpinned by much more detailed strategies for each of the objectives, and this is where individuals in the company can see how what they do helps us to achieve our mission and our vision. Each year we have specific targets that we make clear, sometimes changing them every quarter. Achieving these targets involves everyone, keeps them highly focused and will demonstrate that we are on track to achieve our mission and our vision.

All of this – the vision, mission, objectives and targets – is delivered on a single page so everyone throughout the business can easily understand what it is we are trying to do and what we expect of them.

If we can achieve our goals, the benefits to our patients and to the National Health Service are enormous. For example, if all patients took their medicines properly, there would be at least 40 per cent fewer admissions to accident and emergency (A&E) services throughout the country. At a time when our A&E services are so thinly stretched, when you cannot get hold of GPs after hours, and when you have to wait hours in hospitals, reducing admissions by 40 per cent would make a massive difference. And everyone would benefit – taxpayers, hospital staff, patients, the government, the economy. So we can create value for all.'

So, has the new vision, mission and objectives helped to deliver performance improvement?

Yes, says Natalie:

- Call waiting times are as low as nine seconds, with an average for all customer services teams of 31 seconds.

- We now receive 70 per cent fewer complaints than at the peak of our difficulties and receive 40 per cent fewer complaints than we did prior to that.

- We have also surveyed over 30,000 patients during the last 12 months. Encouragingly, 91 per cent of patients surveyed would recommend Healthcare at Home to their friends and family.

Says Natalie: 'I have no doubt we will continue to improve, mainly because of the passion of our people. To achieve our mission we need to try to change the conversation about home care to focus on the value and not just the cost. This is important to everyone – our patients, the NHS, the government, taxpayers, our pharmaceutical partners, our shareholders and to every one of our employees.'

Like Monarch Group, Healthcare at Home has produced a vision framework on a single page. The strategic priorities they outline are given more detailed substance in terms of plenty of tactical actions they have to deliver, and this is how employees make a connection with the corporate goals. Both have benefited enormously from having their strategy on a single page.

Allow employees to translate the goals to their worlds

At Rio Tinto Group, a British-Australian multinational metals and mining corporation, they are careful to integrate their vision with their values and their strategy. Hugo Bague, group executive, organizational resources, says: 'We have done a pretty good job in defining the values that are important to us, defining the key cultural attributes of the company. But the trick is not to have that identified in an isolated way. The trick is to link it with your business strategy, your vision and then the big acid test of that is execution. For us this means that even if someone delivers great business results, if they have done so in a way that is not consistent with our values, there will be consequences.'

Rio Tinto is a leading global mining group. It supplies metals and minerals to many industries and countries. Its major products are aluminium copper, uranium, coal, diamonds and industrial minerals. With operations on six continents and revenues of around US$35 billion in 2015, the company has 55,000 employees worldwide. Hugo says:

'In a company that needs to keep delivering good results, be safe, work closely with local communities and yet still react to economic forces, it is essential that we create alignment among many and varied operations and cultures. To us, alignment means translation. You need to allow people to translate what is meaningful for them in their own world and in their own way, with all the right checks and balances. This is the only way people get engaged. We believe in asking our people to act as owners of the company. That means you are not owners of the truck you are driving, you are co-owners of Rio Tinto. And that means always looking at the bigger picture and translating it to what you can do as the truck driver to add value to the business. You have to give people the freedom to translate the big strategy goals to actions they can take in their own world.'

How to cascade the goals so they create alignment

OKR stands for objectives and key results. It is a popular method of defining and tracking objectives and their outcomes. The main goal of OKRs is to connect company, team and personal objectives to measurable results, making people move together in the right direction. A big part of OKR is making sure that each individual knows what is expected of them at work. OKRs are kept public in front of everyone so that teams move in one direction and know what others are focusing on. OKRs were invented at Intel, and are today used by many companies, including Google, LinkedIn and Twitter.

Rick Klau, a former senior director of Google, made OKRs accessible by producing a YouTube video when he worked at Google, demonstrating how

OKRs were put to work in the company. He explained: 'As a company grows, it is impossible for the founder or CEO to be a part of every discussion. Simple decisions often don't get made until the CEO weighs in. When OKRs are well defined and communicated broadly, they help everyone in the company understand what matters to the CEO and why. What are the company's priorities? What aren't the company's priorities? How are they measured?'

Though the video goes into more detail, here are a few keys to what make OKRs work at Google:

- Objectives are ambitious, and designed to feel somewhat uncomfortable.

- Key results are measurable and are easy to grade with a number (Google uses a 0–1.0 scale to grade each key result at the end of a quarter).

- OKRs are public; everyone in the company should be able to see what everyone else is working on (and how they did in the past).

- The 'sweet spot' for an OKR grade is 0.6 to 0.7; if someone consistently gets 1.0, their OKRs are not ambitious enough. Low grades should not be punished – see them as data to help refine the next quarter's OKRs.

Objectives are what you want to accomplish, and are aspirational. Key results, on the other hand, are concrete and specific. They describe how you will accomplish an objective, and measure whether you accomplished the objective or not. As an example, I could say that one of my key objectives in the next three months is to significantly raise the profile of my company among prospective clients (senior leaders). To get there I have to outline three key results, a numerically based expression of success or progress towards that objective.

So…

- I will speak at five leadership conferences.
- I will produce a blog on LinkedIn every two weeks.
- I will link up with 100 CEOs.
- I will publish three thought leadership articles in mainstream media.

See how specific and measurable the key results are? It is easy to measure if I'm hitting my targets or not. That is one of the most important parts of setting OKRs.

It is also important to stress that not every employee or team member has to contribute to every single organizational objective. Rick Klau used the example of a US National Football League team. General managers set the organizational objectives to: 1) win the Super Bowl; and 2) fill the stands by at least 80 per cent. The head coach's main focus was to win the Super Bowl, so he does not bother with filling the stands, whereas PR looks into finding innovative ways to attract fans.

It is ideal if a large number of these objectives and key results are driven from the bottom up. Managers want to drive employee engagement by giving people accountability on their contributions. Coaching and nudging to ensure these are truly aligned is encouraged. The main benefit is to keep vision, goals and objectives always in front of employees.

So much research I have seen shows that managers are not doing a good enough job helping employees to see how what they do contributes to the overall vision, yet this is crucial to giving them meaning and a greater sense of purpose. The starting place is to articulate the purpose of your team or organization, your vision and goals on a single page. This is the tool that acts as a catalyst for each and every employee to localize and personalize the vision – and this is what creates alignment, agility and performance.

Next: how leaders truly embed their purpose, values and strategy through purposeful conversations.

Key points from Chapter 10

1 An alignment between vision, values, purpose and goals creates an aligned and agile organization.

2 Research shows that managers are falling woefully short in helping employees to understand the strategic priorities of their organization. The same research shows that employees *want* to contribute to strategic goals.

3 Success depends on ensuring that employees have an understanding of and a commitment to corporate goals, and an ability to set their own goals to align with those corporate goals.

4 Organizations that make it easy for employees to set clear goals are four times more likely to score in the top 25 per cent of business outcomes.

5 Strategic priorities help to form your core culture – when everyone is aligned to a common set of goals this does as much to encourage a winning culture as a strong purpose and a compelling set of values.

6 The best vision, values and goals frameworks all reside on a single page. This becomes a framework for freedom that enables anyone to make a decision and know from this framework the right thing to do.

Purposeful conversations

11

How leaders embed their vision and values and align their organizations

Without alignment, the best strategic plan will never be fully achieved. Alignment is the glue that binds an organization to its purpose, its values and its goals and enables it to get things done faster, with less effort, and with better results. However, you cannot create a fully aligned organization if you don't spend the time aligning and enabling your managers, so that they can have the purposeful conversations that embed a sense of purpose in every employee. Unless you do this, your vision and values break down at the front line. Here, employees see only the gap between your aspirational language and their daily working lives, and they become cynical rather than motivated.

Leaders, at whatever level, often know and can talk about the corporate vision and goals, the corporate values and the corporate purpose, but most of the time they have not interpreted and personalized it for themselves or their teams. They have not thought about their own purpose, their own values, and how those relate to the company they work for. They don't have a personal story to use in their leadership. Often, they also have not explained how what their team does delivers to company goals, or delivers the purpose.

Alignment only comes when managers have understood their own purpose and values, created their own leadership story and aligned it with the corporate story. Only when they have done this can they truly connect their teams with the vision and create 'Our Story' – the team's purpose, values and goals.

My Story. Corporate Story. Our Story – this is the key to alignment.

Bill George is now professor of management practice at Harvard Business School in the United States. He was formerly CEO of Medtronic, a medical device company and the world's largest medical technology development business. He says: 'The most empowering condition of all is when the entire organization is aligned with its mission, and people's passions and purpose are in synch with each other.'

You only have to look at a group of amateurs attempting to row a boat on a lake to understand the impact of a lack of alignment. Oars spinning wildly, the boat going nowhere, much shouting and blaming – sometimes, you see the boat tipping over and sinking. Contrast that with Olympic rowers in an eight – four rowers with an oar on the right side, and four on the left, working in perfect unison to the voice of the coxswain, who is coaxing, motivating, guiding and calming the team. Even here, if team alignment and cohesion is even slightly off, the boat slows, strays off course and loses the race.

Regular conversations are crucial to high performance

The research done for me by YouGov, the online research agency (see Chapter 4), showed that employees want to have a clear line of sight between what they do and the organizational purpose. They are inspired by knowing how what they do provides positive benefits to customers. Understanding this makes them feel more important, and having regular conversations about their performance, and their team's performance, is crucial to their engagement.

Ken Blanchard is famous for his book *The One Minute Manager* (1982). His consulting and training business surveyed 1,400 employees and asked this question: 'What is the biggest mistake leaders make when working with others?' Of respondents 41 per cent identified *inappropriate communication or poor listening*.

When these same respondents were asked to look at a list of common mistakes and choose the five biggest missteps by leaders, two responses stood out:

- *Not providing appropriate feedback* was chosen by 82 per cent of respondents.
- *Failing to listen or involve others* came in a close second, cited by 81 per cent.

Failing to use an appropriate leadership style, *failing to set clear goals and objectives*, and *failing to develop their people* rounded out the respondents' top five of things leaders most often fail to do when working with others.

A 700-person follow-up study conducted by Blanchard in 2013 with readers of *Training* magazine found similar results. In that survey:

- 28 per cent of respondents said they rarely or never discussed future goals and tasks with their boss – even though 70 per cent wished they did.

- 36 per cent said they never or rarely received performance feedback – even though 67 per cent wished they did.

All this points to a simple but worrying truth – managers are simply not having enough of the purposeful conversations with their teams that drive alignment and high performance. As we have seen, all our research shows that this is one of the most important factors in delivering engaged, super-performing employees.

Alignment is a dynamic, ongoing process

The ability to have purposeful conversations is one of the most important factors in delivering an aligned organization. Alignment is not something you do by communicating your vision and values once to employees and then forgetting it. It is an ongoing process that requires managers to be holding a constant dialogue with employees. Only by doing this can employees feel a sense of ownership of the vision, buy in to the values and achieve stretching goals.

Essential to alignment is an understanding among all employees of purpose, values and goals. Managers need to spend time explaining these, talking to the rationale behind the vision, bringing to life where you are going, why you are going there and how you are going to behave along the way. Alignment only comes from plentiful dialogue, and the sad truth is that most leaders are not trained in the art of holding powerful conversations that gain buy-in, build engagement and create alignment.

Why is this so necessary? Because a leader's job is to inspire others, to give people the energy and passion that enables them, encourages them and helps them to see the deeper meaning behind their tasks. But, for this to happen, you have to invest time in your managers to make sure they live and breathe your purpose and values.

Belief in purpose drives performance and commitment

Ivan Menezes is chief executive of Diageo, one of the world's leading drinks companies. Its brands include Smirnoff vodka, Johnny Walker Scotch whisky, and Guinness, the world's best-selling stout. Its products are sold in 180 countries, and it has offices in 80 countries and employs 33,000 people.

I interviewed Ivan in August 2015 a week after he had done a round of investor meetings, reporting on Diageo's latest results. It had been a challenging year, in which conditions affecting the company's emerging markets had been tough, so he was in a reflective mood. 'Under these conditions, you would have thought that morale and engagement scores would drop. Ours went up. The reason, I believe, is because of people's belief in the company, their belief in our purpose and their engagement with our culture and values. This is an incredible asset to have. We have good people here whose hearts are truly in the company and who want it to succeed.'

So what is Diageo's BHAG and purpose? 'Our ambition is to be one of the best-performing, most trusted and respected consumer products companies in the world. Our purpose is to celebrate life, every day, everywhere.'

What that means to Ivan is to make the most of life – to be the best at work, at home, with friends, in the community, and for the community – for Diageo's brands to be part of celebrations big and small:

> 'Our distilleries and breweries and wineries are at the heart of the communities where we work. We have a responsibility to create shared value – for our shareholders, our people, and for the societies that enable our business to grow. We also have to do this in a responsible way and understand our broader holistic impact, not just drive solely for financial success. We are hugely mindful of the fact that we are in a sector where our products, if misused, can cause harm in society. You make sure that you behave in a way that is sustainable and responsible. There is no right way to do the wrong thing.'

Leaders everywhere must bring the purpose to life

Ivan is very clear that it is the responsibility of good leaders in Diageo to bring the company's purpose and values to life. 'It is one of the things we expect our leaders to bring to the company. And when I say leaders, it's not just the senior managers, it's anyone who leads people anywhere in the business.'

Ivan was one of the original team who helped to create the company's purpose and believes that in the years since it was originated it has evolved and deepened – and that his people connect to it in a much richer way than the words initially meant.

Diageo is an invented name created by the branding consultancy Wolff Olins in 1997 when the company was created through the merger of Guinness UOV and Grand Metropolitan. The logic for the name came from combining the Latin root for days, 'Dia', meaning day, and the Greek root for world, 'Geo', meaning world. It was designed as a reference to the company's purpose – celebrate life every day, everywhere. Ivan says:

> 'The leader's job is to create conditions where people are positive about coming to work and wanting to make a difference. Purpose has a very important role in our company – for our people, our brands, in how we perform and how we create value. We each connect to the Diageo purpose in different ways.
>
> Everyone wants to make the most of life and to be the best that they can at work, at home, with friends, in the community. We know that when we are fulfilled we deliver better performance, so it is vital to us that our leaders are able to help everyone connect to the purpose, and that they themselves lead with purpose.'

This means that all leaders in the company are encouraged to live the 'leadership standards' defined by Diageo, and have to spend time reflecting on how their own purpose connects to the company purpose. 'Leaders must be authentic, and you can't be authentic about your purpose if you don't believe in it and you haven't made a personal connection with it', says Ivan. 'To be authentic you have to be transparent, to talk about what makes you tick and what frightens you. It is much easier to do this in a purpose-led organization.'

The Diageo leadership standards are: be authentic; create possibilities; bring the Diageo purpose to life; create the conditions for people to succeed; consistently deliver great performance; and grow yourself. Ivan says:

> 'It is really important to me that all of our leaders get the notion of why the company exists. We live in a world where people have a lot of choices. They can do lots of different things, work in different places, so it's really key that as a leader you can answer the question about why potential employees will get excited every morning if they come to work here. When people talk about work–life balance I always advise them not to think of their life in two halves. You only live one life.
>
> As a leader you personify the business, so it is critical that you connect with the purpose and values and deliver these authentically in your leadership. Knowing this helps you to select the right people and know who is going to thrive in the company.'

Encourage and enable managers to have purposeful conversations

When managers are enabled and encouraged to articulate their own purpose and values, and link those to the purpose and values of the company, you create both authenticity and alignment.

But even this might not be enough. You also have to train your managers how to have the right conversations with their teams, and ensure they do. One company that does this religiously is Unipart Group, a global logistics, supply chain, manufacturing and consultancy company based near Oxford, in the UK. It operates in Europe, North America, Japan and Australia, and serves the automotive, marine, leisure and rail industries.

It was originally a state-owned company, part of British Leyland, but was demerged in 1987 in a management buyout. It is one of the largest privately owned companies in the UK and is partly employee owned.

The chairman and chief executive of the Unipart group is John Neill, who says:

> 'You can't ask people to follow you on a journey if you're not on it yourself and you don't believe in it. To ensure this happens in Unipart, we opened the first corporate university in the country in 1993, in order to train all of our managers and our people in what we call the Unipart Way. This is a comprehensive operational excellence system, which enables us to deliver our purpose, values and goals.
>
> Our purpose and our principles have remained the same for 30 years, and our corporate goal was established in 1987. Everywhere you go in the company you will see our 18 guiding principles, so that if you are unsure of what to do you can just act in accordance with the principles and know that it will be the right thing to do.
>
> When we wrote the company philosophy, it was "to understand the real and perceived needs of our customers better than anyone else, and serve them better than anyone else". In those days, the country was not well focused on customer service but we were clear that the only route to long-term success was to be better than anyone else at understanding customer needs. This means that we give everyone intensive training on what personal customer service means. It is no good setting a goal and sticking it on a plaque in your reception. You have to ensure that it is believed in and lived by the company at every level.'

Unipart people have communication meetings every day, as part of the Unipart Way. This system was designed specifically to engage people to deliver exceptional results for customers. 'We have spent 25 years building the system and now a lot of people buy it from us', says John. 'This system of daily conversations helps people to have a clear line of sight between their jobs and the overall goals of the business. They know what is expected of them, every single day, because of these communication cells.'

Conversations must be structured

Unipart also has a policy deployment process, where key policies and projects agreed by a group executive are then deployed, systematically, down the organization to the individual. 'This is how any individual can see how his or her daily activities connect to the corporate projects', explains John:

> 'What we have found is that you can really only deliver engagement through conversations, but they do need to be structured conversations. We know that if we implement the Unipart Way, it will engage people. Managers are trained to it and their staff are put through it and assessed on it. It takes many years to be trained to coach the Unipart Way, probably 10. If you're very smart, you might get there in five.
>
> This is the way that Unipart delivers empowerment, through managers who understand how to engage the staff and involve them in solution finding. It is only if people cannot solve a problem at their own level that it comes back up through the management chain. Being trained to the Unipart Way enables alignment and empowerment.'

Unipart has produced a booklet entitled: *Conducting Business the Unipart Way*. It is available to everyone in the company but also to anyone who has an interest in the group – customers, potential customers, suppliers and other stakeholders. In it, the company outlines the values that it applies to each and every stakeholder. It is a comprehensive set of commitments to all involved with the company.

'It is important that we are regarded as a responsible, ethical and supportive business in order to earn and retain the trust and confidence of our many stakeholders. This has been the cornerstone of our strategy since we were formed in 1987', explains John. 'This is because we really do believe that corporate responsibility is not just a job for selected people in the business. It defines the way we do business. Responsible business is only a reality if it is practised by all employees at all times.'

Respect for the individual is core to the Unipart group: 'We expect all of our leaders to lead using the Unipart Way. And we check on them. We do this because it is a way of inspiring and engaging people to achieve things they never believed they could achieve, and to feel a great sense of pride and satisfaction from doing it. If they are successful, then our business will be successful, so long as you have got the strategy right.'

(In 2015, Unipart was one of a handful of companies to receive a five-star rating in the corporate responsibility index run by Business in the Community, a charity of His Royal Highness the Prince of Wales (Prince Charles), promoting responsible business by working with more than 800 UK companies committed to improving their impact on society and the environment. In 2016, the Unipart group scored 100 per cent in the corporate responsibility index.)

Purposeful conversations drive better business results

If there is one thing I have learned while speaking to all the leaders I've had the privilege to interview these past four years, it is that conversations are the lifeblood of leadership. When leaders are skilled at conversations, they do much more than communicate effectively – they drive stronger business results, because they are more engaging and inspiring. My own research tells me that we are not doing enough to help our managers to have these conversations, which many actively avoid when things get difficult.

This is borne out by recent research conducted by the Chartered Management Institute (CMI), an accredited professional institution for management, based in the UK. It has more than 130,000 members. The CMI interviewed 2,000 workers in 2016 to understand more about the role that conversations played in the workplace. Their main finding? Difficult workplace conversations are taking a heavy emotional toll on business leaders.

Two-thirds of the 2,000 managers surveyed said they were stressed or anxious if they knew that a difficult conversation was coming, while 11 per cent said they suffered from nightmares or poor sleep in the build-up to a difficult work conversation.

No formal training for difficult conversations

Despite the prevalence of such conversations in the workplace, 80 per cent said they had had no formal training on how to tackle them. As a result,

43 per cent of senior managers admit to losing their temper and shouting when placed in a difficult conversation, while 40 per cent have admitted to panicking and telling a lie. The survey also revealed that 57 per cent of respondents said they would do almost anything to avoid a difficult conversation; and 52 per cent said they would rather put up with a negative situation at work than have to talk about it.

Why? Shouldn't we all be naturally good at having conversations? After all, we do so every day of our lives. Petra Wilton, director of strategy and external affairs at CMI, said it is because managers do not have the support or training needed to deal with work-based conversations, which can often be on very difficult subjects.

'Our survey findings reveal that difficult conversations are really taking their toll on workers', she said. 'When it comes to our home life we often rely on friends and family to support us with tricky discussions. At work, with no advice or training, it can feel like tiptoeing through a minefield. It's no wonder 61 per cent of people told us they would like to learn how to manage workplace conversations with more confidence.'

Middle managers are often the worst affected by the lack of training in handling difficult conversations, as austere times have led to an increase in the work they are expected to handle, and a cut in training budgets to help them.

Purposeful conversations, focused on the triumvirate of purpose, values and goals, enable managers to have much deeper and more meaningful conversations. In most organizations, however, these powerful, courageous conversations don't happen. As we see from the CMI research, hard issues are avoided, and people develop vastly different interpretations about what is needed, about other people's motives, and which priorities do or don't matter. As a result, alignment breaks down, relationships suffer and productivity plummets.

Your managers have to live the purpose and values, and be models of the behaviours you require

'Embedding purpose and values in an organization is not just a matter of communicating them well', says Craig Kreeger, chief executive of the airline Virgin Atlantic. 'It actually takes demonstrating it in a way that enables people to recognize how they should change their own behaviour to be consistent with the purpose and values.'

'Currently ours are not fully baked into the organization', Craig says. 'But that is what we will strive to do. The loop between the engagement of your people and the experience your customers enjoy is a very direct one, so our culture is one of our most precious assets and I will be very focused on how I enhance it.'

On 22 June 1984, Virgin Atlantic operated its inaugural scheduled service between Gatwick and Newark using a leased Boeing 747-200, which they named 'Maiden Voyager'. Many commentators at the time were sceptical that the airline would last until the end of its first year. More than 30 years later, Virgin Atlantic still exists and many of the competitors of the 1980s have disappeared, including Pan Am, TWA, British Caledonian and People Express. The only major competitor of the 1980s that is still around is British Airways. The two airlines have been engaged in a bitter rivalry for more than three decades.

By 2013, that war had taken its toll, and Virgin Atlantic had suffered several years of loss making. Although it had a prestigious presence at Heathrow, and held a significant number of precious landing slots, it was stuck with inefficient aircraft, too few partners to provide access to a wider range of markets, and had been unable to invest in much-needed new IT. It had a disproportionate reliance on one market – with the vast majority of its revenue originating in the UK. For a challenger brand, one that was renowned for superlative customer service, it had become overstaffed and too bureaucratic. Employees felt constrained in what they could do for customers and the airline was in danger of losing the one advantage that it had – a reputation for a superior passenger experience.

At the time, Singapore Airlines owned 49 per cent of Virgin Atlantic and had been disappointed with the return on their investment. They decided to sell their stake, which was snapped up by Delta Air Lines in the United States. Delta is one of the world's biggest airlines and flies more than 160 million passengers every year. In 2013, Virgin Atlantic was flying 6 million passengers a year. Soon after, Virgin Atlantic brought in a new chief executive, Craig Kreeger, who joined from American Airlines after a 27-year career there spanning commercial, financial and strategic roles in the United States and around the globe.

'You can imagine how people at Virgin Atlantic felt. To all intents and purposes, this looked very much like the Americanization of a quintessentially British airline. Even though the Virgin Group still owns 51 per cent of the airline, employees worried that the culture of the airline would become a casualty of all of the changes. This was actually the very opposite of what I had in my mind', says Craig.

Turn around the financials, protect the brand

The mission given to Craig by the Virgin Atlantic board had been very simple and very clear – to turn around the financial performance of the company without ruining the culture or the brand. 'I had to be really straightforward and honest with people in order to get them to buy in to the solutions, which involved having to cut more than 500 people from our number, cut out layers of management and ask people to do without a pay rise until we could return to profitable growth. All of this had to happen without taking anything away from our customers.'

The airline took the decision to replace their fuel-inefficient Airbus A340 fleet and have started taking delivery of new Boeing 787s. It had to exit a number of routes, and take a decision to exit their domestic operation in the UK, which had been branded 'Little Red'.

'Having fixed the business, it wasn't long before we had to turn our attention to planning for the longer term future', said Craig. 'We needed to shift our mind set to a more confident state, improving our balance sheet steadily, so that we are not always threatened every time there is an economic downturn. This means having "a plan to win", which involves building our financial strength, improving customer satisfaction and growing employee engagement.'

Craig and his team started all this with a new mission statement. The old one had been: 'We are here to grow a profitable airline that people love to fly and where people love to work.' Says Craig:

'This didn't really work for me because it could have been that of almost any company. The only word in there that was Virgin-esque was the word "love". Our airline is a place where customers and employees can very much be themselves, in a convivial and embracing atmosphere. We have always had an ethos around making things better for customers and for other stakeholders. Our mission statement had to have much more passion then the existing one.

After much discussion, we agreed on this as our mission statement: "*to embrace the human spirit and let it fly.*"'

To Craig, a mission statement is more than just a set of words:

'We make sure that all the decisions we make, particularly around our customer proposition and how we deal with our people, are consistent with our overarching purpose. We had a very strong culture of valuing our people so that our people would value our customers. We have always hired people who love to be around other people, who want to be individuals and have a sense of fun at work. We've always been true to those values. The trick was creating more consistency in service while creating the space for people to be individuals.'

Share and discuss to embed

Because of the financial constraints of recent years, Virgin Atlantic has not spent as much time worrying about developing the team, which it will be paying much more attention to now. 'When we launched our new purpose statement, for example, we brought our top 400 managers together to share it, discuss it and encourage them to embed it throughout the organization', says Craig:

> 'As I look at the next two to three years, the two big areas remaining for change are technology – where we need to be able to use information better, especially in the service of our customers, and make it available to all the staff who need it – and both empowering and upgrading the skills in the organization, from top to bottom.'

Critical to developing people, is developing leaders. Craig has a clear vision about the type of person he wants:

> 'Some years ago I had a chap working for me who seemed to have very little charisma. He was extremely humble and very quiet, but when I observed the way his team behaved around him and the way in which they grew and developed, I realized that he was terrific at inspiring them.
>
> He was not a great orator but the reason people were so inspired by him was because he genuinely cared and they knew he would always do the right thing. That meant doing the difficult thing rather than the convenient thing. Everyone knew that, because he really cared, some of his decisions were really difficult for him, but they knew what he stood for.
>
> This is what we want from all our leaders in Virgin Atlantic, from managers to onboard leaders of our cabin-crew teams. People who can be humble and have the courageous conversations that inspire their teams to do a brilliant job.'

(Virgin Atlantic posted a pre-tax loss before exceptional items of £128.4 million for the 12 months to the end of February 2013. High fuel prices and the struggling UK economy contributed to the malaise, but competition from British Airways was also a major factor. Craig Kreeger met his first target and posted a £14.4 million adjusted pre-tax profit for the year to the end of December 2014. In 2015, it rose to £22.5 million.)

Hold up a mirror to encourage change

One striking feature of the interviews I have done for this book is how so many leaders have used one simple performance measure to change the culture and focus everyone on the company's purpose. By finding that one critical measure you can align your strategy and your culture, provided the measure is at the very heart of your strategy.

One such company was Yodel, the parcel delivery business whose story I told in Chapter 8. They realized that if they were to change their reputation and improve their long-term viability, they had to focus more on the satisfaction of the people receiving the parcels, and not their customers.

Their customers were the big department stores and online retailers, who wanted the parcels delivered for as little as possible. The people expecting the parcels, of course, wanted a high-quality service and wanted their goods as soon as possible. Yodel understood that if they wanted to improve their reputation and their chances of a long-term future, they had to focus the culture on the end users. When they put in place measures to transparently track end-user satisfaction levels, they were able to drive dramatic shifts in culture by using these measures in real time to recognize good performance and to correct or punish bad behaviours.

Monarch Airline Group wants to be 'Europe's most recommended airline group' – one measure, easy to track, and it drives everything and every discussion in the company. Every conversation can be a preface to the question: 'Will this help or hinder us in getting to being the most recommended airline group?'

Using one critical measure to check purpose is being delivered

Many other examples abound in the case studies I have written about, where that one critical measure has been used to align both purpose and values. It provides a way to check whether you are delivering the promise, and in the right way. By finding this measure you can align your strategy and your culture, and give managers a powerful tool to use to ensure alignment.

When people start to embrace the values and the purpose, you can often get a great deal of anecdotal evidence to show that people are behaving differently. People start talking differently and often customers will comment on changes that they can see taking place. But is everyone aligning to the purpose? How do you really know?

For DFS (one of Europe's leading sofa specialists) that one measure was how customers felt after dealing with them, because customer centricity is the key pillar of growth for the company. Ian Filby, the CEO of DFS, says:

'If you want to be a world-class company, which we do, then you have to keep holding up the mirror to check whether you are truly customer centric, as opposed to customer centric when it suits you.

Everybody thinks they are customer centric until you start pointing out the anomalies. For us, being customer centric means having truly engaged and highly motivated staff, great products for everyone, available in a truly multichannel way, with real expertise in sofas, and a genuine interest in the customer.'

People don't go to work wanting to do a bad job, says Ian, but sometimes you have to help them to understand what a good job really looks like: 'We felt that we had to find out more about how our customers felt after interacting with our sales people in all of our stores. Only our customers or our potential customers would be able to tell us whether we were being customer-centric enough.'

Sorting advocates from detractors

To find this out, DFS introduced a net promoter score programme throughout the company. Net promoter score (NPS) is a management tool that can be used to gauge the loyalty of customers. It was developed by Fred Reichheld, Bain & Co and Satmetrix and was introduced in 2003. The NPS is calculated based on responses to a single question: *how likely is it that you would recommend our company/ product/ service to a friend or colleague?*

The scoring for this answer is most often based on a 0–10 scale. Those who respond with a score of 9 or 10 are called promoters, and are likely to buy more, remain customers for longer and make positive recommendations to their friends and family. Anyone scoring below six is likely to be a detractor, and will not exhibit value-adding behaviours. In fact, they are more likely to do exactly the opposite, which is to speak badly of you. Those who give marks of seven or eight are likely to be passive, neither a detractor nor a promoter. Says Ian:

'We can now track how customers rate every one of our 550 sales personnel around the country every day, every week, every month on a rolling basis. By doing this we can ensure that we are building up more rapport with our customers and, if not, use it as a feedback loop to coach the behaviours we would like to see from our sales people.'

Ian says that more than 90 per cent of purchases in his stores are really driven by women. In an organization that had been built as largely male, apparently very common in the furniture industry, the need for greater empathy and rapport was significant:

> 'I didn't have many female managers and I didn't have a single female in the top 26 senior managers in head office, so, in order to be more customer centric, I set about feminizing the organization. We are still on that journey but at least now more than 20 per cent of our sales staff in the stores are women; we have a growing number of female managers, two women on the board, as well as seven senior women managers. You will not be surprised to know that my female sales staff tend to outscore my male sales people, when we look at the net promoter scores, because they tend to be much more patient in building rapport.'

DFS wanted to take their brand from being the best-known brand in its sector to the best-loved brand. 'This was built on the insight that the sofa is the heart of the home. Being the heart of a home is a far more emotional concept, so we needed to be more emotional and empathetic at every level of the business', says Ian.

Constantly coaching staff on the purpose

Using NPS as the mirror to hold up to all staff has enabled DFS managers to talk to employees about the things they are inadvertently doing that have a negative impact on customers. Because it is measured at the individual level, any negative scores can be tracked back to the exact source. 'If the customer gives us a bad NPS score we can trace it right back to the van driver, to the upholsterer, to the admin person, to the sales person. This enables us to constantly coach everyone on our purpose, to be a truly customer-centric business', explains Ian:

> 'Another thing that has proved to be very powerful is that when we get a score of three or less, we get the store to proactively ring the customer and find out what we can do to put it right. By talking to customers you get a much richer insight. Feeding that back in to staff enables everyone to see how serious we are about this. When we have been able to win back a customer and put it right, we make a big deal of it and call it heroic recovery.'

The DFS purpose statement is: *to make every day more comfortable*. This means having a sofa at the heart of the home that is comfortable, making it comfortable to do business with the company, comfortable if something goes wrong and the sofa has to be repaired, comfortable because it has a long guarantee or comfortable because finance can be provided. 'Our NPS scores also enable us to check that we are truly living the values in the organization, that we are delivering our promise to customers, but most importantly it enables us to ensure that everyone in the business is aligned', says Ian.

Creating an aligned organization means having a clear understanding of stakeholder requirements, but in particular the requirements of customers. It needs a clear statement of strategy, with measurable objectives and well-articulated performance measures. It requires systems and processes, which involve managers talking regularly with their staff, which enables the strategy to be cascaded throughout the organization. It needs regular feedback to ensure that underperformance or overperformance can be identified and remedial action put in place quickly. Threading its way through all of this is the prerequisite that managers understand the corporate purpose, values and goals, have interpreted it for themselves and have taken action to interpret it fully for, and discuss it daily with, their teams. Only then will the measures show positive results.

Next: leading with purpose – what you need to do.

Key points from Chapter 11

1 Alignment is key to achieving strategic goals and delivering purpose and values.

2 Middle managers are key to delivering alignment, but not enough time is spent helping them.

3 Managers rate themselves lowest on their ability to deliver a sense of purpose and strong values within their own teams, even though they understand the corporate purpose and values.

4 Managers must have powerful conversations with their individuals on an ongoing basis, constantly keeping people focused on the organization's purpose and on the behaviours that ensure you are achieving the right outcomes in the right way.

5 Research shows that managers are failing to have these conversations with their staff, because they have been given insufficient training in how to hold the courageous conversations that drive positive change.

6 Leaders at every level should be encouraged to connect with the corporate purpose and values in their own way. This delivers authenticity and consistency and allows them to tell their own purpose story, link it to the corporate story and ensure the team articulates and understands their own purpose and values story.

7 Find one key measure that aligns the whole organization to the purpose and that managers can use to power these conversations and drive performance improvement.

PART THREE
Leading with purpose: what *you* need to do

Define your own purpose

12

You can't inspire your team if you are not inspired yourself

Inspiring managers are passionate, which makes them charismatic. Being around them motivates others to act, because strong emotions are contagious. Link that passion to a cause and some stretching goals, and you have a powerful multiplier effect – and you have great leadership. However, too few managers have thought about their own strengths, beliefs and values – the source of their passion. And even fewer have linked those beliefs to their company's purpose and values. When they do, they think, act and converse in a way completely in line with their corporate purpose, which provides the meaning that employees crave.

The average person is going to spend 80,000 to 90,000 hours at work.

(If you work for all of your adult life, you will be engaged in some form of paid employment from about the age of 18 to 65, which is 47 years. And if you work 40 hours a week, 47 weeks a year, for 47 years, that is 88,000 hours.) That is a huge chunk of time to spend on something you don't love, or don't care about.

The problem is a huge number of managers do exactly that. They are not really engaged with their work, and they don't bother to ensure their employees are engaged either. Day in, day out, managers are tasked with engaging employees, but, according to research by Gallup, a US performance management company best known for its global public opinion polls, a distressingly high number of managers have 'checked out', meaning they care little about their job and their company. In a research project entitled 'The State of the American Manager', Gallup found that, across 190 diverse industries, only 35 per cent of managers were actively engaged, and 51 per cent were not engaged, with 14 per cent actively disengaged.

It goes without saying that this creates a cascade effect – because a manager's engagement or lack of engagement has a direct effect on employees, with dire consequences. The Gallup survey found that managers who were led by highly engaged leadership teams were 39 per cent more likely to be engaged. Employees supervised by highly engaged managers were 59 per cent more likely to be engaged. Of course, the opposite is true, as well. The Gallup survey found that only 30 per cent of US workers were engaged, with 52 per cent not engaged and 18 per cent actively disengaged. The ratio of engaged to disengaged workers is roughly two to one, a ratio that has been constant for a decade. Other studies of global engagement levels back up Gallup – and say that on average 66 per cent of workers are engaged, with one-third or more not engaged – the same ratio!

Until organizations can increase their percentage of engaged managers, they have little hope of increasing their percentage of engaged employees. So where do you start? Gallup learned that a few things had the greatest potential to positively influence leader-to-manager engagement and manager-to-employee engagement. When leaders or managers scored highly on these items, as set out below, their direct reports were more likely to be engaged.

Our purpose makes me feel important

For leaders (defined by Gallup as executives), their managers were most engaged when those managers scored the following two items highly:

- The mission or purpose of my company makes me feel my job is important.
- This last year, I have had opportunities at work to learn and grow.

For managers, the items with the strongest connection to employees were:

- At work, I have the opportunity to do what I do best every day.
- The mission or purpose of my company makes me feel my job is important.

Based on these findings, Gallup believes that leaders should invest in three critical actions to strengthen their managers' – and, subsequently, their employees' – engagement and make the cascade effect work in their favour:

- Clearly and consistently communicate the purpose of the organization, where it has been and where it is going.
- Make learning and development a priority.

There was one additional factor that Gallup identified as crucial to success: whether managers know – and were able to play to – their strengths. Says Gallup:

> 'Organizations that hire managers based on their natural talents and then enable those people to turn their talents into strengths are better positioned for success. Leaders must equip their managers with the tools and resources necessary to identify and develop their individual strengths. But leaders must also understand their direct reports' strengths and know how those strengths play out in specific tasks and responsibilities. They should then mould managers' jobs to best allow them to make the most of those strengths. This approach helps increase the likelihood that managers will be internally motivated and engaged.'

Do you know and understand your own strengths? I doubt it. Not many leaders I have met really do, and there is a good reason for it, which I will come to later.

Why you must liberate your passion through your values

Aon Hewitt is a provider of human capital and management consulting services, based in the United States. It operates out of 500 offices in 120 countries around the world. Aon Hewitt's Global Employee Research Database of 7 million respondents puts it in a unique position to understand the leadership behaviours that drive employee engagement. According to its data, the most critical leadership drivers of employee engagement are the following:

- establishing direction and shared purpose;
- demonstrating character and integrity;
- developing and retaining talent;
- applying knowledge and sound judgement;
- interacting with others.

I would not blame you for thinking that of course leaders should be doing these things. But not all do. One of the reasons is because they cannot link their own passions and beliefs and sense of purpose to that of the organization that employs them. And without this passion, driven by strong values, they are unable to be engaging and therefore simply cannot effectively motivate their employees.

Aon Hewitt says that the most engaging managers have a strong set of guiding beliefs shaped by personality and by early experiences, which steer how they approach work, and influence their interactions with the people they lead. When these behaviours with employees are delivered in day-to-day interactions, you see a positive impact on the engagement of others because these leaders act in a way that shares their own engagement and purpose.

Take ownership of your own engagement

The evidence is clear. You will be a far more effective leader at whatever level in the organization you are, if you are more engaged with the organization's purpose and values. That means you should take ownership of that engagement, and not depend on others to provide it for you. Why?

The main reason is because you want to be a successful leader, to achieve your objectives, get promoted and make even more of a difference in your career. You can only do this if you inspire the people around you to perform. That means you have to engage your team, and your employees. Truly engaged employees have 'bought in'. They are so passionate about solving the problem, delivering the service, or achieving the goal, they willingly invest some of their own time (discretionary effort) to get those results.

If you increase your own engagement you will increase satisfaction in what you do, increase your personal energy by knowing you are doing something worthwhile, and increase pleasure in work well done. And, it means you will create more effective teams, deliver better results and grow your business.

Gallup offers several suggestions on how to go about increasing your own engagement in your work. 'You will be successful because of who you are, not who you are not. By leaning on your unique talents and strengths, you can make the most of each day at work, and engagement will follow. And be sure to celebrate your achievements and keep setting the bar higher.'

Start by finding your strengths

When coaching leaders, I spend a lot of time exploring their careers and asking them to tell me about the seminal moments that changed how they saw leadership, or the way they thought about doing business.

They will tell me about all sorts of moments that had a profound effect on them, whether it was a key insight about how customers behaved, about team dynamics, about the role of incentives or when they hired extremely talented or very bad employees. The reason I encourage leaders to spend time thinking about seminal moments is because those early experiences often manifest later as defining beliefs, which have a profound impact on the way they lead.

I also ask those leaders to do strength-finding tests – using a variety of tools that are available online to look for and understand their personal strengths. One such test, for example, is the VIA Survey of Character Strengths – a simple self-assessment that takes less than 15 minutes and provides a wealth of information to help you understand your core characteristics. Most personality tests focus on negative and neutral traits, but the VIA Survey focuses on your best qualities. It is available at: http://www.viacharacter.org.

Created under the direction of Dr Martin Seligman, author of *Authentic Happiness* (2002) and *Flourish* (2011), and Dr Christopher Peterson, a scientist at the University of Michigan and author of *A Primer in Positive Psychology* (2006), and validated by Dr Robert McGrath, the VIA Survey is regarded as a central tool of positive psychology and has been used in hundreds of research studies and been taken by over 3 million people in over 190 countries.

If you search the internet for other strength-finder sites, you will quickly find a variety of sources to do these tests. One I also often recommend to my clients is the Gallup Strengthfinder test. On the basis that people who use their strengths are SIX times more likely to be engaged, I like clients to have done the test themselves. A book I recommend is called *Now, Discover Your Strengths* (2001) by Marcus Buckingham. It helps you to understand the different talents and strengths, and then (through an online questionnaire) to discover your own top five strengths.

In order to know others, you must first know yourself...

A prerequisite of any effective leadership is that a leader knows themselves before trying to lead others. How can we possibly make judgements about others and select, develop, appraise or motivate people if we don't have an understanding of ourselves, and how we best interact with others?

It is seldom in life that we take time to think about the kind of person we are, how others see us and what impact our behaviour has on others. We can all rise to the special occasion but does that carefully crafted self-image always follow us in our dealings with others?

A fast, easy way to start the journey to understanding the impact of your natural behaviour is to take a personality assessment. There are lots of assessment processes out there – and one I am familiar with and often use is DiSC, a personal assessment tool used by over 1 million people every year. DiSC stands for dominance, influence, steadiness and compliance. DiSC is a tool typically used in business to improve productivity, teamwork and communication via raising self-awareness. DiSC is self-completion and therefore non-judgemental and helps people to discuss their behavioural preferences and differences and to adapt their behaviour to suit different situations. A DiSC assessment asks just 24 questions and will produce a detailed report about your personality and behaviour. DiSC profiles help you and your team:

- Increase self-awareness, for instance how you respond to pressure, what motivates you, what causes you stress and how you solve problems. This helps to facilitate better teamwork and minimize team conflict.

- Develop stronger sales skills by identifying customer types and responding with behaviour that meets their behavioural preferences.

- Manage more effectively by understanding the preferences, motivators, priorities and job emphasis of employees and team members.

- Become a more self-aware, well-rounded and effective leader.

A DiSC consultancy I have used in the past is 'The Personality Profile'. Andrew Sherville, the owner, has used DiSC as an end user and as a consultant since 1987. It's worth trying – www.personalityprofile.com.

Do a 360-degree strengths test

In order to protect against you projecting an overly 'positive' image of yourself, I also insist that leaders also speak to people who know them well, and get a well-rounded view of their strengths from people they trust. Often, they are amazed at what those people say. When they are operating in a strength zone, they find a task easy to do and it makes them happy. The problem is that they think that because it is easy for them, everyone must be just as capable. They therefore don't recognize it as a strength.

The process is simple. Talk to or write to 10 to 20 people you trust, and ask them to use their own words to describe what they see as your strengths. Ask them to give you examples of when you were operating at your best, and why. You will quickly be able to spot patterns from the online tests and from the feedback from your trusted colleagues. From this you will be able to create your own picture of your strengths, and put those strengths into action more often.

You may also get feedback on areas where you need to improve, and being aware of your weaknesses is critical to your leadership and to being authentic. Making sure you have people on the team who can compensate for those weaknesses, and talking to your weaknesses as well, will also be inspiring.

Once my clients have established their strengths, and thought about the seminal moments in their careers, I then ask them to think about what all this means for their beliefs. It is astounding how many 'ah ha' moments they get when they realize they have a deep-rooted value born of one of their strengths or one of their seminal moments. When they then articulate these as their defining values, they are then much more clear about what does and does not matter to them.

Link your values to the way you lead

When you are clear about your strengths and your values and your purpose, you need to think hard about putting in place an action plan to deliver them in the way you lead. It will not happen by accident so you need to think about how you will tell stories around these values, how you will advocate them to others, and how you will employ them in the way you behave and lead every single day.

These values will be your passions, the things you care about deeply. When you talk about these more often you will find it hard not to be passionate. Showing passion is not something you engineer and do in a mechanical way. Talking to what you care about is the trick. When you show passion it is infectious and you pass on that same passion to others. Passion fuels everything.

I recommend that leaders think hard about their strengths and values because I have found that many leaders have simply never thought about what their strengths are, nor have they ever bothered to define their personal beliefs and values. This makes it exceptionally difficult for them to understand their own sense of purpose, and therefore makes it hard to lead authentically.

Finally, I ask leaders to think about what they would like to change in the world. What would they like to do that contributes to some wider social benefit or greater good? It doesn't matter how big or small, but try to find a way to put your talents, passions and values to work to serve people, causes, an organization, the planet, or anything you set your mind to. You should describe not only what you want to do, but be clear about who you want to help and what value you will create by doing it.

Purpose gives you courage

The perfect purpose is the overlap between doing something you love, doing something the world needs, doing something you are great at, and doing something you are paid for. If you can truly get all of these to intersect, that is your purpose. The key is to define it in a way that is about working towards something bigger than yourself in the world, or at the very least making a significant contribution to the world that you inhabit.

Many of the leaders I work with get hung up on trying to define a purpose that can provide direction for every aspect of their lives – work, home, leisure, family, personal or social. What we are talking about here is your work purpose. If that can be applied to all other aspects of your life, that's brilliant, but it is very unlikely.

My own purpose is to help leaders be more inspiring. I believe that more inspiring leaders create better workplaces, enable more people to feel fulfilled in their working lives, enable growth and help to create wealth and thriving economies and communities. In my personal life, I have a different purpose, which relates to family and friends. When I write my crime fiction, my purpose is to thrill and engage my readers. In other words, I have a different purpose for each of the different sides of my life.

My values, however, do not change and I apply them with equal vigour in my personal and professional lives. For example, I believe in the positive benefits of curiosity, and it is one of my main operating values. I will encourage curiosity in the leaders I coach, the teams I work with, and all the young people who come into the companies I work in. I will also do this at home with my friends and family, especially with my grandchildren, and anyone else who cares to listen.

Have a positive impact on others

Finding and articulating your purpose, and linking it to your passions, enables you to be more engaged in your work, realize your interests, and live out your personal values in a way that makes a positive impact on others. Your purpose springs from who you are, which is why it is best to start with the strengths exercise, and by articulating your passions and your values.

Finally, I ask my clients then to map their personal values and purpose on to that of the organization or the team they lead. This means demonstrating how your values fit with the values of the company, and how your purpose contributes to the purpose of the business that employs you. If you cannot do this, you should seriously ask whether you belong in the organization. Frequently, I have seen very talented people fail in organizations where their values simply did not fit the culture. They moved on to different employers, and were able to thrive in a culture where their own values were better suited. If this has happened to you, it is not necessarily a reflection on you as a person, but it can be extraordinarily helpful in thinking about whether to stay in a job or what job to take.

Whatever your values are, they will express themselves in your behaviours. For example, if you value speed, and you come up against someone who values restraint, you could frequently find yourself in a state of tension with that person without fully understanding why. If you value order and planning, people who appear to be disorganized will irritate you and it will show. Understanding what your values are helps you to be more clear about what is going on and then to advocate what you believe in, rather than simply getting stressed about how other people behave.

Not all of your values will be expressed in the same way as your employer's values. However, you will be able to map them on to those values so that you can talk about how something you believe in delivers the desired corporate behaviours. Having purpose and values that match those of your organization is deeply engaging, and is also a deep well of energy that helps you to face up to all sorts of challenges and be resilient in the face of adversity.

Purpose and passion makes you more influential and more charismatic, and also enables you to be courageous. I frequently see people with a strong sense of purpose deal with difficult circumstances and overcome challenges they thought they would never be able to meet, because their strong sense of purpose enabled them to move beyond their fears. Mostly, I see leaders using purpose to engage with others, and have powerful and courageous conversations that enable progress, simply because their sense of purpose overcame personal inhibitions and enabled them to work towards a common cause.

A starting place

Table 12.1 gives a list of common values, nowhere near complete, but it may help you to think about your own. Again, when doing this exercise, it is worth spending time online to find more prompts and lists of values that can help you to identify and describe your own. Don't rely on only one list, and don't hesitate to describe a value in a full sentence, as a belief. You can always shorten it for brevity later.

Table 12.1 List of common values

Acceptance	Brilliance	Conviviality
Accessibility	Briskness	Coolness
Accomplishment	Buoyancy	Cooperation
Accountability	Calmness	Correctness
Accuracy	Camaraderie	Courtesy
Achievement	Candid	Craftiness
Acknowledgement	Candour	Creativity
Activeness	Capability	Credible
Adaptability	Care	Curiosity
Adequacy	Carefulness	Daring
Adoration	Celebrity	Decisiveness
Advancement	Certainty	Decorum
Adventurousness	Challenge	Deepness
Affection	Charity	Deference
Affluence	Charm	Delicacy
Aggressiveness	Chastity	Delight
Agility	Cheerfulness	Democracy
Alertness	Clarity	Dependability
Aliveness	Classy	Depth
Altruism	Cleanliness	Desire
Ambition	Clear-mindedness	Determination
Anticipation	Cleverness	Devoutness
Appreciation	Closeness	Dexterity
Approachability	Coherence	Dignity
Approval	Comfort	Diligence
Ardent	Commitment	Discipline
Art	Community	Direction
Assertiveness	Compassion	Discovery
Assurance	Competitiveness	Discretion
Attentiveness	Complacency	Diversity
Attractiveness	Consistency	Durable
Audacity	Confidence	Dynamism
Availability	Conformity	Eagerness
Awareness	Congruency	Ease
Awe	Connection	Economy
Balance	Consciousness	Education
Beauty	Conservation	Effectiveness
Being the best	Consistency	Efficiency
Belief	Contentment	Elegance
Belonging	Continuous	Empathy
Benevolence	Improvement	Encouragement
Bliss	Contribution	Endurance
Boldness	Control	Energy
Bravery	Conviction	Energetic

Table 12.1 *continued*

Enjoyment	Helping Society	Neatness
Enthusiasm	Heroism	Nerve
Ethical	Holiness	Nonconformity
Equality	Honesty	Nurturing
Exactness	Honour	Obedience
Excellence	Humility	Openness
Excitement	Humour	Order
Exhilaration	Hygiene	Originality
Expectancy	Imagination	Outdoors
Expediency	Impact	Outrageousness
Experience	Impartiality	Partnership
Expertise	Independence	Patience
Exploration	Influence	Passion
Expressiveness	Ingenuity	Patriotism
Extravagance	Inner Harmony	Perfection
Extroversion	Inquisitiveness	Perkiness
Exuberance	Insightfulness	Perseverance
Fairness	Inspiration	Persistence
Faith	Intelligence	Persuasiveness
Faithfulness	Intellectual Status	Philanthropy
Fame	Intuition	Piety
Family	Joy	Planning
Fascination	Judiciousness	Playfulness
Fearlessness	Justice	Plentiful-ness
Fineness	Keenness	Positivity
Fitness	Kindness	Practicality
Flow	Knowledge	Preparedness
Fluency	Lasting	Privacy
Focus	Leadership	Proactivity
Fortitude	Legacy	Professionalism
Frankness	Liberty	Prudence
Freedom	Lightness	Punctuality
Fresh	Liveliness	Purity
Friendship	Logic	Qualification
Frugality	Longevity	Quality-orientation
Fun	Love	Quickness
Gallant	Loyalty	Quietness
Generosity	Making a difference	Rationality
Goodness	Mastery	Reasonableness
Grace	Merit	Recognition
Growth	Mindfulness	Recreation
Happiness	Moderation	Refinement
Hard Work	Mysteriousness	Relaxation
Health	Nature	Reliability

Table 12.1 *continued*

Relief	Shrewdness	Tranquility
Religiousness	Significance	Transcendence
Reputation	Silence	Trust
Resourcefulness	Silliness	Trustworthiness
Restraint	Simplicity	Understanding
Resolution	Sincerity	Uniqueness
Resolve	Solidarity	Unity
Results-oriented	Solitude	Usefulness
Resourcefulness	Soundness	Vision
Rest Restraint	Speed	Vitality
Reverence	Spontaneity	Vivacity
Richness	Stability	Volunteering
Rigour	Strategic	Warm-heartedness
Sacredness	Strength	Warmth
Sacrifice	Structure	Watchfulness
Saintliness	Sturdy	Wealth
Sanguinity	Success	Wilfulness
Satisfaction	Support	Willingness
Science	Tactfulness	Winning
Security	Teamwork	Wisdom
Self-actualization	Temperance	Wittiness
Self-control	Thankfulness	Wonder
Selflessness	Thoroughness	Worthiness
Self-reliance	Thoughtfulness	Youthfulness
Sensitivity	Thrift	Zeal
Serenity	Tidiness	Zen
Service	Timeliness	Zest
Sharing	Traditionalism	Zing

Go through these words and find the ones that most resonate with you. Pick at least 10. Describe, in writing, why these words matter so much. If 'positivity' is important to you, describe why. Start your sentence with 'I believe positivity is important, because...' and complete it with the thought that best explains why this word means so much to you.

Do this for all 10 words, then give each word a rating of between 1 and 10, where 10 is the most important. Now, you should be able to see your top five values, though all will be important to you. Can you rank these in importance? Which value is most central to who you are and what you believe about life?

Your values exist already, but when you recognize and honour them, life becomes more simple, and you become more authentic, predictable and trustworthy as a leader. Which of your top 10 values match the values of your organization? They don't have to be the same words, but should certainly match in spirit. Once you have completed this exercise, you can use your values in all your decision making, and be sure to behave with integrity, approach problems with more clarity, and use them to decide on what feels right to you.

Your values not only reflect who you are, they also reflect who you want to be. When you have to make really difficult choices, start by deciding what you value most.

Below is an example of how one of my clients, Paul Larbey, head of the global video business at Nokia, completed this exercise. First, a list of all his strengths (from 1 to 34) as determined by the Gallup Strengthfinder test. These helped to stimulate a discussion about his beliefs. The last 10 'strengths' are really areas for improvement – but might equally be underpinned by strong beliefs.

Strengths

1 Strategic	**18** Adaptability
2 Arranger	**19** Analytical
3 Restorative	**20** Belief
4 Relator	**21** Command
5 Responsibility	**22** Woo
6 Communication	**23** Activator
7 Futuristic	**24** Input
8 Self-assurance	**25** Deliberative
9 Individualization	**26** Consistency
10 Achiever	**27** Discipline
11 Learner	**28** Intellection
12 Empathy	**29** Competition
13 Developer	**30** Includer
14 Significance	**31** Context
15 Focus	**32** Maximizer
16 Positivity	**33** Connectedness
17 Ideation	**34** Harmony

We used this to discuss the list of 17 beliefs that he held dear. These then translated into 13 values, ranked in importance. This is how he expressed his beliefs, and then his values.

Beliefs – I believe in…

1 Doing what you commit to and by when you commit to do it for.

2 Being accountable for the decisions you make. Being happy to take the blame.

3 Not asking someone (or treating someone) to do something that you would not do yourself.

4 Enjoying what you do. Having fun.

5 Working hard and playing hard.

6 Being loyal to those around you and to expect this loyalty back.

7 Relationships being personal based on mutual benefit.

8 Continuous learning through doing.

9 Being optimistic.

10 Only spending effort on things you can change.

11 Really understanding what the customer wants.

12 Beating the competition is satisfying and fun.

13 Having a real job with clear accountability.

14 Putting things in perspective.

15 Solving problems is fun.

16 Things being organized.

17 Getting on with things.

Once he was clear on his values, he was able to succinctly express his purpose, which he says is to make a difference, to grow faster.

Values:

1 Be accountable.

2 Be passionate.

3 Just do it.

4 Be an example.

5 Focus your energy on things you CAN change.

6 Relationships matter.

7 Be loyal.

8 Choose to be positive.

9 Embrace challenge.

10 Winning together is fun.

11 Understand, create, solve.

12 Never stop learning.

13 Keep life tidy.

Purpose:

1 Make a difference.

2 Grow faster.

Having made clear his own values and articulated his purpose, his next job was to map his personal values to the values of the company he leads. He did this by using a matrix that showed how his values could be used to talk to the five values of his company (Table 12.2). For example, he was able to talk about how the corporate value of achievement was delivered by being accountable, passionate, focused on things you could personally do, making sure that you kept relationships in good order, and the idea that winning together was fun.

Table 12.2 Personal value map

Values	Challenge	Simplicity	Achievement	Respect	Renewal
1. Be accountable			X	X	
2. Be passionate	X		X	X	
3. Just do it	X				
4. Be an example				X	
5. Focus your energy on things you CAN change			X		
6. Relationships matter			X	X	
7. Be loyal					
8. Choose to be positive	X				
9. Embrace challenge	X				X
10. Winning together is fun			X	X	
11. Understand, create, solve		X		X	X
12. Never stop learning		X			X
13. Keep life tidy	X	X			X

Having mapped these to his organization's purpose and values, he is able to be more passionate, more purposeful and more persuasive about the things he believes are necessary, and how he wants his people to behave.

Where his personal values do not map to the organization's he simply does not talk of these. If he had values that ran counter to the company's, he would have to question whether he was in the right place.

Finding and describing your purpose and values is challenging, and requires a great deal of effort and commitment, but the rewards are considerable.

The process

1 Reflect on the seminal moments in your career/life – what beliefs derive from these?

2 Do a strengths and talents questionnaire – then think about the beliefs that underpin your strengths.

3 Ask colleagues to help you with a 360-degree strengths test – how do they see you?

4 Find and describe your values – why are these important to you?

5 Prioritize your top 5–10 beliefs/values.

6 Describe your purpose – how do you want to change the world?

7 Map your purpose and values to that of your team/organization.

8 Speak and behave to your beliefs in a way that supports your corporate values/purpose.

Bringing out your best

Ivan Menezes, CEO of Diageo, the global premium drinks company, says that finding his own purpose was not easy. When he did, it powered his leadership style: 'I define my purpose as "fulfilling the potential of people and businesses". That means I'm always looking for the best in people, and ways to grow the business. When I am at my best or enjoying myself the most, I am delivering my purpose and it both motivates and fulfils me.'

Nick Varney, CEO of Merlin Entertainments, a visitor attractions company that operates across 23 countries on four continents, is a great example of what many leaders have told me about leading from their own passion. He says: 'I just love the business we are in. I find putting people into an alternative magical reality the most rewarding thing about what we do, and I love it. As a result I've made sure that our leaders throughout the business are equally passionate about it. As a result we have a strong culture of people doing what they say they will do, and just getting on with delivering memorable experiences to our visitors.'

Nick and his team are providing all of his employees with a great sense of meaning, which we have already seen is a crucial element of inspiring leaders. A sense of working towards something meaningful is central to happiness and well-being, both of which power productivity and high performance.

Sadly, a lot of leaders can inadvertently deny their people any sense of meaning – because they haven't thought about it. Instead of providing a big hairy audacious goal that is out of reach but not out of sight, they make goals seem so extreme as to be unattainable or so vague as to seem empty. Or, they behave inconsistently, sometimes pulling people up for tardiness, and sometimes not. When they are not clear and consistent about their expectations and their standards, they send signals that confuse and disorientate people, and have a negative affect on motivation.

As we have seen, it is really important to employees that they are making progress in delivering meaningful work. When leaders behave inconsistently, and show a lack of respect, they will, for example, dismiss the importance of a subordinate's work and ideas, shift goals frequently, or cause people to feel that their work might never see the light of day and therefore not make any difference to anyone, ever. How motivating is that?

Purpose makes you charismatic

When you are passionate about your purpose, you become charismatic and your passion is contagious. People really do catch the emotions of others. Just think about people you have had to work with who have been constantly negative, and reflect on whether you became more pessimistic around them. Being around someone who is passionate and optimistic is a far better place to be. Every leader should aspire to create a positive and optimistic aura. When leaders talk about ideas that are bigger than themselves, something they care about deeply, they are inspired by that idea and it is the cause that animates them.

Most employees value jobs that let them contribute and make a difference. You should not rely solely on incentives such as bonuses or raises to incentivize people. The YouGov research I conducted showed that so long as employees felt they were being paid fairly, it was the behaviours of managers that had a far greater impact on their willingness to commit to the job and give of their discretionary effort. To do that, you have got to inspire them with your vision, set challenging goals and pump up their confidence so they believe they can actually win.

I believe that one of the great training shortfalls in most organizations is that of helping new and middle managers to have powerful conversations centred on purpose and values. Not only do managers need help with how to hold these conversations, but they also need help in relating their own purpose and values to that of the team and the company.

First-time managers, particularly, need help. For them, the challenge of leading a team is tough, especially if they have achieved that position by being very good at what they do and have been elevated from the ranks of the people they previously worked with. Often, new managers find themselves inhibited in showing who they really are. When their passion is liberated, they become more authentic, more authoritative and people are more willing to follow.

Sir Rocco Forte, chairman of Rocco Forte Hotels, says that the one thing he is always looking for in managers he recruits to run his hotels is passion for the business:

> 'I want someone who is driven to run the best hotel in the world, because then it will become the best hotel in Frankfurt or in Berlin, but only if they care deeply about the detail and care deeply about our guests. I get involved in lots of detail in all of the hotels when I visit them, caring about every little thing that makes a difference to our guests. This passion shows itself to the general managers and to all the staff. Unless you pay attention to the detail and show that you care, then your staff won't do it themselves. What they care about and take a lead from, is how passionate you are.'

Be visible, be consistent and be true to your values

Philip N Green, CBE (not to be confused with Sir Philip Green of the Arcadia Group) is chairman of Carillion plc, a leading international integrated support services company, and chairman of Baker Corp, a global market leader in tank, pump and filtration equipment rentals. He is also chairman designate of Williams and Glyn, the UK challenger bank set to spin off from the Royal Bank of Scotland. He was previously the chief executive of United Utilities, the UK's largest listed utilities company, and before that he was chief executive of Royal P&O Nedlloyd, an Anglo-Dutch container shipping line, now owned by Maersk. He says:

> 'Passion is central to leadership. I have led a wide range of businesses and
> I cannot say that I was passionate about each and every one of them before
> I joined. Before I was running a shipping business, for example, I can't honestly
> say that I had been passionate about container shipping. However, I wouldn't
> have taken the job if I didn't believe that I could become passionate about it.
> I have turned down some very senior jobs because I felt I couldn't behave with
> authenticity and passion in that job.'

You cannot expect people at the front line to be passionate about their jobs if the whole of the leadership team is not passionate and aligned on the values. He says: 'It starts with the leader, but the whole leadership team must be aligned and must be prepared to go out and preach the gospel.'

As evidence of that commitment, Philip talks about the time he set himself the objective of being seen by 80 per cent of a 20,000 people global workforce, in the first 12 months of becoming CEO: 'That didn't mean that they saw me on a video, it meant they saw me personally in town hall meetings, or in their workplaces. It was a huge commitment and meant a great deal of travel. It is really important that as the leader you spend a lot of time out and about meeting your people and talking about vision and values. That is a central part of leadership.'

Philip believes it is crucial that the whole leadership team sits down to clearly define and articulate values and purpose, and not in a glib way: 'They have got to be owned by management, easy to understand, and lived and breathed every day. I'm really clear that employees want to work in organizations where there is a clear purpose statement, a clear vision and a clear set of values. If management doesn't live by them, they will lack authenticity, and therefore fail.'

You also have to check that you are living the values in the right way, says Philip:

> 'I believe it is important to be a good listener and for a long time I believed
> myself to be a very good listener. But then I got feedback from someone who
> said that there were several people in the organization who didn't believe I was.
> When I explored it, I came to understand that my problem was that I quickly
> understood the points that people were making because I listened intently

to what they were saying, but as soon as I had got the point I switched off and it was clear to them that I wasn't listening. I wasn't being intentionally disrespectful, because I had already clocked their point, but my mind went somewhere else. I had to be a lot more attentive thereafter, and curb my inclination to let my mind wander once I had understood people.'

As a leader you are being scrutinized all the time and people will micro-analyse your every behaviour, says Philip: 'If you are not living your values in the way that truly demonstrates what you believe, people will see it and you will lose credibility. You've just got to realize this. It goes with the turf of being a leader.'

The right values create value

Lady Susan Rice, CBE, is a Scottish banker and head of the Scottish Fiscal Commission. She is the chair of Scottish Water and a member of the Banking Standards Board. Having been managing director of Lloyds Banking Group Scotland, and previously chief executive then chairwoman of Lloyds TSB Scotland, Lady Rice was the first woman to head a UK clearing bank, in 2000:

'Having worked in an industry that has been under such fire for bad behaviour, I'm really clear that as a leader you have to make decisions that are for a common good and not just for an individual good. It is crucial to communicate the *how* as well as the *what*, to every single member of your staff.

You only have genuine value if that value is created and delivered against a set of values. I say this all the time because it is so important. Values enable people to be committed to a task and understand the true purpose of what they are doing. Unless you can show that what you are doing creates wider value, and is being done the right way, you leave yourself open to interpretation and create wriggle room for people who might try to exploit things for their individual advantage. Commonly held values bind your people to the mission of your organization – the mission beyond the actual numbers that we measure. It is only by a focus on this that you can ensure good behaviours.'

These values are important because they are an indicator of cultural strength, and the ability of an organization to deliver in the future, she says. Too often, she adds, companies are measured only on their last quarterly results, with too few indicators of their ability to continue to deliver value in the future: 'How you behave will determine the quality of your relationships inside and outside the organization, and therefore your impact on the wider community and it is this that will determine whether you succeed or fail in the future. Your values are central to making sure everyone in the organization behaves in the right way.'

The role of leaders is to programme values into employees, so that they all share unwritten rules that allow them to trust each other and work together and feel a sense of belonging, says Lady Rice. The right values create a control mechanism to counteract the tendency for people to put themselves ahead of other people.

Manage who you are, not just what you do

As a leader you manage who you are being, not just what you are doing. This was one of the key pieces of advice that I received from many of the leaders I have interviewed. If you manage both who you are being and what you are doing, this will help you to inspire, engage and enable people by consciously developing the right mind sets and behaviours, not only in yourself but also in your team.

Whether you lead a team of leaders at the top of business, or a team operating at the front line, it seems crucial to your effectiveness that you properly define the purpose of the team, within the context of the organizational purpose. Understanding your own purpose helps you to speak passionately to both the team's purpose and the organization's purpose, because it unlocks your passion and enables you to deliver it without having to think about it.

Defining your own values and using those to guide and articulate the values of your team enables everyone to understand how to work together and how to behave with everyone they come into contact with. It will also tell them what they can expect of you and how to generate the trust that is so crucial to effective teamwork. When you have engaged yourself in purpose and values, you are far more easily able to engage everyone else.

Next: the tool to help you bring together purpose and values, vision and goals.

Key points from Chapter 12

1 Charismatic managers are passionate, and they are passionate because they unlock their own sense of purpose and believe passionately in their values – but very few have thought about or understand what their own strengths, purpose and values are.

2 Unless managers are engaged, they cannot engage their employees. Research shows a cascade effect when leaders are not engaged – which manifests in large numbers of front-line employees being disengaged, and in low levels of productivity and effectiveness.

3 Leaders at all levels should take ownership of their own engagement, by taking the time to articulate their own purpose and values, and mapping those to the corporate purpose and values.

4 Your real purpose comes from who you are, and who you are comes from the things that you believe truly matter.

5 Map your own purpose and values on to the organization you represent, so that you can create the alignment that is so crucial to being an authentic leader.

6 Leaders must constantly advocate their purpose and values, talking frequently with every member of the team, to ensure alignment.

7 Always check that people understand the values in the way you intend, and that you are living the values in a way that delivers the right signals.

The purpose framework 13

How to create the tool that gives everyone in your team a sense of purpose

When you combine purpose, values and goals into an integrated framework, and articulate it all on a single page, you create a powerful tool that enables you to deliver a more agile, empowered, energized and aligned organization – the prerequisites of high performance. Once you have done that, the tool becomes the vehicle by which you facilitate the conversations that need to happen up, down and across the company to create understanding, commitment and alignment.

For most companies, improving productivity is the number one economic challenge. In Europe, after Britain voted in mid-2016 to exit the European Union, it has become an even more significant issue. For both Britain and member countries of the EU, improving productivity is one of the most important ways to tackle the challenges that will arise from Britain's exit from the single market. Improving productivity is not only a challenge in Europe. It is a challenge in most economies and countries.

One of the ways to improve productivity is to improve employee motivation, and unlock greater discretionary effort from millions of employees. Discretionary effort is something we hold back unless we feel really motivated or inspired to give more, and when most employees are giving it, this enables exceptional performance.

As we saw from the YouGov research in previous chapters in this book, there are four management behaviours that have a uniquely important relationship to unlocking more productivity and higher performance from employees.

These four key management behaviours are:

- helping employees to understand the purpose and vision of the organization, and understand where it is headed;
- making employees feel like they make a contribution to this;
- valuing employee input and perspectives;
- communication skills that enable managers to have good conversations and to be good when addressing large groups.

To do any of this, managers need to localize and personalize the organization's purpose, values and goals for every employee. And they cannot do this if it is not written down and articulated in a way that enables this process to take place.

When articulated and communicated the right way, a compelling purpose, truly shared by all employees, delivers significant business value, for large and small companies alike. When also aligned to strong and true values, the right purpose enables leaders to create cultures that will help them to thrive now and well into the future. Shared purpose and powerful values help to deliver mutually beneficial relationships, strong reputations and more trust and credibility – all endangered species at a time of hyper-transparency and lightning speed, brought about by the digital revolution and social media.

When embedded, purpose and values liberate people to lead

A powerful purpose, strong values and clear goals liberate people throughout your organization to be leaders. It enables them to make decisions when their own leaders are not around, confident that they are on mission and sticking to the principles of the organization. They need this framework in order to perform at the very highest level. With such a framework, your people will be more engaged, more committed and much more likely to give of their discretionary effort to help you achieve your goals. So, how should you think about purpose, values and goals and then best deliver them in your team or organization? How can you best give your people what they need to help you succeed?

You have to start at the top. If the top team is not aligned, then it will be impossible to align the organization. Yet, it often amazes how few top teams truly are aligned, and are able to speak to the purpose and strategic objectives of a company in a coherent and consistent way.

Perhaps it is unfair, but I often submit management teams to a test that exposes this lack of alignment. It happened recently at a dinner for the executive management team of a large technology business. At the end of a dinner that focused on their strategy for the next three years, I handed out a blank card to each of the 10 people present and asked them to write on the card – without conferring with their colleagues – what they thought was the purpose of the organization they led.

After they had handed the cards back to me I then asked them to fill in another blank card, this time stating what it was they thought was the most important priority that they should all focus on in the coming year.

Finally, I asked them to articulate their long-term vision, in a single sentence. I didn't bother to ask them about their values because they had recently spent time focusing on the three values they thought were most important for the culture of their organization.

As I read out their answers, they first appeared puzzled, then amused and finally alarmed. Why? On the matter of their purpose, only two people wrote down the same answer. One was the CEO. The other eight wrote eight different answers. They didn't need me to explain the problem, which is why they were becoming more alarmed. As they realized how they were misaligned, they understood how that lack of alignment would permeate throughout the organization they led, and how that in turn would create competing agendas, a breakdown in trust and a lack of collaboration that was essential to their progress. Worse, as a team, it meant they would often be working at cross purposes, with all the danger of conflict and divisiveness that this would bring.

One of the problems that became apparent was that each of them had a different meaning in their heads when they thought of the words purpose, vision and mission. To each of them, they meant different things. Worse, they had never had a discussion about what these words meant to them and how they would be using them so that they could all use them in the same way.

Be sure you all understand and agree the terminology

The more research I have done into the subject, the more I have seen that this is a problem afflicting business people in general. Even in my research for this book, I have found that leaders have different things in mind when they talk about purpose. It has become abundantly clear that if you are to articulate a purpose, vision and values framework for your organization, the first task is to agree what you mean by each word so that you can properly define your own purpose, your own mission and your own vision in a way that is meaningful and aligns everyone in the room.

In my research of company vision statements, they use terms such as:

- purpose, principles and ambition;
- why, what, how;
- vision, mission, objectives, goals, targets, delivery plans, values;
- vision, values, principles, culture;
- our vision, our values, our DNA.

The list of possible permutations goes on and on.

In the model that I am going to propose you use as a template to facilitate the creation of your own purpose framework, I have offered up some meanings for each of these words. You can choose to adopt or adapt these. You will need to ensure that you pick the word and the meaning that most suits your purpose, and then ensure that the whole team understands exactly what those terms mean and why they are important.

To be clear, I have come to the strong view that your company purpose is not its vision or its mission. Each of these is different, as you will see when I will lay out a suggested framework to use when developing your own.

Balancing people with purpose and profit

In any organization, managers will tend to be very focused on delivering goals and financial results. They manage by the numbers – profits, sales and other numerical targets. The people side of the business, however, can often be found wanting. Managers tend to neglect or avoid how people are feeling, avoid dealing with emotions, and find it easier to be logical and rational. Yet, how their people feel will determine how well they perform and whether any of those targets and objectives are actually ever met.

However, it is also clear to me that most of the leaders I have worked with are constantly fascinated by the future, and are always dissatisfied with the status quo and hungry for change. Because they are impatient for progress, they always seem determined to set and achieve demanding goals.

In Chapter 1, Richard Boyatzis, the American organizational theorist and professor of organizational behaviour at Case Western Reserve University in Ohio, says that advances in functional magnetic resonance imaging (fMRI) have made it possible to venture physiologically inside leaders and followers to understand what is happening in their brains during leadership interactions.

Professor Boyatzis hopes these insights may move the primacy of a leader's actions away from the often used 'results orientation' leadership towards a greater focus on relationships: 'This does not preclude a concern with the results, but is focused first and foremost on one's relationships that enable others to perform better and more innovatively – and lead to better results.'

How to balance a results focus with a relationships focus

The purpose of this book is to enable you to bring together the softer people issues with a hard results focus, in a way that integrates and clarifies: people *and* performance; culture *and* results. To be able to do this, I believe you need to focus on the following:

1 Clarify and articulate a compelling purpose, a long-term future and stretching goals for your team/ department/ organization.

2 Identify and encourage a strong set of values that inspire a shared culture.

3 Ensure your own passion and purpose is delivered in a way that integrates with that of the corporate purpose and values. This is only possible if you are clear on your own values so that you can behave consistently with the corporate values.

4 Drive up your own ability to engage, by being a more inspiring leader who communicates in ways that motivates people to perform at the highest level.

5 Personalize and localize purpose, vision and values so that they are meaningful to each and every person in the organization. This is what creates alignment and agility.

6 Measure not only how you are progressing towards your key goals, but also how you are managing your intangible assets, such as levels of engagement among employees, the quality of your relationship with your key customers, your reputation, your ability to innovate, or the quality of

your relationship with other key stakeholders. You need to ensure that you are making progress to your long-term and short-term goals, while ensuring that you are progressing in a way that is mindful of your role in society, your dependence on external relationships, your use of resources, your impact on the planet and the need to create an environment that enables long-term viability.

7 Regularly report on your progress and enter into dialogue on how to further improve performance, both internally with your team, and externally with customers and other stakeholders.

If you get all of this right, I am convinced that you will perform better as a leader and get more from your team and organization. Your people will be more engaged, and will be liberated to make not only good decisions but the right decisions that will ensure you can maintain and build the relationships inside and outside the organization that you need for long-term success. You will be able to engage better with staff, with more purposeful conversations, and you will be able to engage better with customers and other stakeholders. You will build your brand value and your reputation, improve operational effectiveness and reduce your risks. All of this will have a direct financial impact, enable growth and create more business opportunities.

People expect more of business

As we have seen in various chapters of this book, people expect more of business today, and society demands that leaders have a wider sense of purpose and a new morality. So do prospective employees, especially millennials. Purposeful companies engage their people better, creating nicer places to work, and happier employees, who return the favour with higher levels of commitment and efficiency, innovation and customer service.

But do not think that simply articulating and communicating a purpose and some values is enough. You have to make every leader more purposeful, and every person in the organization more inspired by the purpose, sharing not only the purpose but also the values, so that you create a common culture.

To do all that, you need a tool to help you articulate your purpose, your values, your vision and your key goals – all on one easy-to-read page. Once you have done that, the tool becomes the vehicle by which you facilitate the conversations that need to happen up, down and across the company to create understanding, commitment and alignment.

The purpose framework

Figure 13.1 overleaf is a composite of all that I have seen and read over the past three years. I have worked with this diagram with a number of management teams, and it has been a wonderful catalyst that provokes debate on each and every one of the key areas, resulting in greater clarity around purpose, greater focus on key strategic priorities, and much debate on the values that can help to build an appropriate culture. It is not just a catalyst to use to articulate strategy – the conversations it provokes can often help to formulate strategy.

In each and every case, the leaders that I have worked with have subtly changed the model to suit their own ends, sometimes choosing different words to describe different parts of the model. I am not precious about holding them to this model. So long as what they produce is something that they all own and understand, my mission has been achieved. They become a team with much greater alignment and an ability to talk to their vision in an aligned way, more able to deliver it uniformly throughout the company they lead.

Let me explain the various components of Figure 13.1, one by one.

1. Purpose – the beating heart of your organization

Very deliberately, as you can see from Figure 13.1, purpose is at the centre of everything. As Ann Francke, chief executive of the Chartered Management Institute, says: 'Without purpose, you are nothing. Purpose creates meaning and is essential for engaging your employees. It gives your customers a connection to your company and creates ties to communities.'

Purpose is why you exist, and explains what you are doing for someone else, mainly your customers. By delivering your purpose, it shows how you create value for customers, how you answer their needs and should connect with the heart as well as the head. You have to find a way to express how what you do has a positive impact on the lives of your customers, your clients, your patients or whomever else you are trying to serve. My advice is to keep your purpose statement as short as you can. This is not easy. You need to capture all of the above in as few words as possible.

Moss Bros, the men's outfitter, says their purpose is to 'make men feel amazing'. This is a wonderful statement that not only explains who their customers are, but how, through clothing, they will make their customers feel. Trust Ford, the Ford motor car dealership, says their purpose is to 'drive

Figure 13.1 The purpose framework

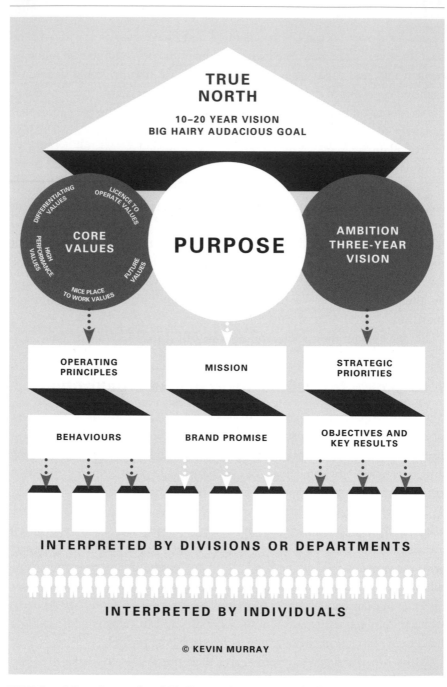

© KEVIN MURRAY

NOTE: For a fuller, colour version of this diagram, please go to www.leadershipcommunication.co.uk

the standard in customer care'. They want to be the envy of their competitors and be recognized as the benchmark in all of their operations, identified not just by the cars they sell, but mostly for the service they provide. The implicit benefit to customers is clear.

Southeastern, the train operating company, says their purpose is to 'achieve 85 per cent by 2018': this is shorthand for attaining their highest ever customer satisfaction rating, aligned with their vision of delivering their best ever passenger experience. Again, it is focused entirely on their customers and what they are trying to do for them. Virgin Atlantic, the global airline, says their purpose is 'to embrace the human spirit and let it fly'. The company believes strongly in individualism, and freeing people to be themselves. It is highly emotional and highly effective.

Furniture retailer DFS says their purpose is to 'be famous for creating and making quality sofas that every home loves and can afford'. This statement is really clear, with both emotional and rational benefits. Diageo, the global drinks company, says its purpose is 'to celebrate life, every day, everywhere'. Who doesn't like the idea of celebrating life? Every one of these provides a benefit statement for customers.

I put the purpose section of Figure 13.1 at the heart, because a powerful purpose statement is the beating heart of your organization. It drives everything, which is why every other part of the framework must connect to the purpose directly. Your long-term vision will be an expression of how much impact you can have by delivering your purpose. Your ambition statement will describe how well you see yourself delivering your purpose in three years. Your strategic priorities will articulate the key goals you need to achieve to ensure you deliver your purpose, profitably. Your values will enable your purpose to be delivered in the right way, consistent with the ethos behind the purpose. Your purpose is front and centre of everything you do, and should be embedded in every conversation you have as a leader.

When you start thinking about how to express your purpose, think about the problem you are solving for your customers. Defining the problem often leads to breakthrough solutions in providing a compelling purpose statement. What is the problem or need that you are solving or answering? What is the benefit you are delivering to them, preferably that only you can deliver? What is the business opportunity you see? Is there a service or a product you can provide that better answers customer needs than anyone else? Keep focused on this and you will arrive at the right purpose statement.

I don't believe that a purpose statement should be about making a profit. Of course, a business always needs to make a profit, and in many ways this is its first responsibility, because without profit you cannot deliver your purpose, nor can you be a responsible citizen taking an active role in helping your local community to thrive and prosper. But profit is a measure of your success at delivering your purpose, and is not the purpose itself.

As you have seen in earlier chapters in this book, it is increasingly important that companies explain their wider social purpose, in order to demonstrate that they are mindful of their social and environmental obligations, both now and in the future. They also need to demonstrate that they seek to build long-lasting relationships with all stakeholders, relationships that are mutually beneficial. I believe that these do need to be stated, but not in the purpose statement.

You can state how you will be a responsible business in your long-term vision, in your strategic priorities or even your values and principles. But not in your purpose statement. I am strongly of the view that this needs to be focused on your customers, and unless you can serve them profitably, well into the future, you will not be able to deliver on your social purpose, your wider purpose, your higher purpose or whatever else you choose to call it.

It is, however, really important that you explicitly talk to your wider purpose somewhere in this purpose framework. As we have seen, recognizing that you have environmental and social responsibilities is a critical element, one increasingly demanded by the citizens of countries all over the world. People believe that companies can both make a profit and help to build a thriving planet and thriving communities. It is not something they desire, it is something they expect. Companies that do not do this will suffer reputational damage, harm their relationships and risk their long-term future. Companies that do it create competitive advantage.

2. The power of a breathtaking long-term vision – your True North

And what of your vision statement? In Figure 13.1 I prefer leaders to differentiate between their long-term vision and their short-term vision. The short-term vision is usually expressed in the three-year planning horizon that is their business plan. I call this their ambition, and I call the long-term vision their True North.

The reason I call it True North is because this is usually a goal that becomes a guiding light for decades to come. I know that great leaders always have a long-term vision, usually expressed as a big hairy audacious goal of some sort. This goal can be 10 to 20 years in the future, or even longer, but it must create a sense of urgency among employees because it is so stretching that they will never get there if they don't begin with some urgency now. It is an expression of what you want to become, or what you want to do, or what impact you want to have on the world.

Here are some examples from some famous brands and organizations:

- **Nike**: to be the number one athletic company in the world.
- **Pfizer**: we will become the world's most valued company to patients, customers, colleagues, investors, business partners and the communities where we work and live.
- **Oxfam**: a just world without poverty.
- **Save the Children**: a world in which every child attains the right to survival, protection, development and participation.
- **Coca-Cola**: our vision serves as the framework for our road map and guides every aspect of our business by describing what we need to accomplish in order to continue achieving sustainable, quality growth:
  - *People*: be a great place to work where people are inspired to be the best they can be.
  - *Portfolio*: bring to the world a portfolio of quality beverage brands that anticipate and satisfy people's desires and needs.
  - *Partners*: nurture a winning network of customers and suppliers, together we create mutual, enduring value.
  - *Planet*: be a responsible citizen that makes a difference by helping build and support sustainable communities.
  - *Profit*: maximize long-term return to shareowners while being mindful of our overall responsibilities.
  - *Productivity*: be a highly effective, lean and fast-moving organization.
- **Amazon**: to be earth's most customer-centric company; to build a place where people can come to find and discover anything they might want to buy online.
- **Google**: to provide access to the world's information in one click. (Google's mission statement is *to organize the world's information and make it universally accessible and useful*. It is closely connected to their vision.)
- **Walmart**: to become the worldwide leader in retailing. (Mission: *to help people save money so they can live better*.)
- **Ford**: to become the world's leading consumer company for automotive products and services.

- **Samsung**: to lead the digital convergence movement.
- **Facebook**: to make the world more open and connected.

In every case, the organization has set themselves an incredibly stretching goal that will take many years to achieve. As you will see from these statements, they provide real guidance on what to focus on, a compass for all of their decision making – a True North. It is an explanation of the difference you will make to the world by delivering your purpose, brilliantly.

3. Defining your short-term vision – your three-year ambition

Leaders have to simultaneously achieve both short-term goals and put in place the planks that they can build the future on. They will often be taking actions today to help them prepare for tomorrow. If they are focused too much on delivering short-term goals, at the expense of investing in the future, they put in jeopardy their long-term future.

However, they must achieve short-term goals. For this reason I also like for leaders to define what success looks like in a reasonably near-term future – usually the future they have envisaged in their business plan.

Too few leaders try to turn those three-year goals into a picture of success that not only describes in numerate terms what you will achieve, but also what that means for all of the relationships you will depend on for success. To earn more revenue and achieve more profit ultimately means changing the behaviours not only of employees, but probably also customers, suppliers, financiers and other stakeholders, including regulators and NGOs.

That requires high-quality relationships that are mutually beneficial. Describing those relationships in the state that you hope they will be is what needs to go into this part of the diagram – what I call the three-year ambition. You may want to double your profits, but what will that mean people will be doing at the time when profits have doubled? Your employees? Your customers? Your suppliers? Where will you be operating? How many more customers will you have and why will they be coming to you, or remaining loyal? How will employees be feeling? (A great example of this is the Coca-Cola statement on page 237.)

This is where you can talk about the state of your relationships in a way that demonstrates your commitment to all stakeholders. It is here that you can also talk about your environmental and ethical commitments, as well as your commitments to local communities and other key communities, such as students and future employees.

4. Strategic goals bring your plan to life

To achieve your three-year ambition requires you to focus on no more than about five strategic priorities – fundamental things you have to get right in order to achieve your revenue, profit and relationship goals. These will be high-level tasks that will take you at least three years or longer to achieve, but which are the building blocks of success.

All subsequent operational or tactical planning and resource allocation decisions will be based on these strategic priorities. Defining these will enable you to decide which projects or initiatives to continue and which to stop or delay. If this or that project does not help you to achieve one of your five strategic priorities, then why are you doing it? Defining these goals is to bring your strategy to life, and enables employees to understand the various initiatives that are under way in the organization. When done well, they will also explain what those goals will contribute to the vision, and why they are of value to the organization.

Success, however, depends on ensuring that employees have an understanding of and a commitment to corporate goals, as well as an ability to set their own goals to align with those corporate goals. And they must be regularly reviewed. Understanding goals is one thing, but feeling that you can do something about them is even more important. The YouGov research showed that it was critical to motivation that employees felt they were making a contribution to organizational goals.

In the Monarch Airlines example in Chapter 10, we saw that Monarch talks about six strategic goals, including introducing a new fleet of aircraft, building a strong balance sheet and a competitive cost base, and developing a profitable all-year-round flying schedule.

You will understand that each of the strategic goals outlined by Monarch will only be achieved if they successfully deliver a series of objectives underneath each strategic goal. To introduce a new fleet of aircraft, for example, requires the training of pilots and cabin crew, new equipment, new processes, integration with marketing and other departments, and many other tasks, if it is to be done successfully. This is where employees begin to understand how what they do helps to deliver to the long-term vision of the company. They can see how their daily actions help to achieve the objectives that help to achieve the strategic priorities, which in turn help to achieve the three-year ambition, which is but a step en route to the long-term vision.

Every division in the organization should align itself to these high-level goals, and translate them into local actions through the OKR system I outlined in Chapter 10.

5. Objectives and key results

OKR stands for objectives and key results. It is a popular method of defining and tracking objectives and their outcomes. The main goal of OKRs is to connect company, team and personal objectives to measurable results, making people move together in the right direction. A big part of OKR is making sure each individual knows what is expected of them at work. OKRs are kept public in front of everyone so that teams move in one direction and know what others are focusing on. OKRs were invented at Intel, and are today used by many companies, including Google, LinkedIn and Twitter.

6. Core values – beliefs in action

While the right-hand side of Figure 13.1 is all about performance and goals, the left-hand side is all about culture. Culture is the way we do things around here and, at its most simple, is all about behaviours. What we do is influenced by a number of things, not least of which are the things that we think are important and which therefore drive our own leadership behaviours. We think something is important because of what we believe about the world, and what we believe so deeply (that it has an effect on our behaviours) represents our values.

Most organizations that I have researched use no more than about five high-level values to help to shape and influence the culture they desire. Companies with rich and healthy cultures achieve fast income growth and are better at attracting the talent that enables them to keep growing and generating value. Leaders who pay attention to culture, as I have said, achieve superior results.

As I described in Chapter 5, many companies lay claim to exactly the same values. Two of the most commonly used values are innovation and integrity. Aren't those fairly fundamental values that every company should have? I believe companies lay claim to these because they have not thought hard enough about the real purpose of values, and how best to use them. Some of the companies I have researched have used a few key values, and then gone on to describe their operating principles and desired behaviours, elaborating on a few key values to enable them to provide a better understanding about the DNA of the organization.

The 'purpose' framework above prompts you to look at the different types of values you need:

- your licence-to-operate values;
- your future values – the values you will need in order to achieve your objectives and that currently you may not have;
- current values that describe your DNA as it is;
- your differentiating values that describe your unique selling proposition (USP);
- your high performance values;
- the values that make your organization a nice place to work.

All of these have a place, but you cannot use all of them in the same way. You have to look at the most important values that are fundamental to your success, and I describe these as your core values. Normally, you should limit these to about five. If you need to elaborate, you can do so in your operating principles, or in the section called behaviours.

7. Operating principles – your beliefs explained

As we saw from the medical devices company BTG, featured in Chapter 9, they not only describe the key values that are important to them, but they also have a list of 10 statements about their DNA. These are more like operating principles, which many companies use to elaborate on their values and to give them a better definition.

These principles should elaborate on the values you express (usually one-word values), which need to be brought to life in an interesting and exacting way. The reason is because they should make clear and lead to a common set of behaviours. What you do, and how you behave, *is* your culture.

Wouldn't it be brilliant if you could sum up your four or five values in one sentence? A sentence that makes it utterly clear what you expect of your people. For example, instead of saying our values are about creativity, customer care, teamwork and innovation, you could say: 'We want people to have fun together and bring to our customers solutions to their problems and a constant stream of ideas that add value to them and to us.'

8. Behaviours

Your values should be your beliefs in action – manifesting as behaviours that are expected of all employees, if the values are real and meaningful. Sometimes, depending on where you sit in the organization, you have to describe these behaviours slightly differently. For example, while being customer focused might appear to be self-evident to salespeople on the shop floor, it might not be that evident to a member of the IT department who provides a helpdesk to members of staff. How will the IT department demonstrate customer focus? Sometimes these things need to be spelled out in a way that is most appropriate to the team or department, and can be very different from the finance department to the sales desk, from marketing to warehousing. These should be an expression of how you want everyone to act, in order to deliver to the values and help us achieve our goals and vision – in the right way.

9. Mission

Your purpose should not be a description of what you do. In Figure 13.1, you will see that this is what I describe as your mission. Your purpose may not always clearly explain your business activities, and you do need to define these to both internal and external audiences. It is helpful to explain what business your organization is in, and sometimes even what it is not in, and thus provide a focus for management and staff. I have seen some powerful examples of companies using their mission statement to send a clear message to staff about lines of business they will no longer pursue. A good mission statement would describe the type of work you do, the clients you cater to, where you provide your products and services, and possibly what areas you aim to be in for the future.

10. Brand essence – the public promise to customers

Ideally, your brand promise would mesh perfectly with your purpose statement. Perhaps it might be a shorter, punchier version, written more as a slogan than a purpose. Watch out for the slogans that do not match with your purpose, or connect with your values. That's when you fall into the gap between expectation and delivery. This should talk to the place that you want your brand to occupy in the minds of your target customers – and how you are unique.

In summary

A team or company is truly agile when every member of the team is able to make decisions that connect with your purpose, values and strategy. With this knowledge, your people have all the context they need in order to know how to behave in all the challenging situations they might find themselves in. In one page, with a simple purpose and a set of principles well defined, you will, as former Visa founder Dee Hock says, 'give rise to complex, intelligent behaviour'. Your people will know how to act, what to say, what to allow, what to refuse, and they will do the right things even when you are not in the room.

In summary, the key steps you need to take are:

- *Develop your purpose framework*:
  - Clarify and articulate a compelling purpose, and a strong set of values that combine to inspire a shared culture and manifests as behaviours that help you to achieve your goals.
  - Identify a long-term future and stretching goals that inspire the team. Demonstrate how you will fulfil a social purpose.
  - Write up these ideas on a single page.

- *Define your personal passion, purpose and values*:
  - Ensure your own passion and purpose is delivered in a way that integrates with that of the team. This is only possible if you are clear on your own values so that you can behave consistently with the corporate values. You must map your personal purpose and values to the corporate values and purpose.

- *Work on your inspiration quotient and communicate to engage*:
  - Drive up your own ability to engage, by being a more inspiring leader who communicates in ways that motivate people to perform at the highest level. Understand what most motivates and moves employees to perform. (For more guidance here, see my previous books – *The Language of Leaders* and *Communicate to Inspire*.)

- *Create alignment by cascading purpose, vision, values and goals*:
  - Personalize and localize purpose, vision and values so that they are meaningful to each and every person in the organization, right to the front line. This is what creates alignment and agility. Facilitate powerful conversations on purpose, values and goals. Ensure managers are capable of holding these purposeful conversations.

- *Use integrated reporting methods to measure your progress*:
  - Measure not only how you are progressing towards your key goals, but also how you are managing your intangible assets, such as levels of engagement among employees, the quality of your relationships with

your key customers, your reputation, your ability to innovate, or the quality of your relationships with other key stakeholders upon whom you depend for success.

- *Communicate, communicate, communicate*:
  - Regularly report on your progress and enter into dialogue on how to further improve performance, both internally with your team, and externally with customers and other stakeholders. Put in place a continuous improvement process that encourages people to bring you bad news, so you can rapidly fix problems and improve performance.

People with Purpose perform better. Leaders who have purpose, and who give people purpose, are able to create teams and organizations that are fully aligned, with employees who are more engaged and more productive. *People with Purpose* liberate leadership and enable agility. They facilitate trust and collaboration. As a result of their purpose and their values, they engage better with their external audiences, especially customers, and build strong reputations, which enhance relationships and create the conditions for long-term success.

Leaders who make purpose the beating heart of their organizations create more engaged employees, more committed customers, more supportive stakeholders and greater value, because they create thriving businesses, communities and environments. Giving people a sense of purpose *is* a leader's role – no matter whether you lead a small team or a global organization. It is, perhaps, a leader's most important role. I wish you every success with your own team, as you strive to make all members of your team *People with Purpose*.

The resources

Your guide to the purpose framework

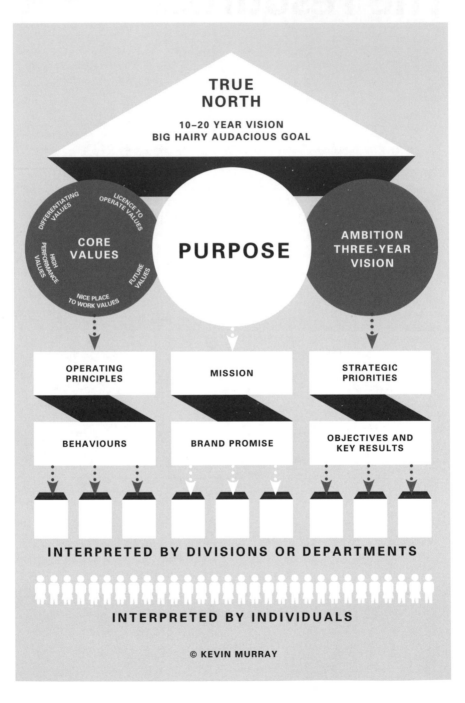

TRUE
NORTH

10–20 YEAR VISION
BIG HAIRY AUDACIOUS GOAL

DIFFERENTIATING VALUES

LICENCE TO OPERATE VALUES

CORE
VALUES

HIGH PERFORMANCE VALUES

FUTURE VALUES

NICE PLACE TO WORK VALUES

PURPOSE

AMBITION
THREE-YEAR
VISION

OPERATING
PRINCIPLES

MISSION

STRATEGIC
PRIORITIES

BEHAVIOURS

BRAND PROMISE

OBJECTIVES AND
KEY RESULTS

INTERPRETED BY DIVISIONS OR DEPARTMENTS

INTERPRETED BY INDIVIDUALS

© KEVIN MURRAY

PURPOSE

Why you exist, always expressed as a positive benefit to customers or stakeholders, one they would all agree is a benefit to them. The beating heart of your organization.

TRUE NORTH

Our guiding light – what steers every decision and goal, expressed as a major positive impact on the world or your community of interest. If you deliver your purpose brilliantly this is the impact you you will have on the world.

CORE VALUES

Our core beliefs in action, these help us drive our behaviours in order to deliver on our purpose and our promises. Drawn from:
a. *Differentiating values*
b. *Licence to operate values*
c. *Future values*
d. *Nice place to work values*
e. *High performance values*

AMBITION

What success looks like in 1–3 years, in numbers (profit/ margin/revenues) and in terms of all internal and external relationships.

STRATEGIC PRIORITIES

The 5–6 fundamentals you have to get right to deliver your purpose and your short- and long- term vision. These will last as projects for years.

OPERATING PRINCPLES

Your values, explained.

TRUE NORTH
10–20 YEAR VISION
BIG HAIRY AUDACIOUS GOAL

a. b.
e. CORE VALUES c.
d.

PURPOSE

AMBITION
3 YEAR VISION

OPERATING PRINCIPLES

MISSION

STRATEGIC PRIORITIES

BEHAVIOURS

BRAND PROMISE

OBJECTIVES AND KEY RESULTS

INTERPRETED BY DIVISIONS OR DEPARTMENTS

BEHAVIOURS

The behaviours you expect from everyone in the organization, measured and rewarded.

OBJECTIVES

The key tactics that will deliver each strategic priority, with measures.

MISSION

A brief factual explanation of what you do.

BRAND PROMISE

The slogan that promises a benefit to customers, usually a USP.

The questions that will help you to understand your own inspiration quotient

Mark yourself on a scale of 1–10, where 10 is excellent.

1 Can I say that I genuinely inspire our people by communicating with passion and integrity? (Does my leadership team do the same?)

2 Am I confident that everyone (at all levels in the organization) has a clear view of our values and our purpose so that all the decisions they make are aligned with these?

3 Do all our people understand what each of them needs to do to help achieve our goals, and are they inspired by our vision?

4 Is everyone in the organization committed to constantly improving our key relationships – with each other, our suppliers, partners, stakeholders and, most importantly, our customers?

5 Are we having enough meaningful conversations with our employees so they feel engaged, motivated and committed to what we are doing? Am I recognizing good work when I have those chosen conversations?

6 Can I truly say that I understand what things are like for our people so that I can talk about issues that are important to them?

7 Do I make it a priority to get feedback and input from our people across the organization and respond to their concerns? Am I a good listener? Do I make it easy for people to bring me bad news?

8 Can people in the organization look at me and say that I speak out strongly and clearly on the issues that are important to me and to our organization?

9 Am I known as a leader who inspires and engages people by using stories to communicate the messages I want to convey, or do I only use charts with facts and figures?

10 Am I confident that the way I act, and the signals I send, communicate the right messages to our people? □

11 Am I and all the leaders in the organization properly prepared and trained for speaking publicly so we can ensure that every word we say counts? □

12 Is communication a fundamental leadership priority within the organization, ensuring that we develop all of our leaders to become inspiring communicators? □

13 Above all, am I doing everything I can to ensure that our people, our customers and all of our stakeholders trust who we are and what we do? □

Once you have completed your marks you can compare your total with 1,000 leaders whose results can be found at the beginning of Chapter 4.

Average mark:

ACKNOWLEDGEMENTS: MEET THE PEOPLE FEATURED IN THIS BOOK

Special thanks must go to all the leaders, scientists and specialists who so kindly gave their time and their wisdom to this project. They include:

Hugo Bague, Group Executive, Rio Tinto

Hugo Bague joined Rio Tinto in August 2007 and is Group Executive, Organizational Resources with overall responsibility for Human Resources, Health, Safety, Environment and Communities, Media Relations, Corporate Communications, External Affairs, Procurement, Information Systems and Technology, Shared Services, and Group Property. Previously he worked for six years for Hewlett Packard, based out of Palo Alto, California, as well as Compaq Computers, Nortel Networks and Abbott Laboratories, based out of Switzerland, France and Germany.

Dr Duncan Banks, Director, Work-based Learning, Open University

Duncan Banks's first degree was in Medical Physiology from Leeds University and later a PhD from Sheffield University on the action of anaesthetics on the nervous system. He is a neuroscientist whose current research interest is in Alzheimer's disease and neurodegeneration. He has been a trustee of the British Neuroscience Association since 1995. He has been a government advisor since 2000, including advisor to the Cabinet Office, and has spent several years as a consultant to the Home Office. Duncan has been with Open University since 2000.

Richard Boyatzis, Professor, Case Western Reserve University

Richard Boyatzis is Professor in the Departments of Organizational Behaviour, Psychology and Cognitive Science at Case Western Reserve University. He is the author of books on leadership, competencies, emotional intelligence and change, including: *Primal Leadership* with Daniel

Goleman and Annie McKee, published in 28 languages; and *Resonant Leadership*, with Annie McKee, published in 18 languages. Prior to becoming a professor in 1987, he had been President and CEO of McBer and Company (a research-oriented human resource consulting company) for 11 years.

Julie Deane OBE, Founder and CEO of The Cambridge Satchel Company

An unlikely fashion entrepreneur, Julie Deane OBE graduated from Cambridge University in 1987 and worked as a chartered accountant before returning to the university, where she was the Fellow for Development for her college – the first female to be appointed to this role in the 650-year history of the college. In 2008 she launched The Cambridge Satchel Company to fund her children's education. Julie invested just £600 to get the idea off the ground. In December 2014 she received an OBE for Services to Entrepreneurship.

Paul Donovan, CEO, Odeon and UCI Cinemas

Paul Donovan (1958) is CEO of Odeon and UCI Cinemas, the leading European cinema operator. He is also Director of Upstream S.A., a mobile e-commerce solutions provider. He started in the fast-moving consumer goods industry before transferring to the technology sector where he worked for Apple and BT Cable and Wireless. He joined Vodafone in 1999, and from 2004 was a member of Vodafone's Executive Committee. He is a former director and CEO of Eircom, Ireland's leading telecommunications company. He holds a master's degree in Business Administration from the University of Bradford.

Natalie Douglas, CEO of Healthcare at Home Ltd

Natalie Douglas has spent over 20 years in the pharmaceutical industry, most notably at Johnson and Johnson, and in the health-care services sector. She is CEO of Healthcare at Home Ltd, the UK's largest clinical home-care company. Previously she was CEO of IDIS, a specialist health-care services company with operations in Europe, India and the United States. From 2009 to 2014 Natalie served as Non-Executive Director for Shield Therapeutics, a Swiss-based pharmaceutical company. Natalie holds a master's degree in Marketing Management from Middlesex University, London and a Chartered Institute of Marketing Diploma from Thames Valley University, London.

Vernon Everitt, Managing Director, Transport for London

Vernon Everitt is responsible for Transport for London's customer and technology/data strategies and their delivery, which put customers at the heart of the organization's operations. This includes accountability for fares and payment operations, contact centres, customer information, marketing and customer insight, media relations, public affairs and travel demand management. Prior to joining TfL in 2007, Vernon spent 10 years at the Financial Services Authority (FSA) and 18 years at the Bank of England. This included leading the FSA's national work to improve the financial capability of consumers.

Paul Feeney, CEO, Old Mutual Wealth

Paul Feeney has been CEO of Old Mutual Wealth since July 2012, having joined the group in January 2012. Prior to joining Old Mutual, Paul was Head of Distribution and Executive Director at BNY Mellon Asset Management, Group Managing Director and Global Head of Distribution at Gartmore Investment Management, Chief Executive of NatWest Private Banking, Global Marketing and Sales Director of Coutts Group and Chief Executive and President of NatWest Investments USA. He has a first-class honours degree and PhD in Financial Economics from the University of Wales.

Ian Filby, CEO, DFS

Ian Filby joined DFS in 2010 and has 34 years of retail experience. As CEO of DFS, Ian champions the importance of marketing and has a focus on the customer being central to everything he does. Ian joined Boots as a retail marketing trainee and subsequently joined the Boots Executive 10 years ago, as Trading Director. Ian was Interim CEO of Groupe Aeroplan London (Nectar) in 2009–10 and remained a non-executive member of their Group Advisory Board for a further three years. In 2015 Ian became Chairman of both the BRC Policy Board and the newly listed Shoe Zone plc. Ian is married and lives in Grantham, Lincolnshire.

Sir Rocco Forte, Chairman, Rocco Forte Hotels

Sir Rocco Forte is Chairman of the luxury hotel company Rocco Forte, which he founded in 1996. Sir Rocco joined Forte plc in 1969, becoming CEO in 1983 and Chairman in 1992, when he succeeded his father the late Lord (Charles) Forte. Forte plc was sold in 1996 following a hostile takeover bid and has since been broken up. Sir Rocco was knighted in December 1994 for services to the UK tourism industry. He qualified as a chartered accountant in 1969. A keen sportsman, Sir Rocco represented Britain at the World Triathlon Championships in 2001, 2002, 2003 and 2007.

Ann Francke, CEO, CMI

Ann Francke is CEO of the Chartered Management Institute (CMI) and author of: *Financial Times Guide to Management: How to make a difference and get results*. Prior to CMI, Ann was Global General Manager at the British Standards Institution; she held executive board positions at Boots and Yell and was European Vice President at Mars, with responsibility for the pet-care portfolio. Ann began her career at Procter & Gamble, rising to Global General Manager.

Mark Goyder, Founder Director, Tomorrow's Company

After 15 years as a manager in manufacturing businesses, Mark initiated the Royal Society of Arts and Commerce (RSA) Tomorrow's Company Inquiry and consequently founded the business-led Tomorrow's Company think tank. Over the past 10 years he has inspired and challenged the boards, leaders and managers of leading large and small companies with practical insights into the changing agenda for leadership, governance and stakeholder relationships. Mark holds a number of other positions, including on the British Airways Corporate Responsibility Board; BT Leadership Advisory Panel; and Camelot Advisory Panel for Social Responsibility.

Philip N Green, CBE, Chairman of Carillion plc

Philip N Green is Chairman of Carillion plc, the international construction and service business, and holds the same role at BakerCorp, the Permira-owned industrial services company in the United States. He is Chairman Designate of Williams & Glyn, the UK 'challenger' bank that is being divested by RBS, planned for late 2017. Philip was appointed to the board of Saga as Senior Independent Director in May 2014. He was CEO of United Utilities plc from 2006 to 2011. In 2003 he was appointed CEO of P&O Nedlloyd. He was previously Chief Operating Officer at Reuters Group plc, which he joined in 1999. From 1990 to 1999 he was at DHL, becoming Chief Operating Officer for Europe and Africa. He holds an MBA from the London Business School and a BA (Hons) from the University of Wales.

Debbie Hewitt MBE, Non-Executive Chairwoman of Moss Bros Group plc

Debbie Hewitt is Non-Executive Chairwoman of Moss Bros Group plc, private equity-owned Evander Group, fashion retailer White Stuff Ltd and Visa UK. She has a portfolio of other non-executive director roles, including the plc boards of NCC Group and Redrow, where she is Senior Independent Director, and Non-Executive Director of The Restaurant Group plc, Domestic and General, a business backed by the private equity house CVC, and of BGL, owners of ComparetheMarket.com. In her executive career Debbie started as a management trainee with Marks & Spencer and, after working in a variety of different roles in the motor industry for Lex plc, she ultimately became the MD of RAC plc, a role that concluded in 2008 after the acquisition of RAC by Aviva.

Steve Hood, Chairman and CEO, TrustFord

Steve Hood is a graduate of Leeds University and has worked in the automotive industry for over 30 years. He has had a number of senior positions with Ford Motor Company in both the UK and Europe and has also worked in the retail world, having spent seven years in the Ford retail group. TrustFord was recently recognized as one of the Top 25 large companies to work for in the *Sunday Times* 100 best companies to work for.

Stephen Howlett, Chief Executive, Peabody Group

Stephen Howlett has been Chief Executive of Peabody since 2004. Founded in 1862, Peabody is one of London's oldest and largest social-housing charities. Stephen was previously Chief Executive of Amicus, a group of housing associations in London and south-east England, and Director at Notting Hill Housing Trust. Before this he worked for the National Housing Federation and the Housing Corporation. From 2009 to 2011 he was Chair of g15, the group of London's major housing associations.

Killian Hurley, Co-Founder and majority shareholder of Mount Anvil

Killian Hurley is the Co-Founder and majority shareholder of Mount Anvil, Central London's specialist residential-led developer. He has worked in the London property market since 1988. Under Killian's leadership, Mount Anvil has seen almost tenfold growth. Mount Anvil has been named as one of the *Sunday Times* 100 Best Small Companies to Work For in each of the last nine years. Killian received a degree in Commerce from University College Cork and qualified as a chartered accountant with Pricewaterhouse-Coopers in 1983.

Valerie Keller, Global Head, EY Beacon Institute

Valerie Keller is Global Head of the EY Beacon Institute and an Executive Director of Ernst & Young LLP in its strategy practice. As a former CEO she has established health-care facilities, housing developments and social enterprises. Valerie was also founder of Veritas and two US coalitions focused on housing and health-care system reform. She has advised US congressional committees and facilitated public–private partnerships across businesses, government agencies and NGOs. She is an Associate Fellow of the University of Oxford Said Business School, where she designs and leads executive education programmes.

Craig Kreeger, CEO, Virgin Atlantic

Craig Kreeger was appointed CEO of Virgin Atlantic Airways on 1 February 2013. He joined from American Airlines (AA), where he had a 27-year career spanning commercial, financial and strategic roles in the United States and around the globe. Craig holds a Bachelor of Arts degree in Economics from the University of California at San Diego, and a Master of Business Administration degree from the University of California at Los Angeles.

Dame Louise Makin, CEO, BTG

Dame Louise Makin, MA, PhD (Cantab), MBA, DBE, joined BTG as CEO in October 2004. She is a non-executive director of Intertek Group plc and the Woodford Patient Capital Trust, a trustee of the Outward Bound Trust and an Honorary Fellow of St John's College, Cambridge. From 2001, she was President, Biopharmaceuticals Europe of Baxter Healthcare, where she was responsible for Europe, Africa and the Middle East. Before joining Baxter, she was Director of Global Ceramics at English China Clay and prior to that she held a variety of roles at ICI.

Ian McCaig, CEO, First Utility

Ian McCaig joined First Utility in 2011 from lastminute.com where he was CEO. He is a trustee of English Heritage, sits on the board of VisitBritain and is a member of the ChildLine board at the NSPCC. Ian is particularly proud that First Utility started its own charitable foundation in 2014, which supports those who help some of our society's most vulnerable groups.

Ivan Menezes, Chief Executive, Diageo plc

Ivan Menezes has been Chief Executive, Diageo plc since 1 July 2013. He was previously Chief Operating Officer, Diageo plc. Ivan joined Diageo in 1997. Before Diageo, he worked across a variety of sales, marketing and strategy roles for Whirlpool in Europe, Booz Allen & Hamilton in the United States, and Nestlé in Asia. He serves as a non-executive director of Coach, Inc. in the United States, is a member of the Scotch Whisky Association Council and sits on the Advisory Council of the China-Britain Business Council. Ivan holds an MBA from Northwestern University's Kellogg School of Management, a postgraduate degree from the Indian Institute of Management, Ahmedabad and a BA Economics from St Stephen's College, Delhi University.

Helena Louise Morrissey, CEO, Newton Investment Management

Helena Louise Morrissey, CBE, has been CEO at Newton Investment Management Ltd since July 2001 and also serves as its Chairwoman. She joined the firm as Fund Manager in 1994. Previously, she was Global Fixed Income Manager at Schroder Investment Management. She serves as a panel member of The Takeover Panel (UK). She was appointed CBE in 2012 and holds an MA in Philosophy from the University of Cambridge.

Dennis M Nally, Chairman, PricewaterhouseCoopers International Ltd

Dennis Nally is Chairman of PricewaterhouseCoopers International Ltd. He has served as Chairman since 2009. Prior to that, he was Chairman and Senior Partner of the US firm of PricewaterhouseCoopers. Dennis joined the PwC US firm's Detroit office in 1974 and became a partner in 1985. He is a member of the American Institute of Certified Public Accountants and the New York State Society of CPAs. He also serves as Vice Chair and board member of the US Council for International Business.

John Neill, Chairman and Group CEO, Unipart Group

John Neill joined Unipart Group of Companies from General Motors in 1974 in what was then British Leyland's Parts Division. In 1987 he led the management buyout of the company. He was educated at George Heriot's

School, Edinburgh and the University of Strathclyde. He is Chairman of Atlantis Resources Ltd and was also formerly a director of the Court of the Bank of England and a non-executive director of the Royal Mail, Charter International plc and Rolls-Royce plc.

Saker Nusseibeh, Chief Executive, Hermes

Saker is Chief Executive of Hermes. He was appointed CEO in May 2012, having been acting CEO since November 2011. Saker joined the firm in June 2009 as Head of Investment. Prior to joining Hermes, he was Global Head of Equities at Fortis Investments USA. Before this he was CIO Global Equities and Head of Marketing for SGAM UK. He started his career at Mercury Asset Management in 1987. In 2015, Saker was named CEO of the Year at the Global Investor Investment Excellence Awards.

Paul Polman, CEO, Unilever

Paul Polman has been CEO of Unilever since January 2009. Under his leadership Unilever has an ambitious vision to fully decouple its growth from overall environmental footprint and increase its positive social impact through the Unilever Sustainable Living Plan. He is Chairman of the World Business Council for Sustainable Development, a member of the International Business Council of the World Economic Forum, and sits on the Board of the UN Global Compact and the Consumer Goods Forum, where he co-chairs the Sustainability Committee.

Christine Porath, Associate Professor, MBC Faculty, Georgetown

Christine Porath's research examines incivility and its effects. Her research focuses not only on the effects of bad behaviour, but also how organizations can create a more positive environment where people can thrive; and how individuals and organizations benefit in terms of individual well-being and performance. In addition to her book *The Cost of Bad Behavior*, her research has appeared in many other journals and books. Her work related to incivility has been featured worldwide in over 500 television, radio and print outlets.

Lady Susan Rice CBE, Chairwoman of Scottish Water

Previously Managing Director, Lloyds Banking Group Scotland, and before that Chief Executive then Chairwoman of Lloyds TSB Scotland plc, in 2000 Lady Rice became the first woman to head a UK clearing bank. In July 2014 she became the first Chair of Scotland's new Fiscal Commission. Alongside her roles as a commercial banker and currently a non-executive director of J Sainsbury's and the North American Income Trust, Lady Rice is a lay member of court of Edinburgh University. In the arts, she chairs the boards of the Edinburgh International Book Festival and Edinburgh's Festivals Forum.

Hilary Scarlett, Director, Scarlett & Grey

Hilary Scarlett is a consultant, writer and speaker, and Director of Scarlett & Grey. Her work has spanned Europe, the United States and Asia and concentrates on the development of people-focused change management programmes, coaching and employee engagement. She is currently conducting research into applied neuroscience with four major organizations in the private and public sectors. Hilary has also been working with Professor Walsh of University College London to apply cognitive neuroscience to practical management tools.

Phil Smith, Chairman, UK and Ireland, Cisco

Phil Smith is the UK and Ireland Chairman of Cisco. Additionally, Phil is the Chairman of Innovate UK and Chairman of The Tech Partnership. He sits on the board of the National Centre for Universities and Business (NCUB) and the Business Disability Forum. Phil has a 30-year track record in the Technology industry in leading companies such as Philips Electronics and IBM. In Cisco, he leads around 5,500 people in the UK and Ireland. He works closely with government ministers, industrial leaders and top thinkers in business, politics, academia and society to orchestrate life-changing innovation.

David Statham, Managing Director, Southeastern

David Statham is Managing Director of Southeastern. Previously, he held appointments as Customer Service Strategy Manager at Great Western and in management of the ScotRail franchise in 2004. A key player in First Capital Connect's successful bid for the Great Northern and Thameslink franchise, he mobilized the franchise to combine the Great Northern and Thameslink businesses in 2006. In September 2014, David joined Southeastern as Managing Director. He is leading the company to focus on passenger satisfaction and has overseen investment of £4.8 million in major station improvements and maintenance on the majority of the company's trains.

Dick Stead, Executive Chairman, Yodel

Dick Stead became Executive Chairman of Yodel in September 2012. Dick joined Yodel from Parcelforce Worldwide where he was Marketing Director and subsequently became Managing Director, spending five years at the company. Dick previously worked for the Royal Mail and Post Office, which together with Parcelforce gave him great insight and experience across the sector. He studied Fuel and Energy Engineering at Leeds University and began his career at Yorkshire Chemicals Ltd. Dick spent a number of years working in the energy sector for British Steel Corporation, NCB and British Coal.

Andrew Swaffield, CEO, Monarch Airlines Group

Andrew joined Monarch Airlines in 2014. Prior to his appointment at Monarch Airlines, Andrew held the position of Managing Director of Avios Group Ltd, part of IAG. Prior to that, Andrew held positions at Thomas Cook and British Airways, where he headed leisure sales in the UK and Ireland, as well as running its travel agency and tour-operating subsidiaries.

Anthony Thomson, Founder and Chairman, Atom Bank

Anthony Thomson is Founder and Chairman of Atom Bank, Chairman of the Financial Services Forum, Chairman of the National Skills Academy for Financial Services, and NED of Agiliti, a company providing banking software as a service. Previously Anthony was Founder of Metro Bank and served as the first Chairman from 2009 until 2012. In 1987 Anthony founded City Financial Marketing, which by the time he sold it to Publicis in 1997 was Europe's largest financial services marketing and communications group.

Charles Tilley, immediate past Chief Executive, Chartered Institute of Management Accountants

Charles Tilley (who, at the time of going to press, announced his departure from CIMA) is a prominent advocate for global reform of corporate reporting and the critical importance of management accounting to sustainable business. Amongst other roles, he is a member of the International Integrated Reporting Council. Chief Executive of CIMA since 2001, Charles has spearheaded a partnership with CIMA's US counterpart, the American Institute of CPAs. Charles is a former partner of KPMG and Chief Financial Officer of the investment bank Hambros plc.

Nick Varney, CEO, Merlin Entertainment

Nick has over 25 years' experience in the visitor attractions industry and was appointed CEO of Merlin Entertainments in 1999. He started his career in consumer goods marketing, first with Rowntree and then with Reckitt & Colman. He went on to hold senior positions within the Tussauds Group (Pearson plc), including Marketing Director of Alton Towers and Head of Group Marketing, before becoming Managing Director of Vardon Attractions and a main board Director of Vardon plc. In 1999 Nick led the management buyout of Vardon Attractions to form Merlin Entertainments, guiding the company to successful IPO in November 2013. Nick is increasingly active in the wider tourism agenda, particularly in the UK, but also worldwide.

SPECIAL MENTION

Finally, special thanks also to the people who gave me advice and help in the production of this book: Libby Elderfield, my always enthusiastic PA; Paul Larbey and Andrew Sherville, for their chapter-by-chapter feedback; Matthew Gould for the design of my purpose framework; Stefan Kaszubowski at YouGov for the care he put into our employee–manager research; Anna Moss, my patient editor at Kogan Page (and all at Kogan Page who have helped to produce and publish this work); and especially to my wife, Elisabeth, for her endless support when I go into writing mode.

ABOUT THE AUTHOR

Kevin Murray has been advising leaders and leadership teams for the past three decades. He has worked across a wide variety of sectors, often helping leaders deal with significant change programmes as well as a range of other business challenges including, sometimes, managing crises. He has also provided personal coaching for many of these leaders, helping them to become more inspiring.

Kevin is author of the bestselling books *The Language of Leaders* and *Communicate to Inspire*, both of which are published by Kogan Page and featured as finalists in the Chartered Management Institute Management Book of the Year Awards. The books have been published in many languages around the world.

He has interviewed more than 120 CEOs for his research, and commissioned ground-breaking studies to investigate what most inspires employees. As a result of his books and his research, Kevin now gives talks and workshops on leadership around the world.

Kevin has himself been a successful businessman, having led the biggest public relations and communications group in the UK for more than 15 years. He has 40 years of experience in communications; first as a journalist, then in corporate communications, and now in consultancy. Previously, he was Director of Communications for British Airways, and before that Director of Corporate Affairs for the United Kingdom Atomic Energy Authority (AEA).

He started his career as a crime reporter for *The Star* newspaper in South Africa in 1973, and has also written a chart-topping crime novel, *Blood of The Rose*.

For more information, visit www.leadershipcommunication.co.uk.

INDEX

Also available from **Kogan Page**

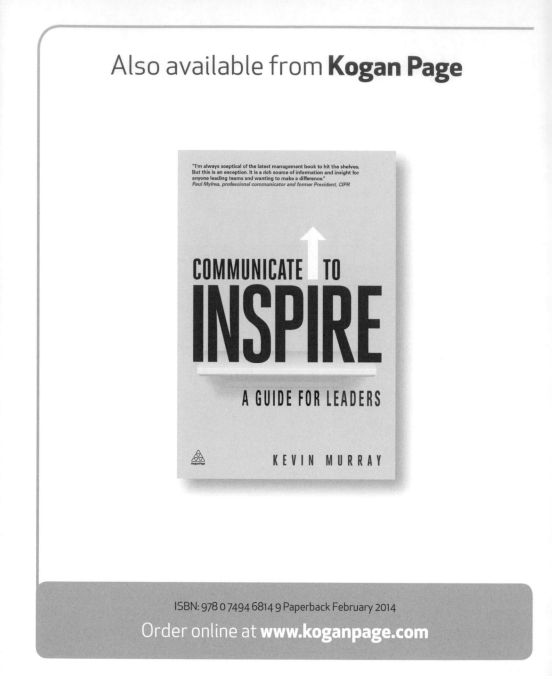